THE BALLAD IN SCOTTISH HISTORY

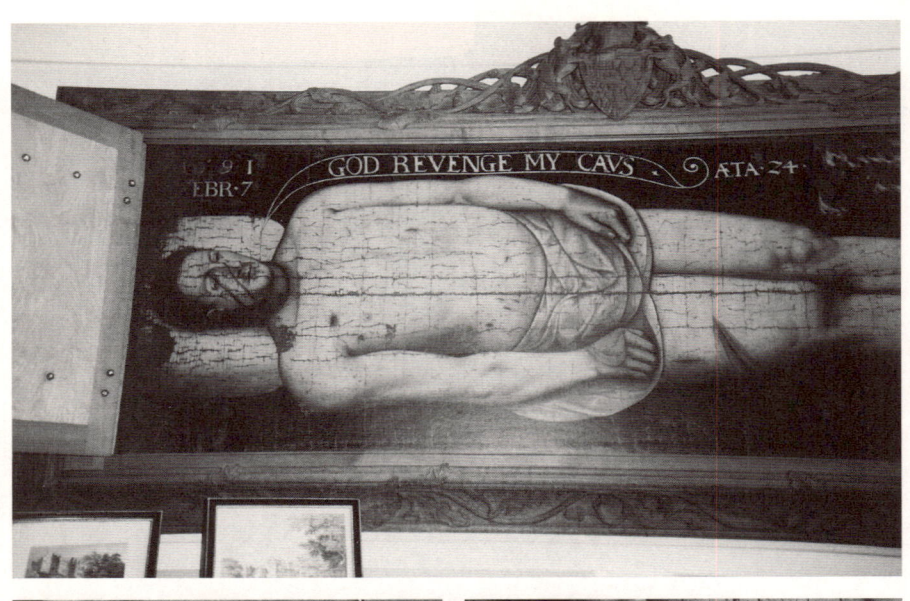

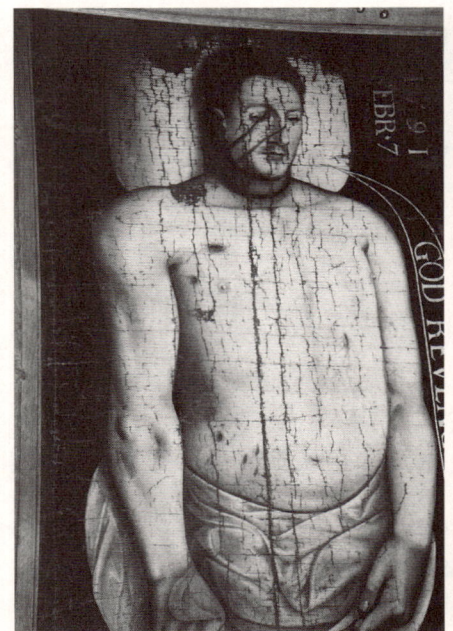

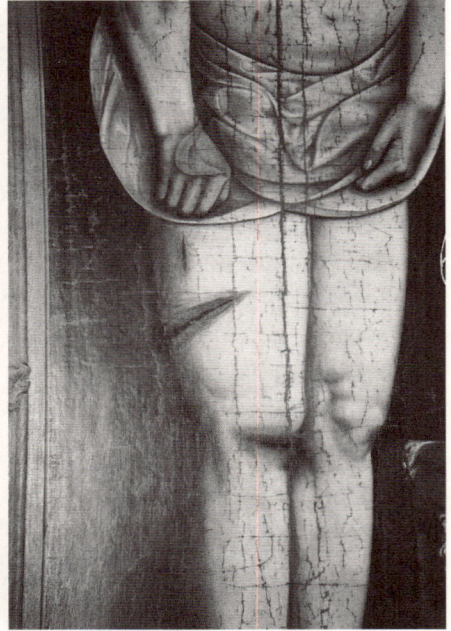

The death portrait of the Earl of Moray
(see pp. 42–3)

THE BALLAD IN SCOTTISH HISTORY

edited by

EDWARD J. COWAN

TUCKWELL PRESS

First published in Great Britain in 2000 by
Tuckwell Press Ltd
The Mill House, Phantassie, East Linton, East Lothian, EH40 3DG
Scotland

ISBN 1 86232 008 X

British Library Cataloguing-in-Publication Data. A catalogue
record for this book is available on request from the British Library

Typeset in 10.5/13 Garamond by
Aligra Lancaster
Printed and bound in Great Britain by
The Cromwell Press, Trowbridge, Wiltshire

Contents

Contributors

VALENTINA BOLD is Lecturer in Scottish Studies at Crichton College of the University of Glasgow, Dumfries.

EDWARD J. COWAN is Professor of Scottish History, University of Glasgow.

CHARLES DUFFIN recently completed his Ph.D. at the University of Glasgow.

LIZANNE HENDERSON, a graduate of the universities of Guelph, Ontario and Memorial, Newfoundland, is currently studying for her Ph.D. at the University of Strathclyde.

ROBERT A. LAMBERT is a member of the teaching and research staff at the Institute for Environmental History, University of St Andrews.

KAYE MCALPINE is an Independent Scholar and Ballad Historian.

IAN A. OLSON is a retired Aberdeen medical practitioner with an interest in Scottish traditional culture and history. He is editor of *Aberdeen University Review*.

CHRISTOPHER A. WHATLEY is Professor of Scottish History at the University of Dundee.

1

Introduction: The Hunting of the Ballad

EDWARD J. COWAN

> The historical ballads are often a guide to
> what History is not.
>
> Hamish Henderson[1]

This collection of essays was conceived with at least two aims in mind. First, most, but not all, of the papers published here, were presented at a conference to commemorate the death of Francis James Child (1825–96) whose *English and Scottish Popular Ballads,* third edition, 5 vols. (Boston and New York, 1882–98) has attained near-canonical status during the past century. Secondly, in celebrating Child's achievement, contributors were invited to consider a question which, with the exception of a very few notable investigators, has been somewhat unfashionable during the past century or so, namely, how valuable are the ballads for the recovery of the social history of pre-industrial Scotland? There can be little doubt that ballads currently find little favour with Scottish historians concerned with the period before 1800. Record-thirled historiography has scant regard for oral or popular tradition; the 'story' of history depends on the written, rather than the spoken, word. All kinds of nonsense, once committed to parchment or paper, is revered, orality reviled.

It has become a truism that a ballad is a folk song that tells a story but further elaboration of that definition has engendered ferocious scholarly dispute and the sacrifice of many forests of trees, while in the torrent of criticism the defined invariably becomes the described:

> The ballad may be described as a popular and primitive short-story – religious, historic, romantic, tragic, gnomic, fairy, or even humorous – told simply, succinctly, and dramatically – partly in the form of elliptic and repetitive dialogue, and with complete suppression of the narrator's personality – in rhymed, often irregular verse, generally in short-line quatrains or in octosyllabic or anapestic couplets.[2]

In laconic style, minimalist description, and lack of subjectivity the ballads have much in common with the Icelandic sagas, the great vernacular prose narratives first committed to vellum in the thirteenth and fourteenth centuries which gave rise to similar contentious debates on the subject of orality and literacy. The essence of the ballad is in the singing or the telling, 'the peculiar mode of narration',[3] something which cannot, unfortunately, be recovered from the printed page. Nor, so far as I am aware, are their any references to ballad performance in the pre-1800 period, apart from the bald and unsurprising information that they were sung, but were they also on occasion chanted or recited and how important was audience participation which might have acted to check the freedom or inventiveness of the performer? While certain ballads may appear to have a recognisable theme, they may well have originated in England or the Gàidhealtachd, or even further afield, for variants are often to be found all over Europe, and beyond. Pre-literate folk, like modern journalists, had a bag of motifs ready to hand to describe eventualities as they occurred. Scottish ballads, in turn, flowed easily across the border, or, for that matter, the North Sea or the Atlantic. Certain it is that a large proportion of what became the Child corpus was collected in Scotland[4] which, in the eighteenth century, was already regarded as the country par excellence for the hunting of the ballad. Throughout this book square brackets thus [306] after a ballad title indicate the ballad number allocated by Child.

Francis James Child graduated from Harvard in 1846 when he secured a post as a mathematics tutor, transferring to history, political economy and English after a couple of years. He studied in Germany from 1849 to 1851 and returned to the Chair of Rhetoric and Oratory at Harvard. In his hunt for ballads Child owed much to a network of Scottish informants; Emily Lyle's excellent article on his 'Scottish Harvest' lists thirty-one of them including such luminaries as John Francis Campbell, Norval Clyne, George Kinloch, David Laing and Andrew Lang, all of whom were authorities in their own right and each of whom enjoyed access to a wider circle of singers, reciters and individual owners of texts and manuscripts.[5] The most influential of Child's Scottish acquaintances was William Macmath (1844–1921), a legal assistant in Edinburgh who acquired a considerable reputation as a scrivener and copyist; a native of Galloway he grew up in a household of tradition-bearers, the custodians not only of ballads, but also of riddles and tales. The two men met briefly in Edinburgh in 1873, on which occasion Child made an utterly fruitless visit to Abbotsford. Macmath eventually secured copies of the Abbotsford MSS as well as the Glenriddell MSS and the Kinloch MSS for Child, and he negotiated the purchase of several other collections on behalf of Harvard which, pirate-like, plundered an invaluable part of Scottish heritage at this period. He was particularly interested in the historical origins of individual ballads, more so than Child. Believing the latter to be overly concerned with questions of arrangement and classification, he once threw Child's own words back at him: 'Strictness is offensive as well as useless. Perhaps it is impossible. Ballads are not like plants or insects, to be classified to a hair's breadth.'[6]

Child, who had produced editions of Spenser, Chaucer and Gower, was in some respects an unlikely editor of popular ballads and the great project with which his name will forever be associated frequently represented a source of considerable frustration to his literary and aesthetic sensibilities. Such disappointment was not unusual. In an article which he contributed to James Hogg's journal, *The Spy* (no. 50), one J. C. Robertson deplored the way in which 'the simple lays of our ancient bards' had been superseded in his own day 'by the vilest trash'. For good measure he traduced ballad hawkers as well as low and debased listeners:

> If ballads and songs can no longer be made the channels of
> morality and patriotism it is surely at least in the power of
> those who should exert some care over the public manners
> to prevent them from being openly prostituted to the sub-
> version of these important purposes. Magistrates should
> silence the venders of such nonsense, smut and blasphemy.[7]

Child too was often alienated by what he called the 'vulgarity' of the ballads – 'by which I mean always the *essentially* vulgar, the absolutely mean and stupid'. He described the great collections of broadside ballads as, on the whole, 'veritable dunghills, in which, only after a great deal of sickening grubbing, one finds a very moderate jewel'.[8] He communicated this reaction despite the fact that the distinguished ballad scholar, Svend Grundtvig, had already told him that vulgarity was the best proof of material authenticity. The Dane went on to soberly lecture the New World scholar.

> It must be remembered – and is well known to ballad collec-
> tors of the old world, where the tradition of bygone days
> still lingers on – that in the recent traditions of the common
> country people [peasantry] the old ballad cannot always
> appear in a stately and knightly form and apparel, but must
> in many instances exhibit the traces of a long dwelling in
> humble company. Very often what now to delicate eyes and
> ears may seem 'vulgar' is in fact of the old stamp ... Let us

have the old national ballads as antique and genuine as possible,
and let us not prefer or substitute the bastards of modern
forgers, however gifted and elegant and polished. The old
times shall be seen in their *best*, but in their *own clothes*, and
be judged by their own standard.[9]

Nevertheless, five years later, Child still deplored some of the 'trash' he
received from Scotland.

Part of Child's problem derived from his conviction that the ballads
actually did represent a debased form of literature – that of medieval
romance.[10] Ever since the seismic impact of the Ossianic phenomenon,
through Percy's *Reliques* and Scott's *Minstrelsy*, critics and commentators
had been obsessed with the notion that ballads were composed by
'minstrels', who were always imagined as individuals with lutes and
pointy boots rather than vagrants with a song to sell, or farm servants
with a creative bent. The preferred representative of the craft was
generally 'the last' of his kind (and it invariably was a 'he' rather than a
'she' despite the contemporary evidence of female preponderance among
informants).[11] As the 'jockies' and bards were consigned to the fringes of
society by successive legislation so their compositions degenerated, a
relentless (and critically invidious) process of downward dilution and
dissipation, from the privileged to the deprived.[12]

Child's disdain for his informants did not stop him fantasising, against
his better instincts and contrary to type, about playing a more pro-active
role in collecting. In 1879, convinced that Shetland must harbour many
undiscovered specimens, he confided that if he were 'on the spot' he
'could be continually prodding up the people – there *must* be ballads
there',[13] blissfully oblivious that if he had visited the Northern Isles he
would probably have proved to be the one unsalted herring in the barrel.
Later he became convinced that the ministers had destroyed every last
vestige of ballad and tradition.[14] The great collector J. F. Campbell of Islay
told Child in no uncertain terms that he should dirty his feet in the field –
'If you will do in Yankeedoodledom as I did here, you may gather a bigger
harvest orally than I did, for *the people* of this old country are now in the
New World; legends, stories, ballads, and all'; otherwise, 'come over
yourself'.[15] Child confessed a weariness with his attempts 'to stir up
Scotsmen to an interest sufficient to induce them to exert themselves to
save things that may still be left. It is in vain. The Scot loves his ballads,
but is incurious about them.'[16] The objects of his criticism might well
have riposted that while Child undoubtedly loved his ballads he was
comparatively incurious about the Scots. He seems to have been rather
disinterested in performance or context preferring the more clinical and

more remote transmission of ballads through the medium of manuscripts processed by the learned – a venerable tradition in ballad collecting – hence his heavy, and (for posterity) fortuitous, reliance upon the likes of William Macmath.

A further complicating factor in assessing Child's contribution is that he never produced a rationale for his research nor even a clear definition of what he thought a popular ballad was. As a result, a fair amount of ballad criticism since the publication of his monumental work, especially by a devoted and dazzled band of American scholars, has taken the form of what amounts to Childean exegesis.[17] The great man's sole article on balladry appeared in *Johnson's Cyclopedia* of 1895. Despite all the words that have been written on the subject of definition it is clear that Child relied upon instinct; whatever he decided was a ballad *was* a ballad, though he admitted that 'the chemistry' of the ballads seemed as 'indeterminable as that of Greek myths'.[18] The first edition of his *Ballads* was published 1857–9, the second in 1861, and he was planning the third from about 1871. It is apparent from his correspondence with Grundtvig that the latter unduly influenced him in the matter of Scandinavian variants and versions; Child's prefaces to individual ballads frequently consist of highly learned discussions of supposed parallels from Scandinavia or further afield, which upon examination, sometimes cannot be sustained. The cognate dominates the context and the universal diminishes the distinctive. On Child's terms a study of the ballads becomes a study of the European psyche, the response of a sixteenth-century Scot being no different from that of an eighteenth-century Croat. The professor may have been correct but we are not told why he should have been so. To indicate an exotic analogue for a Border tale may be fascinating from a folkloristic or anthropological point of view but it is not of special interest historically; the historian is concerned about what the story selected, out of all the hundreds in circulation, tells us about the people and the circumstances of the time which preserved it. Not that Child is to be criticised for having been influenced by the ideas of the contemporary historic-geographic school which was primarily concerned with questions of origins, simply because, today, the quest for an Ur-text is regarded as futile.

Some of the foregoing remarks may appear unduly critical in a volume of commemoration but this shy, retiring and mostly diffident scholar has already been the subject of a surprising amount of hagiology. According to Gummere he wished his *Cyclopedia* article 'to be neither quoted nor regarded as final'.[19] As it happens he elsewhere recorded his greatest ambition, 'I want to live long enough to put the world in possession of all the English [and Scottish] ballads, and find it frequently necessary to say to myself that this is the only matter of essential importance.'[20] In that endeavour he may be deemed to have succeeded admirably.

* * *

The Scots had, of course, been discussing and debating the nature of ballads for some considerable time before Professor Child addressed the subject. In his *Minstrelsy of the Scottish Border* (Kelso and Edinburgh 1802–3) Scott described a completely integrated historical and literary microcosm. His primary interest, however, was in history, that of the landscape and his own people. The first part of the publication was devoted to historical ballads, the second to the romantic variety, those which by implication derived from medieval romances; and the third part comprised imitations. In foregrounding history with such emphasis Scott essentially initiated a debate which would rumble on for a century or more. He believed that if the entire corpus of Scottish song had survived 'there is no doubt a very curious history might have been composed by means of minstrelsy only, from the reign of Alexander III in 1285, down to the close of the Civil Wars in 1745'. That such ballads and songs had once existed was attested by the statements of successive chroniclers and historians who referred to them 'as authorities for general tradition'.[21] As the true heir of the Scottish Enlightenment Scott revered the ballads as providing a window on the manners of a past era; all specimens were, to some extent, historical. He proceeded to give a potted history of ballad publication. Originally, of course, they had been confined to the oral tradition in the 'well-exercised memories' of the minstrels.

> Nor was it a difficult task to acquire a sufficient stock-in-trade for their purpose, since the Editor has not only known many persons capable of retaining a very large collection of legendary lore of this kind, but there was a period in his own life, when a memory that ought to have been charged with more valuable matter, enabled him to recollect as many of these old songs as would have occupied several days in the recitation.[22]

His account continued with a poetry miscellany produced by Scotland's first printers, Chapman and Millar, who set up in Edinburgh in 1507. He credited John Watson's *Choice Collection* (1706) but allowed that Allan Ramsay was the first to take a serious interest in balladry even though some of his examples were modernised. A breakthrough came in Bishop Percy's *Reliques* (1765) which had so impacted upon Scott as a boy at

Sandyknowe. While deploring Joseph Ritson's 'eager irritability of temper' and his attacks on Percy, he could nonetheless applaud his critical rigour. David Herd produced his *Ancient and Modern Scottish Songs* in 1776, his brief introduction noting the fierce attachment of the Scots to their music – 'Such is the character of the pathetic and sentimental songs of Scotland, which may with truth be termed, *the poetry and music of the heart*'.[23] The balladic adventures of John Pinkerton were briefly noticed though some of his specimens 'smelled of the lamp' which was to say that they were the author's forgeries. More satisfactory in terms of scrupulous accuracy were the assorted publications of Ritson who as Scott's immediate predecessor reflected well, by implication, on his own work although the youthful Walter was not guiltless of the odd embellishment. By 1830 the works of William Motherwell, arguably one of the most gifted and sensitive of collectors, and George Kinloch,[24] had also appeared. The *Minstrelsy* would prove to be, and would remain, one of the most influential works ever published on the ballads. Scott, however, was intent upon rendering the ballads more historical than their contents warranted, utilising a plethora of learned notes in sharp contrast to the bald minimalism of folk performance, in order to construct a process of mystification surrounding ballad scholarship which would outlive Child and which is not yet quite dead even today.

Nineteenth-century Scottish ballad publication is worthy of a study in its own right. Robert Jamieson, originally from Morayshire, had actually anticipated Scott in contemplating a ballad collection, but his *Popular Ballads and Songs, From Tradition, Manuscripts, and Scarce Editions* did not appear until 1806. The publication was noteworthy as the first to include 'popular' in the title. The word may have been intended to signify inclusion, to widen the audience to everyone irrespective of birth, background or education, a notion in which he had been pre-empted some three and a half centuries earlier by the author of *The Complaynt of Scotland* (1550). In that remarkable encyclopaedia of Scots learning and lore, following a learned disquisition on history, physics, astronomy and geography, the shepherd's wife advocates 'joyous comonyng' which involved tales, songs, music and dance, in which all could participate.[25] It was part of this heritage which Jamieson was keen on communicating, the garb of Old Scotia, in the form of traditional poetry, for his expatriot contemporaries, among others. There is more than a hint in Jamieson's work that he was as interested in the source as he was in the ballad, that is to say, in the Scottish people at large. He was also the first to indicate Scandinavian parallels which were later of such interest to Child.[26]

Allan Cunningham, who would later produce his own *The Songs of Scotland* (1825), provided Robert Cromek with much spurious material for his *Remains of Nithsdale and Galloway Songs* (1810) while Charles Kirkpatrick Sharpe, a wealthy dilettante, published *A Ballad Book* (1824). William Motherwell reminded his readers that 'the old people who recite these legends attach to them the most unqualified and implicit belief'. Any 'audacious sceptic' who 'dared to question their being matter of incontrovertible fact' would find the lips of his informants implacably sealed. When working in the field the suspension of belief was essential:

> ... from sheer ignorance of this important article of belief, I have, unfortunately for myself, once or twice notably affronted certain aged virgins, by impertinent dubitations touching the veracity of their songs, an offence which bitter experience will teach me to avoid repeating, as it has, long ere this, made me rue the day of its commission.[27]

The somewhat eccentric Peter Buchan of Peterhead, whom Child detested on account of his allegedly sloppy working methods, published *Gleanings of Scotch and English and Irish Scarce Old Ballads* (1828). Another worthy and willing participant in this ballad craze was William Maidment who began publishing ballads as early as 1824; he was to produce three more collections culminating in his *Scottish Ballads and Songs* (2 vols., 1868). He introduced the potentially useful classification of 'traditionary' ballads, meaning those traditionally connected with a historical event, but, though it enjoyed some currency in nineteenth-century criticism, it never really caught on.

While Child was between editions a number of ballad collections[28] and ballad studies by Scots appeared, mostly saying much the same thing and sharing the same assumptions, one of which was a belief in the historicity of the ballads. Professor J. Clark Murray of McGill University coped with the problem of whether ballads were genuine or not by ignoring it in his rather curious investigation of 'the influence which the ballads and songs may be shown to have exerted on the character of the Scottish people',[29] a somewhat skewed study which might better have explored the texts as exemplars of Scottish characteristics. William Gunnyon, in pursuit of a similar quarry, proclaimed that

> the humbler classes of Scotchmen, especially in rural districts, are so saturated with the spirit of their country's Muse, that they hasten to chronicle in verse any access of passion, pleasing or the reverse, and thus live their bliss over again, or lull the demon of disappointment to rest.

He was less flattering to Scotswomen asserting that marriage was 'in a man's life an episode, in a woman's the *Ultima Thule* of her hopes' and that 'a woman like a well-broken horse, likes to find her master'.[30] Small wonder that the female role in balladry was underplayed and misunderstood. This misogynistic production was followed in turn by William M'Dowall's *Among the Old Scotch Minstrels*,[31] rather a whimsical production which, nonetheless, attempted a ballad history of his native land. All three believed that the ballads were co-eval with the events they described; all detected an 'artlessness' which indicated the genuineness of the ballads; and all worshipped at the shrine of Scott whose *Minstrelsy* continued to be regarded as the bible of the subject. Each of these writers also harked back to Alexander III, Thomas the Rhymer, William Wallace and the battle of Otterburn in order to prove the antiquity of the ballad tradition in Scotland, just as each approvingly cited the references to earlier ballads in *The Complaynt of Scotland* and demonstrated the vitality of the tradition by pointing to the Reformers' use of the medium in *The Gude and Godly Ballatis*,[32] in which the protestants wrong-headedly substituted religious words in popular ballads in order to promote their cause. Furthermore all three were quite eclectic in their use of texts, cheerfully using 'improved' or 'polished' versions when it suited them to do so. Indeed, throughout the nineteenth century, the collation of ballad variants was approved,[33] and Quiller-Couch followed the same model in editing *The Oxford Book of Ballads* (1910).

Dave Harker has provocatively charted the emergence of ballad scholarship, arguing that bourgeois collectors from the early eighteenth century onwards were intent upon the gentrification and sanitisation of the ballads.[34] There is undoubtedly much substance in his thesis, although he rather plays down the vitality of the oral tradition which paralleled and survived the collecting mania while it was undeniably subject to continuous reinforcement and influence from chapbooks, song-books and collections; Alan Lomax, after all, remarked, 'the Scots have the liveliest folk tradition of the British Isles, but paradoxically it is the most bookish'.[35] It might also be suggested that at least some of the collectors, in modifying and 'improving' their texts were acting in a rather similar, if slightly more sophisticated and self-conscious fashion, to that of the singers. Such editors may have altered words and polished stanzas but they seldom completely changed the shape or essential substance of the ballad. There is also the awkward and incontrovertible evidence that lyrics which might be deemed unfit for, or offensive to, polite sensitivities quite frequently slipped through the editorial net.

Nonetheless there are blatant examples of total fabrication. Scott himself famously wrote, with reference to ballad forgery, or as he preferred to describe it 'a beautiful poem under the guise of antiquity', that 'the public is surely more enriched by the contribution than injured by the deception'.[36] James Hogg who was himself steeped in the ballad tradition thought that no one would 'think an old song the worse of being somewhat harmonious'.[37] The current consensus is that however refined the versions actually published, both Scott and Hogg frequently worked from originals derived from oral informants, but given the backgrounds of a number of Scott's informants, such as John Leyden or Mrs Anna Brown of Falkland[38] to name but two, it is easy to detect with Harker a kind of bourgeois conspiracy. John Veitch discovered a 'complete' version of 'The Dowie Dens of Yarrow', and he attempted to scrupulously document the circumstances of collection from William Welsh, 'an old man in Peebleshire ... a worthy type of what is best in our fast-decaying old-world character – its simplicity, homeliness, and steady uprightness'. But suspicions are raised when it is revealed that Welsh was the author of a volume of poems and tales relating to local topics.[39] As Lieut.-Col. the Hon. Fitzwilliam Elliot soberly remarked, 'it is really amusing to note how eagerly ballad-collectors invoke the memory of old people and ignore the possible ingenuity of others',[40] and it is true that young people do not seem to rate as informants. Even those upon whom age conferred authority were more often than not anonymous.

Much ingenuity is to be detected in the efforts of Scott and his disciples to prove the historicity of the ballads. Sir Walter, as usual, pointed the way by seldom hesitating to confidently indicate a location, context, or genealogical information about the main participants, on the slimmest of evidence. Indeed, under Scott's tutelage ballads were made to dictate historical events otherwise unknown, as well as to illuminate those well documented. A prime example is 'Sir Patrick Spens' [58] which became one of the best known and most often anthologised of the corpus. It was deemed to describe events surrounding the marriage of Eric of Norway and Margaret, daughter of Alexander III in 1281 or, alternatively, the death in Orkney of their daughter, the 'Maid of Norway', in 1290. T. F. Henderson suggested that the ballad's eponym was Sir Patrick Vans of Barnbarroch who was involved in the marriage negotiations between James VI and Anne of Denmark in 1589 when severe storms detained the bride at home. In both suggestions the ballad as prophecy is to be detected since there is absolutely no evidence for the catastrophe it laments. Further obfuscation was generated by William Maidment's 'discovery' of Spens's grave in Papa Westray, Orkney.[41] Another ballad which spawned much speculation was 'Mary Hamilton' or 'The Four Marys' [173], a story allegedly involving four maids of honour of Mary Queen of Scots, all named Mary – Beton, Seton, Fleming and Livingston – though the ballad's Marys, Carmichael and Hamilton, have been dismissed as 'mere poetical myths'. John Knox records the execution for infanticide of a French woman, 'not far from the queen's lap' in 1563; although she is unnamed, that incident alone probably suffced to inspire the ballad implicating the queen's husband, Darnley, so serving to smear the court in general.[42] Maidment, however, found another candidate: one, Miss Hamilton, at the court of Peter the Great of Russia, who also suffered the capital penalty for infanticide.[43] It is not impossible that rumours of the later incident reinforced interest in the existing ballad.

At the same time the possibility that ballads preserved events of local significance that have otherwise been lost should not be totally dismissed. Major episodes such as battles at places like Otterburn, Harlaw[44] or Philiphaugh,[45] would long be remembered while interest in less momentous incidents would evaporate when transposed from their locality. The world, after all, has long been fascinated by the interminable squabblings and trivial altercations between a handful of tiny Greek city states. It was part of Scott's genius to indicate that in the investigation of the historical process the parochial was potentially as significant as the portentous. Until recently the local superseded the national in the way in which historians approached the battle of Otterburn (1388), regarding it as little more than a border skirmish between the Douglases and the Percies whereas its true significance in the context of the ongoing wars of independence has now been established.[46]

By the time Child's great five volume work was published academic historians were uncomfortable with the ballads, as indeed with oral sources of any kind, and they largely remained so despite the publication of the late David Buchan's seminal study which was firmly rooted in a historical context.[47] For their part, ballad scholars retreated from the past, becoming much more interested in text, style and performance. It is diagnostic that a recent publication on Child's legacy contains not one contribution on the ballad as history.[48]

Principal Robert S. Rait of Glasgow University provided a brief introduction to John Ord's *Bothy Songs and Ballads of Aberdeen, Banff & Moray, Angus and the Mearns* (Glasgow 1930) in which he commended the contents for providing 'a living picture of Scottish rural life, absolutely sincere and free from any form of affectation'. Ord, Superintendent of Glasgow City Police, was, not surprisingly, much influenced by the work of Gavin Greig and the Rev. James B. Duncan who collected over 3,000

texts and over 3,100 tunes in the north-east,[49] so furnishing an invaluable
assemblage of material for the history of nineteenth-century bothy life.
The late Alan Bold was one critic who clearly found the concern with
historicity to be tiresome, pithily asserting that 'a good ballad has a poetic
independence unthreatened by historical fact' and that 'history, in the
ballads, provides only raw material for rousing narratives'.[50] He was
largely echoing A. L. Lloyd who dismissed 'the sport of tracing ballad
stories to some literal historical source ... The fact is, well substantiated or
ill, this kind of historical attribution tells us nothing essential about the
ballads.'[51] The point is, however, that such attribution may inform us
about history. It may be permissible to suggest that the period from *c.*1400
to *c.*1800 constituted a kind of Scottish *longue durée*, or 'long duration' to
borrow a term from the French *Annales* school.[52] This is to suggest that
although the various generations experienced a good deal of turmoil and
upheaval, the deep structures remained pretty much intact, that a person
living in 1750 had more in common, generally speaking, with an ancestor
in 1450 than with a descendant in 1850. Shelter, diet, clothing and
environment were little altered over a period of several centuries. Of
course people were subject to some change but everyday existence was
essentially static; in 1800 the vast majority of the population still lived on
the land. Too often we visit the past in search of the familiar rather than
the strange, looking for connections with the present rather than focusing
on attitudes and ideas that bound our predecessors to their pasts. To cite
something of an analogue, the philosophers, historians, and to some
extent the literary critics of the Enlightenment, were engaged in a dialogue
with the ancients of Greece and Rome; they were emphatically not
anticipating a debate with the twentieth or twenty-first centuries.

Collectors have always believed that they were preserving what was on
the verge of extinction but in a real sense men like Robert Burns and
Hogg – and Scott vicariously – were part of a living tradition which would
soon disappear in the final capitalisation of land, a process in which the
two first named were thoroughly caught up, to their respective detri-
ments, while Scott pursued neo-feudal tendencies as a defence against
dreaded change, seeking shelter from present reality in an enchanted world
in which he was both minstrel and patron. It was almost as though the
collectors could step through a curtain to visit a medieval world in their
own back-yards, yet safely retreat to the material comforts of the present.
At the same time, though it may have been no part of their intent, the
balladists demonstrated, in every successive collection of surviving ballads,
that Scotland was a remote and static country thirled to superstition and
the vestiges of pagan belief. Such was, and is, the danger of all folk studies,

namely, that we describe the primitive in order to reinforce our own modernity. The protestants in 1560 declared war on superstition of every kind while their disapproval and condemnation embraced virtually all aspects of folk culture and belief. However, it was not the Reformation which sounded the death knell of such entities as witches and fairies and ballads, as might have been expected, and as many reformers hoped, but the inexorable economic forces of agrarian transformation and industrialisation. As long as the survival of ballads and the beliefs they reflected could be demonstrated, so the corollary that Scotland was a backward country was sustained. Throughout the eighteenth and nineteenth centuries travellers and visitors to Scotland sought the archaic and the ancient.[53] Even F. J. Child was disappointed when he could not find the evidence he sought, and for that, ironically, he blamed the unreconstructed folk themselves.

Further validity for the historical approach to ballads is to be distinguished in their themes, many of which are incontrovertibly medieval, thus furnishing some proof for the idea that they were transmitted by means of the oral tradition over a fairly lengthy period of time. A certain recognition factor must have ensured their perennial appeal; many people in the Borders or in Aberdeenshire and in many other parts of Scotland still had landlords who lived in castles, who had almost total control over their lives and who occasionally provided spicy nuggets of scandal which were promptly balladised to the detriment of the great and the good. Variants from other parts of Europe constitute further evidence for the antiquity of individual ballads since no theory of spontaneous combustion could account for the sudden appearance of similar stories, in different places, in the nineteenth century. Historians soberly analyse saints' lives written hundreds of years after their subjects flourished, just as they scrutinise medieval chronicles which must incorporate much material which was originally oral. With care and by using rigorous methodologies, there is no reason why the world of the ballads cannot be reconstructed. With more scholarly input there is also the chance of new discoveries. It has recently been suggested that the eponym of 'Sir Cawline' [61] was Sir Colin Campbell who accompanied Edward Bruce to Ireland, 1315 to 1318.[54]

In the final analysis historians must handle ballads like any other historical source, testing the evidence and finding corroboration. If a recognisable ballad title appears in a compilation such as *The Complaynt of Scotland*, it surely indicates, at the very least, that some version was then extant even though it cannot now be recovered. True, it may bear no more similarity to existing versions than do American variants of say,

'Barbara Allan' [84], to what we may think of as a Scottish or English 'original', but it is more convincing as evidence than some of the nonsense which has been presented as ballad criticism. A number of ballads appear in chapbooks and more, almost certainly, await discovery.[55] It is quite perverse to continue to argue that the more obviously historical ballads are somehow not contemporary with events they describe. Hamish Henderson has convincingly made the point that '"the true ballads" for the historian as well as for the folksinger' were composed by individuals who were not only virtuosos in the techniques of their craft, but also 'literate persons with a certain amount of knowledge of their country's written poetry'.[56] Some of our Scottish historians would certainly benefit from a hefty injection of poetry. They could do worse than return to the world of the ballads.

The contributors to this volume all address various aspects of the ballad in Scottish history. Charles Duffin examines the relationship between song collectors and the material they collected in order to show how tradition 'imparts meaning to the historical message'. Ian Olson utilises his medical knowledge to provide considerable evidence for the contemporaneity of 'The Bonny Earl of Moray' [181]. Lizanne Henderson demonstrates the value of the ballads in exploring popular *mentalité* or mindset in relation to fairy belief. Kaye McAlpine advances a fresh and original reconsideration of several Border ballads, long contentious in the debate about improvement and forgery, by rooting them firmly in their historical context. My own contribution seeks to test the validity of ballad evidence through comparison with 'establishment' sources in the context of sex and violence. Valentina Bold investigates the vexed question of the relationship between Sir Walter Scott and the best known of his informants, James Hogg, the Ettrick Shepherd, by rigorously scrutinising the manuscript evidence. Chris Whatley finds new, and important, evidence of early nineteenth-century protest songs. If it is so difficult to recover material from a comparatively recent period, how much more so to rediscover ballads which are now some 400 years old. Robert Lambert celebrates the vital survival of the ballad form with reference to lovers of the mountains in the more recent past. The editor wishes to record his thanks to all of the contributors for their patience, to Dorothy Mallon for her invaluable assistance with the typescript, to Alison Grant for her excellent page-setting skills, and to John and Val Tuckwell for their faith in the project.

David Hume of Godscroft (1560–1630), whose *History of the Houses of Douglas and Angus* was published in 1644, had much of interest to say to those engaged in the hunting of the ballad, including the quotation of examples known to him personally. Writing of 'Chevy Chase' [162] or 'The Hunting of the Cheviot' he noted that it was not 'the musick of the rough singer' that gave the ballad its force, nor yet the 'virtue of the gross rhime ... It is the matter that gives the efficacy & the virtue of the man that begetteth a resembling virtue in the heart.' The heroes of ancient Ireland believed that the finest sound in the world was 'the music of the thing as it happened'. We must be grateful for the survival of the ballads and their preservation of the echo of the happening.

NOTES

1 Quoted from Hamish Henderson at 'The Ballad in Scottish History' conference, University of Glasgow, Mar. 1996.

2 W. Power, *Literature and Oatmeal. What Literature has meant to Scotland* (London 1935), 61.

3 T. Pettitt, 'Introduction: the ballad as narrative', in F. G. Andersen, O. Holzapfel and T. Pettit (eds.), *The Ballad as Narrative. Studies in the Ballad Traditions of England, Scotland, Germany and Denmark* (Odense 1982), 2. See also F. G. Andersen, *Commonplace and Creativity. The Role of Formulaic Diction in Anglo-Scottish Traditional Balladry* (Odense 1985); B. H. Bronson, 'The interdependence of ballad tunes and texts'; and 'On the union of words and music in the "Child" ballads', both in his *The Ballad as Song* (Berkeley 1969).

4 It is sometimes difficult, and rather pointless, to try to decide which ballads are Scottish given the international dimensions of the subject. The University of Glasgow's SCRAN (Scottish Cultural Resources Access Network) Project entitled 'Traditional to Digital: The Scottish Ballad Project' has distinguished approximately 216 of the Child ballads as 'Scottish' on the basis of theme or informant. When completed the project will provide a complete text, an introduction, an image, and an audio clip for each ballad selected. The material will be stored by SCRAN but a selection should be available on the web and a CD-ROM of the entire collection will be available for purchase. For further details contact University of Glasgow, Department of Scottish History, 9 University Gardens, Glasgow, G12 8QH, or Fax 0141 330 4576.

5 E. B. Lyle, 'Child's Scottish harvest', *Harvard Library Bulletin*, xxv (2) (1977), 125–54.

6 S. B. Hustvedt, *Ballad Books and Ballad Men. Raids and Rescues in Britain, America, and the Scandinavian North since 1800* (Cambridge, Mass. 1930), 218n. See also J. D. Reppert, 'William Macmath and F. J. Child', *Publications of the Modern Language Association of America*, lxxi (1956), 510–20.

7 J. C. Robertson 'On the decay of lyrical and ballad poetry in Scotland', *The Spy*, no. 50 (1811), 347–8. Quoted in E. J. Cowan, 'Scottish History and Scottish Folk', Inaugural Lecture, University of Glasgow, Mar. 1995 (Glasgow 1998), 12.

8 Hustvedt, *Ballad Books*, 254.

9 Ibid., 249–50.

10 For a useful discussion, see H. O. Nygard, 'Popular ballad and medieval romance', in D. K. Wilgus (ed.), *Folklore International. Essays in traditional literature, belief and custom in honour of Wayland Debs Hand* (Hatboro, Penn. 1967), 161–74.

11 Two important studies which address this issue are W. B. McCarthy, *The Ballad and the Matrix. Personality, Milieu and the Oral Tradition* (Bloomington 1990), and

D. A. Symonds, *Weep Not for Me. Women, Ballads, and Infanticide in Early Modern Scotland* (Pennsylvania 1997).

12 E. J. Cowan, 'Calvinism and the survival of Folk', in *The People's Past* (Edinburgh 1980, 1991), 32–3. See, too, C. Lindahl, 'The oral undertones of late medieval romance', in W. F. H. Nicolaisen (ed.), *Oral Tradition in the Middle Ages* (Binghampton, NY 1995), 59–75, and F. C. Sautman, D. Conchado, and G. C. Di Scipio (eds.), *Telling Tales. Medieval Narratives and the Folk Tradition* (New York 1998), *passim*.

13 Lyle, 'Child's Scottish harvest', 140–1.

14 Hustvedt, *Ballad Books*, 283.

15 Lyle, 'Child's Scottish harvest', 143.

16 Hustvedt, *Ballad Books*, 283.

17 See, e.g., 'Introduction', in *English and Scottish Popular Ballads Edited from the Collection of Francis James Child*, ed. H. C. Sargent and G. L. Kittredge (Boston and New York, 1904); W. M. Hart, 'Professor Child and the ballad', *Publications of the Modern Language Association of America*, xxi (4), new ser., xiv (4) (1906), 755–807; F. B. Gummere, *The Popular Ballad* (Boston 1907); L. Pound, *Poetic Origins and the Ballad* (New York 1921); L. C. Wimberly, *Folklore in the English and Scottish Ballads* (Chicago 1928); G. H. Gerould, *The Ballad of Tradition* (Oxford 1932); T. G. James, 'The English and Scottish popular ballads of Francis J. Child', in M. Leach and T. P. Coffin (eds.), *The Critics and The Ballad* (Carbondale, Ill. 1961). For a clear-eyed view of the subject by 'a haunter of unquiet graves', see M. J. C. Hodgart, *The Ballads* (London 1950).

18 Hustvedt, *Ballad Books*, 272.

19 Hart, 'Professor Child and the ballad', 756.

20 Hustvedt, *Ballad Books*, 283.

21 Walter Scott, *Minstrelsy of the Scottish Border*, ed. T. F. Henderson (4 vols., Edinburgh 1932), i, 23, citing 'Introductory remarks on popular poetry' which Scott wrote for the 1830 edition to supplement the original introduction which was 'rather of a historical than a literary nature'. His dates, as usual, are a little wild. He is presumably thinking of Alexander III's death at Kinghorn in 1286 which is commemorated in an oft-quoted 14th-century lament. The Jacobite cause came to grief at Culloden in April 1746.

22 *Minstrelsy*, i, 21.

23 D. Herd, *Ancient and Modern Scottish Songs, Heroic Ballads etc.* (2 vols., 1776; Edinburgh 1973), i, p.xi.

24 G. Kinloch, *The Ballad Book* (Edinburgh 1827); G. Kinloch, *Ancient Scottish Ballads* (Edinburgh 1827).

25 A. M. Stewart (ed.), *The Complaynt of Scotland (c. 1550). By Mr Robert Wedderburn* (Scottish Text Soc., 1979), 49.

26 On Jamieson, see the illuminating observations of Dave Harker: D. Harker, *Fakesong. The Manufacture of British 'Folksong' 1700 to the Present Day* (Milton Keynes 1985), 42–3, 49–50, 70–1. Jamieson was part of the influential Thorkelin circle of septentrionalists: see E. J. Cowan, 'Icelandic studies in eighteenth and nineteenth century Scotland', *Studia Islandica*, xxxi (Reykjavik 1972), 114.

27 W. Motherwell, *Minstrelsy, Ancient and Modern* (Glasgow 1827), 36–7. See M. E. Brown, 'Mr Child's Scottish mentor: William Motherwell', in T. Cheesman and S. Rieuwerts (eds.), *Ballads into Books. The Legacies of Francis James Child* (Bern 1997), 29–39. Motherwell inspired Andrew Crawford's important manuscript collection of ballads; see E. B. Lyle (ed.), *Andrew Crawford's Collection of Ballads and Songs* (2 vols., Scottish Text Soc., 1975, 1996).

28 R. Chambers, *The Romantic Scottish Ballads: Their Epoch and Authorship* (Edinburgh 1859); N. Clyne, *Ballads from Scottish History* (Edinburgh 1863).

29 J. Clark Murray, *The Ballads and Songs of Scotland, in view of their influence on the character of the people* (London 1874), ix.

30 W. Gunnyon, *Illustrations of Scottish History, Life, and Superstition from Song and Ballad* (Glasgow 1879), 178, 197, 205.

31 W. M'Dowall, *Among the Old Scotch Minstrels studying their ballads of war, love, social life, folk-lore and fairyland* (Edinburgh 1888).

32 *The Gude and Godlie Ballatis*, ed. A. F. Mitchell (Scottish Text Soc., 1897). See also Cowan, 'Calvinism and the survival of Folk', 36–9.

33 E.g. *The Ballad Minstrelsy of Scotland. Romantic and Historical. Collated and Annotated* (Paisley and London 1893).

34 Harker, *Fakesong, passim*.

35 Quoted in H. Henderson, 'The ballads', in *Alias MacAlias: Writings on Songs, Folk and Literature* (Edinburgh 1992) 24.

36 *Minstrelsy*, iv, 10.

37 Quoted in T. Crawford, *Scott* (Edinburgh 1982), 24, one of the most illuminating brief discussions of Scott as balladist.

38 Although much has been written about Anna Brown, one of the most useful discussions remains B. H. Bronson, 'Anna Brown and the ballads', in *Ballad as Song*, 64–78.

39 J. Veitch, *The History and Poetry of the Scottish Border. Their Main Features and Relations* (2 vols., Edinburgh 1893), ii, 174–201.

40 F. Elliot, *Further Essays on Border Ballads* (Edinburgh 1910), 50. See also F. Elliot, *The Trustworthiness of the Border Ballads* (Edinburgh 1906).

41 T. F. Henderson, *Scottish Vernacular Literature. A Succinct History* (London 1898), 350–5.

42 L. A. Barbé, *In Byways of Scottish History* (London 1912), 26–7.

43 E. K. Wells, *The Ballad Tree. A Study of British and American Ballads, their Folk-lore, Verse, and Music* (London 1950), 50–2. It should be noted that a mary, or marie, was a maid.

44 D. Buchan, 'History and Harlaw', in E. B. Lyle (ed.), *Ballad Studies* (Folklore Soc. 1976), 29–40.

45 E. J. Cowan, *Montrose For Covenant and King* (London 1977; repr. 1995), 231–8. Attributions should not be rashly or idly made. See ibid., 171, where the present writer confidently identified the skirmish at Fyvie in 1644 as the inspiration for the 'Bonnie Lass of Fyvie', whereas it clearly derives from an English song entitled 'The Irish Dragoons or Pretty Peggy of Derby O'. See J. Morris, 'A bothy ballad and its chapbook source', in P. Isaac and B. McKay (eds.), *The Reach of Print* (London 1998), 85–102. I am indebted to John Morris for kindly drawing his article to my attention.

46 A. Grant, 'The Otterburn War from the Scottish point of view', in A. Goodman and A. Tuck (eds.), *War and Border Societies in the Middle Ages* (London and New York, 1992), 30–64. See also in this volume J. Reed, 'The ballad and the source: some literary reflections on *The Battle of Otterburn*', 94–123.

47 D. Buchan, *The Ballad and the Folk* (London 1972; repr. East Linton 1997). For a sympathetic critique, see H. Henderson, 'The Ballad, the Folk and the Oral Tradition', *The People's Past*, 65–101.

48 Cheesman and Rieuwerts, *Ballads into Books*.

49 *The Greig-Duncan Folk Song Collection*, ed. P. Shuldham-Shaw and E. Lyle (7 vols., Aberdeen and Edinburgh, 1981–95). One more volume of this incomparable collection is forthcoming. See also A. Keith (ed.), *Last Leaves of Traditional Ballads and Ballad Airs collected in Aberdeenshire by the late Gavin Greig* (Aberdeen 1925), an engrossing work of much sense which can be seen as a last-ditch attempt to wrestle control of Scottish ballad scholarship from the Child school.

50 A. Bold, *The Ballads* (London 1979), 58, 62.

51 A. L. Lloyd, *Folk Song in England* (London 1967; repr. St Albans 1975), 129.

52 '... a history of constant repetition, ever-recurring cycles ... the slow unfolding of structural realities ... in the perspective of the very long term': F. Braudel, *The Mediterranean World in the Age of Philip II* (2 vols., London 1972), i, 20, 23.

53 E. J. Cowan, 'Burns and superstition', in K. Simpson (ed.), *Love and Liberty. Robert Burns: A Bicentenary Celebration* (East Linton 1997), 229–38.

54 H. Henderson, 'The ballad and popular tradition to 1660', in R. D. S. Jack (ed.), *The History of Scottish Literature*, vol. I: *Origins to 1660 (Medieval and Renaissance)* (Aberdeen 1988) 264–5.

55 The Glasgow-Strathclyde Chapbook Project is now underway. Its first task is to establish a catalogue of existing chapbooks, something which has never been done. It is hoped that some of this material will be available on a website in the course of 2000.

56 Henderson, 'Ballad, Folk and Oral Tradition', 99–100.

2

Fixing Tradition: Making History
from Ballad Texts

CHARLES DUFFIN

As the idea behind this collection of essays is to celebrate one of the great ballad collectors, this seemed like a good opportunity to examine the relationship between song collectors and the material that they gather. Given that the main focus is directed towards early collectors who were processing traditional songs in order to produce 'modern' texts for an emerging mass literary audience, it is perhaps inevitable that what follows is, to a limited extent, a history of ballads as texts. The authority of such a history does not rest on a literary perspective alone, but demands an understanding of the kind of oral history contained within the ballad text and the nature of the history which flows through the performance of the ballad.

One of the most intriguing aspects of dealing with ballad texts is that, even though they have been removed from their proper context, in the reduction of song to the printed page, what remains is still a powerful cultural product. As a written or printed text it is evidently some kind of literary product but it is not clear to what extent that product derives its cultural potency from a literary process because, as a text, it is a frozen form of an evanescent, oral tradition.

> The expression 'oral tradition' applies both to a process and to its products. The products are oral messages based on previous oral messages, at least a generation old. The process is the transmission of such messages by mouth over time until the disappearance of the message. Hence any given oral tradition is but a rendering at one moment, an element in a process of oral development that began with the original communication. The characteristics of each rendering will differ according to its position in the whole process.[1]

The performance contains both the oral process and the history of oral process and the product is tradition, a social product which cannot be condensed into print. What can be said is that the ballad text gives a kind of substance to that process which can help make tradition comprehensible to a literary culture although revitalising the oral process through texts alone will always have its limitations.

An oral ballad is a unique creation in performance which depends on both performer's and audience's shared conception of the message contained in the ballad and of the history of that message, through which the culturally significant past is ushered into the present. If we try to raise an interpretation of this message from an exclusively literary perspective we are re-creating something which is other than a ballad and denying the complexity of the oral process from which the text is derived.

It would be convenient to a literary interpretation of this process if we were able to consider a ballad text as the final embodiment of a series of lost historical documents passed along an unbroken chain of oral transmission and interpretation but, as with other forms of oral tradition, there is no single line of transmission through which a ballad can be traced. The performer is heard by the audience, and the ballad, along with the historical message it contains, is repeated by others to a different audience who have not witnessed the original performance. They, in turn, pass it on and down through the tradition. What is remarkable about this process is the degree of stability which can attach to the historical message as it works through this complex generational matrix.

The ballad is not, however, simply a historical document; any historical message it contains is being processed through an artistic medium. On the face of it, the stability of the message would suggest a trenchant artistic conservatism in the oral process but this is not borne out by the rich textual differences that we find in related ballad versions. If the historical message remains stable, then the ways of relating that message appear to be diverse in the extreme. The critical control of the message, however, lies with the traditional audience – they are not simply auditors, but authorisers, of the message and whatever individual artistic skills the performer demonstrates are, above all, subject to that critical authority.[2]

> Just as the story of the Fall of Troy and the other Greek epic legends were not themselves the original fictions of certain authors, but creations of a whole people passed through one generation to another and gladly given to anyone who wished to tell them, so the style in which they were to be told was not a matter of individual creation, but a popular tradition, evolved by centuries of poets and audiences, which the composer of heroic verse might follow without thought of plagiarism, and indeed without knowledge that such a

thing existed. This does not mean that personal talent had no effect on style, nothing to do with the choice and use of the medium whereby an author undertook to express his ideas: Aristotle points out Homer's superiority to other writers of early epic verse in the organisation of his material. It does mean, though, that there were certain established limits of form to which the play of genius must confine itself.[3]

Milman Parry's observations on the Greek oral epic can be fairly applied to any artistic oral tradition. In an oral culture, where human memory is the only means of storing and retrieving information, any message has to be memorable to ensure its survival. To be memorable, it has to have some current significance which means it must accommodate and reflect social change. In order to fully appreciate the artistic expression of the ballad, the audience must be familiar with that message. Familiarity allows the audience freedom to contemplate innovations in the telling of the tale while anticipating, with certainty, the events to come. The audience demands a predictable, but not a static, world. This predictability also allows the artist to demonstrate creative originality in conveying the information; a process through which the historical message is re-interpreted for, and by, a contemporary audience, guaranteeing its continued significance. The history contained in the oral ballad is a history of the contemporary situation in relation to the message, as well as a history of the events that the message describes. That being the case, to what extent is the object of that message historical?

If we look for objective historical 'truths' in the ballad texts we are likely more often than not to be disappointed, but we could expect to find the kind of culture-bound 'truths' that emphasise group consciousness and cement the worldview of a traditional, oral community. This seems to be particularly relevant to the ballads where there is a high degree of artistry involved in transmission. Contemporary oral historians, like Vansina, have concluded that the more artistic any narrative form is, the less likely it is to reflect a reliable succession of events or an accurate rendering of an actual historical situation.

This leaves the problem of how to contextualise the historical information that ballads contain and, in the absence of a living oral tradition, it is the ballad text that is our primary resource. By examining a text we can look not only at the information itself but at the way in which that information is presented. By studying the structures and language that ballad singers used we can hope to gain some insight into the modes of expression and reception through which tradition imparts meaning to the historical message.

Oral societies verbalise their shared sense of reality in recurrent formu-
laic clusters like those commonplace phrases that infest and characterise
the ballad language. Ballads, in common with other complex forms of oral
verse making, utilise a subtle array of organising principles that are
recognised by an orally attuned audience.[4] These may be overtly struc-
tural forms of narrative and stanzaic organisation, or they may appear as
discrete messages which contextualise and enhance the value of narrative
information to an informed oral audience. This value-laden information is
amalgamated into the narrative body and helps contextualise action and
events for an educated ballad audience.

Ubiquitous, variable, commonplace phrases tend to be characterised in
a literary world, which prizes originality, as redundant formulas or
clichés. Fused together in an oral narrative they are the essence of
tradition. The manner in which they are disposed in relation to one
another allows the artist creative freedom and the audience to extract
valuable conceptual information which accrues to the narrative through
each unique performance.

> 'O is my biggins broken, boy?
> or is my towers won?
> Or is my lady lighter yet
> Of a dear daughter or son?'
> 'Your biggin is na broken, sir,
> Nor is your towers won;
> But the fairest lady in a' the lan
> For you this day maun burn.'
>
> 'O saddle me the black, the black,
> Or saddle me the brown;
> O saddle me the swiftest steed
> That ever rade frae a town
> Or he was near a mile awa,
> She heard his wild horse sneeze:
> 'Mend up the fire, my false brother,
> It's na come to my knees.'

This extract from 'Lady Maisry' [65A], which shows how the narrative
function of the 'saddle' formula – to signify a transitional move from one
scene to another – also provides a means by which the audience can draw
further information by relating the sense of urgency in the ballad actor's
response, which is built up through the incremental dynamic of this
formula, to the events described in the preceding formulaic stanza. That
stanza is itself a formulaic response to a 'question' formula and the

culmination of a formulaic narrative process which contextualises future action and events as they are revealed in the final stanza of this cluster. These same formulas used in another ballad, or another ballad version, might carry similar conceptual messages but, differently disposed, they create new layers of meaning and interpretation for both artist and audience.

The absence of written sources poses particular problems in recalling knowledge for non-literate societies. There is nothing outside the individual to verify accuracy of recall except another individual – recollection is communication in oral society. The oral culture is sound driven and the dynamic of sound shapes oral thought and expression in distinctive ways. The only method of recalling and retaining thought in oral societies is to shape it in mnemonic patterns which lend themselves to oral retrieval. Rhythmically balanced, conceptually loaded, phrases and expressions are fused together, through a process described by Albert Lord as a tension of essences, to create a thematic setting which informs and contextualises the narrative and the history it contains.[5] Formulas make up the complex, intellectual organisation systems of the oral world and those forms of thought and expression that we find in ballad texts display distinctive formulary characteristics.

Even where the effects of literary encroachment reveal texts to be transitional, these characteristics are pockmarks of authenticity which underwrite the origins of the ballad in the oral tradition. So, when we come to interpret information from ballad texts, it is more than useful to be aware of these processes because that allows for a literary interpretation which can, to some extent, draw a distinction between the apparent or literal meaning of the text and its intended meaning for an educated oral audience.

Formulas are not only, as David Buchan has shown, functional in terms of form and structure but also essential to the aesthetic relationship between the oral performer and the traditional audience.[6] Parry, in his study of the Homeric texts, demonstrates how, so called, 'redundant' phrases in oral tradition are repositories of common sensibility which carry discrete conceptual messages between audience and performer. Their disposition in performance is crucial to the relationship of situation to events in the narrative, and this ultimately appears as the defining relationship in any contextualisation of history in the ballad tradition.

The blend of consciousness which enables the artist to present the same information in a unique way each time it is performed to an audience that is simultaneously interpreting the information critically, is the consequence of a mutually comprehensible formulaic discourse which lies at the heart of tradition. Through that formulaic discourse, history is re-established for an oral culture each time the ballad is performed. The history contained in the oral ballad is a vital history.

Ballad texts are, as we noted earlier, a literary product and if we are to usefully reconstruct the oral process from texts we should also be aware of the literary process as it affects the translation and the historical interpretation of the oral ballad. The central question for those who are trying to understand tradition through texts is that of authenticity. What is an authentic ballad text? For a literary culture that question coalesces around mediation.

The importance of the publication of *A Collection of Comic and Serious Scots Poems* in 1706 lay not so much in the editor and printer James Watson's choice of materials, which were largely sourced from readily available broadside versions rather than the folk tradition, as in his recognition that there was a literary market for popular verse in Scots.[7] The work may have been prompted by his own nationalist agenda but that was allied to a sound commercial sensibility which was shared by Allan Ramsay and accounted, in no small measure, for the latter's success as a popular cultural figure. Ramsay was the first mediator to deal exclusively in Scottish song, although he confined his interest mainly to popular songs. Ramsay's successful mediation of these works for a popular literary audience excited a general interest in collecting from traditional sources and this was to have a profound influence in the mediation of ballads as they were received into the literary culture.

Ramsay's detractors rely on his inaccuracies and interpolations to fuel their accusation that he is an unreliable mediator, but they generally base this on criteria of authenticity that were not an issue in his own day. Ramsay viewed the popular oral tradition as a genuine cultural contender. His song collections may have been aimed at an emerging urban literary audience but his own roots were in a rural community where traditional song still held its own against encroaching literary products. Whatever Ramsay's sins as a collector it is difficult to sift through his original literary work without disturbing the spirit of tradition. Ramsay was a creative collector who revitalised the popular tradition by translating it for a popular and modern literary audience. That audience was part of a new literate and commercial class but for many, like Ramsay, only one generation removed from traditional agrarian communities, the rhythms and accents of tradition provided some psychological cushion against the demanding and exclusive sophistication of the neo-classical literary prospectus. For Ramsay, the critical imperative was the commercial judgement of a popular audience and it was to the demands of that judgement that the material was tailored. Ramsay was building on Watson's foundations with his collections of Scottish traditional material, but he was doing so in an artistic as well as a commercial sense. Ramsay's mediation was not authentic in an antiquarian sense, but it shared with tradition a democratic regard for audience sensibility and it envisaged a genuine role for tradition in the literary consciousness.

Kinghorn and Law claim that with the publication of *Evergreen* in 1723: 'Ramsay's chief aim was to furnish his contemporaries with a readable text'. In confirming his success they point out that, with the exception of those mistakes which arose from his ignorance of Middle Scots, he was a relatively faithful transcriber.[8] Working from various literary sources, including the Bannatyne manuscript, Ramsay delivered a more considered and faithful representation of older Scots poetry than Watson. He was not, however, driven, by the antiquarian impulse so much as the popular demand for a modern text that was actually readable to the contemporary audience: an audience identified by the success of the *Choice Collection*. Kinghorn and Law have argued that the *Evergreen* was a 'preservative work'.[9] While that may, incidentally, hold true, there is evidence that preservation was not the sole concern in Ramsay's mind. This is most clearly illustrated by the deliberate plant of his own composition, *The Vision*, in a collection that purported to be *written by the ingenious before 1600*, and in this case specifically dated by the introductory remark: '*Compylit in Latin be a most lernit Clerk * in Tyme of our Hairship and Oppression, anno 1300, and translaitit in 1524*'.[10]

On the face of it, this work is a less than remarkable attempt by Ramsay to mimic the style and form of medieval Scots poetry but, as with many of Ramsay's re-creative works, it is his strategic intention that is noteworthy. Re-creating the dream allegory for its own sake would be an amusing, if essentially worthless, occupation for Ramsay as a poet. It is the vital connection he makes between the synthetic allegory and a contemporary set of political circumstances which revives the spirit of the past through its relevance to the historical perspective of a contemporary audience. Deliberate deception is an essential element in the process of manipulating a contemporary sensibility so as to engage it with the spirit of the older Scots poetry which Ramsay, for commercial, political and historical reasons, is trying to promote.

With the publication of his song collections, *Scots Songs* in 1718 and his *Tea-Table Miscellany* in 1723, he was addressing a broadly based, modern market for Scots songs and was making no attempt to consider the authenticating procedures that he would later be criticised for failing to observe. Ramsay was involved in a re-creative process geared towards a popular audience. Where later antiquarian critics insisted on a fixed and 'accurate' text, which allowed them to disempower traditional culture by historicising the texts through their connection with older Scots language, Ramsay viewed Scots as a vital and contemporary vehicle that was adaptable and culturally significant – a position that was fundamentally undermined by the linguistic prospectus of the Enlightenment.

Adam Smith's main focus on literature fixed on English texts as models of language. He recognised a value in approved 'authentic' Scots poetry among which he included 'Hardyknute' and the recent translations of Ossianic 'Erse' poetry, despite the fact that these were works of creative deception. These works co-exist, canonically, according to Smith's programme, with 'The Cherry and the Slae' and 'Wallace Wight'. Blair would later try to broaden this canon by advocating a value to popular works in Scots like Ramsay's 'Gentle Shepherd'. Cultural value, however, is strictly contextualised by the random nature of Smith's historicisation of any work in Scots. There is an implied obsolescence, noted by Crawford in *Devolving English Literature*,[11] in the phrase 'old Scots Language', with which Smith qualifies his attention to these works; more significant, perhaps, is the way in which Smith consigns them, via that qualification, to a rudimentary stage of cultural activity where 'Poetry is cultivated in the most Rude and Barbarous nations, often to a considerable perfection ...'[12] Ramsay's strategy is less distanced from the aesthetic priorities of a traditional audience than it is from a post-antiquarian literary critique. Ramsay's re-creative approach was, however, something quite other than traditional. He was re-creating the traditional format as popular song by writing new, as well as editing old, texts attuned to the aesthetic priorities of a popular literary audience. The accents of tradition that we find in Ramsay's work highlight the poet's identification with the spirit, rather than the letter, of the ancient poetry and song. They also imply a recognition of his audience's psychological dependency on the materials of tradition, albeit modernised to suit their contemporary cultural priorities and aspirations. Ramsay's achievement, however, is even today undermined by a failure to fully understand the competing aesthetic priorities in a transitional culture.

As with *Evergreen*, *Tea-Table Miscellany* provided for a need and filled an emotional gap in the make-up of the educated Scot in London as well as in Edinburgh. Unfortunately for his reputation among genuine antiquarians like Hailes and Herd, he failed to recognise the long-term results of his purging and pruning to suit contemporary tastes.[13]

This conclusion reinforces every prejudice that those 'genuine antiquarians' ever generated. Ramsay met an emotional need for his culture as a whole, testified by the popularity of the work which ran to twenty-four editions in the course of the century. His, so called, failure in adapting the materials of tradition to a contemporary aesthetic was a genuine attempt to re-invest traditional oral culture with contemporary relevance for a literary culture. The long-term results of his 'purging and pruning' were visible through the works of Fergusson and Burns and the continuing effort to revitalise Scottish culture through the vernacular. Ramsay was not an antiquarian; he was a popular poet and adaptor who respected the priorities of a contemporary literary culture and recognised the potential for change in tradition through an evolution of the popular aesthetic.

The publication of David Herd's *Ancient and Modern Scottish Songs* in 1769 marks a significant step in the translation of traditional materials for a Scottish literary audience. Herd's own observation, in the Preface of the first edition of his collection, throws light on his relationship to Ramsay through an attempt to distance himself from the *Tea-Table Miscellany*. He claims:

> The only collection upon our plan consisting entirely of Scots songs, is the *Orpheus Caledonius*, Published by William Thomson in 1733, but this is confined to a small number, with the music, and now become very scarce; for Allan Ramsay's *Tea-Table Miscellany* cannot be termed *A complete Collection of Scots Songs*; they are, as he himself entitles them, *a Choice Collection of Scots and English*.[14]

This backhanded slight of Ramsay's work fails to recognise the debt which Thomson's own volume owed to the *Tea-Table Miscellany* but it also highlights aspects of contextualisation which were not so significant for Ramsay. Thomson's work is raised above its own sources because it consists 'entirely' of Scottish material and Ramsay's work is relegated because it is not a 'complete' collection. Two critical criteria have emerged in the forty-five years that separate Herd's and Ramsay's editions of popular Scots song: firstly, that the work should consist of exclusively Scottish material; and, secondly, an expressed desire to include as much of that material as can be had. The element of editorial 'choice' has been critically undermined here in favour of comprehensiveness.

To account for this critical shift we have to note the influence of English anthologists like Ambrose Philips and Bishop Percy. Ian Haywood notes that these 'anthologists' were interested in 'the transmission of the past through oral poetry', and collected traditional 'poems' for their historical value, but they were not interested in the oral process of transmission.[15] They relied on anonymity of authorship and confused chronology to re-construct tradition in a literary light. Percy, in particular, utilised the growing authority of the manuscript in contemporary historiography to present ballad texts as units of actual historical knowledge. As manuscript sources came to be increasingly regarded as an empirical measure of history notions of traditional authenticity became centred on the manuscript. Percy could work this to his advantage while no one questioned his sources but, as the power of the manuscript as historical source became accepted, a developing concern over the authenticity of manuscript sources emerged.

Joseph Ritson, a dyspeptic vegetarian with a taste for Bishops' blood, hounded Percy relentlessly over the authenticity of his collections. Percy's refusal to allow proper access to his manuscript sources left him vulnerable to the charge that he was a dishonest editor who tampered with his sources and consequently with historical 'truth'.

The accumulation and preservation of the noetic materials of an oral culture in printed textual form make it possible to analyse that stock in specific ways. Ritson's approach to the historical analysis was categorical and conservative. The materials of the past were to be preserved in the 'authentic' state from which their cultural value was drawn. Ritson argued for a moral form of mediation which, on the face of it, was designed to secure respect for traditional materials by encouraging collectors to present those materials exactly as they were found in manuscript form or, perhaps more importantly, as they were delivered from performance in a traditional context. Ritson's approach relied on a literary sense of authority which excluded oral tradition from the process of creativity. There are two additional critical factors here. The first is that Ritson's moral prospectus was founded on a neo-classical sensibility which coloured his notion of what was and was not authentic tradition. This manifested itself in a preference for supposedly authentic ballad versions that assumed a literary polish. The second factor is that Ritson was no less keen to secure a literary reputation than Percy. There was a tremendous market for these materials in printed form and one method of reinforcing the authenticity, and subsequent marketability, of your own product was to accuse rivals of falsehood.

This battle reflected a broader search for a means of authenticating the past which had its origins in historiographical concerns about the relationship between history and fiction. This eventually resolved around a Humean notion of feeling. Authentication became a matter for the educated reader who, it was assumed, could discern authenticity on an instinctive level and so convey legitimate authority to the text.

If we briefly remind ourselves here that, in the oral tradition, authorisation of the historical message is a shared responsibility between performer and audience, we can recognise a fundamental shift not only in the aesthetic conception of the ballad but also in the attitude towards the history it contains – now authorised by the educated reader. The driving force behind that change in Scotland is the underlying desire, implied by Herd's preface, for a view of traditional history that bolstered the discerning reader's sense of national identity. There is a tendency to assume that Herd's editorial indifference signifies an absence of ideology, but the 'mild nationalism' which underpinned the work fronts an analytical perspective that fundamentally altered the creative and interactive literary approach to tradition in Scotland, personified by Ramsay. Herd claims that:

> Every nation, at least every ancient and unmixed nation, hath its peculiar style of musical expression, its peculiar mode of melody; modulated by the joint influence of climate and government, character and situation, as well as by the formation of the organs.[16]

The critical differentiation between Herd's and Ramsay's approach is marked here in the contextualisation of history. For Ramsay, history in song is a vital cultural store to which the poet has legitimate creative access. For Herd, history is an analytical measure of progress underwritten by the consuming ideologies of the Enlightenment.

Attempts to identify an emerging conception of national identity through indigenous sources had to constantly engage not only with the difficulties of authenticity (the true age and validity of texts) but also with the relationship between history and fiction that were found in traditional materials. The obvious course was to displace those materials and the anomalies they contained into a reconstructed past. The traditional ballad, viewed at this historical remove, becomes something quite other than a ballad. It begins the transition from the vital fluidity which Ramsay both recognised and utilised creatively to the mordant functionality which the literary ballad, viewed as a historical unit, displays.

This 'authorised' literary culture did not directly address tradition on its own terms but filtered the material of tradition through a conversation about the past.[17]

Once tradition was consigned to the museum it could be analysed by the literati, self-appointed curators of the cultural imagination. Under the scrutiny of that authority, the traditional corpse could be worked into a mythical clay from which the dreams of the cultural movers and shakers of the day might be realised. Appropriation of tradition in eighteenth-century Scotland meant that the literary language of Romance was designed to be an exclusive discourse which, although it drew on the materials of oral tradition as an imaginative resource, refused to admit the critical priorities that had sustained those materials and so denied the popular audience a vital role in the contemporary literary culture. The arrival of 'authorised' literary notions of authenticity on the cultural agenda signalled an eclipse of the popular aesthetic which is critical to the traditional process. The transfer of authority from the oral audience to the 'educated' literary reader made it impossible for that relationship to reflect the dynamic of oral history contained in the formulaic discourse of the ballad. Nationalist determination, allied to a spirit of literary invention, allowed the literary culture to redefine the relationship between history and fiction in such a way as to produce the desired outcome – a supplementary history of customs and manners which could override what they viewed as factual anomalies.

The vehicle of this transformation was Macpherson's adoption of the bardic voice. This represents a completely new approach to literary creativity as it applies to oral tradition. Where Ramsay utilised the verbal, syntactic and ideological possibilities of tradition to make discrete, synthetic commentaries on history, Macpherson 'imaginatively recreated oral culture from the inside'.[18] The bardic voice was the voice of 'authorised' tradition.

The literary figures of the Scottish Enlightenment did not invent the figure of the bard but they seized on the notion of the bard as community historian and the original 'author' of national history. The collusion between the Scottish literary establishment, most notably Hugh Blair and James Macpherson the creator of Ossian, to remodel tradition in their own image and likeness was a remarkable literary event. Blair, with the support of his peers, prescribed the theory from which Macpherson conjured virtual history from the mouth of a virtual bard. The creative complex which emerges from the relationship between the preface and the text of the *Fragments of Ancient Poetry, Collected in the Highlands of Scotland, and translated from the Gaelic or Erse language in 1760* reduces, essentially, to a pair of mutually regenerative factors: Macpherson's capacity for deception in the interest of creativity, and Blair, in his role as spokesman for the literati, for self-delusion in the interests of cultural wish-fulfilment. Contemporary anxieties about the inherent dangers of this combination are contained by the desire to believe in the existence of a genuine, national, epic poetry and are reflected in the urgent tone of Hume's communication with Blair about the growing scepticism concerning the origin of the *Works of Ossian*:

> It is in vain to say that their beauty will support them, indepen-
> dent of their authenticity: No; that beauty is not so much to
> the general taste, as to insure you of this event; and if people
> be once disgusted with the idea of a forgery, they are thence
> apt to entertain a more disadvantageous notion of the
> excellency of the production itself. The absurd pride and
> caprice of Macpherson himself, who scorns, as he pretends,
> to satisfy anybody who doubts his veracity, has tended much
> to confirm this general skepticism; and I must own, for my
> own part, that though I have had many particular reasons to
> believe these poems genuine, more than it is possible for any
> Englishman of letters to have, yet I am not entirely without
> my scruples on that head.[19]

Hume goes on to question the internal evidence of the poetry which Blair finds so convincing, and urges him to set about an independent authentication of sources. That Blair made some attempt to do so might indicate that he addressed these concerns once they had been raised. Without his initial willingness to accept Macpherson's work at face value, however, the shared process of wish-fulfilment focused on the notion, to which Hume implicitly subscribes, that 'the ancient poetry of Scotland *ought* to have been epic' could never have been realised.[20] In order to sustain the faith in a national epic a sense of a continuous sensibility had to be underwritten by history, literature and reason. The myth of progress had to be encoded here in order to satisfy reason, or at least dazzle it. In drawing attention to the superstition that both characterised a bygone era and was consistent with empirical studies of contemporary primitive societies, Macpherson maintained continuity while establishing a sense of difference. That continuity consists in the establishment of a tradition of cultural class. The druids are characterised by Macpherson as the 'ancient' arbiters of a primitive sensibility. The difference, Macpherson implies, is that his age is above all that – it is a scientific, empirical age and they, the literati, were the rightful heirs of the cultural mantle. Continuity, for the literati, consisted in the smooth transition of power through history from one cultural élite to another.

But the facilitator of that transition is the bard whose genius, long after the Druids have died out, continues to refine the primitive sensibility to the point where the eighteenth-century 'man of feeling' recognises his inheritance in the moral, ethical and aesthetic manners of contemporary 'virtue'. Through the virtual bard, whose literary programme had been validated by the existing cultural authorities in order to allow them to impose their own values on tradition, Macpherson creates the mythology of a cultivated class which distinguished the Caledonian Celts and explained the origins and identity of the literati to themselves.

The process of tradition where aesthetic arbitration consists in the immediate relationship between the performer, audience and the tale to be told is subverted and invested with self-fulfilling, literary values which support the notion of a 'natural' cultural hierarchy and reinforce the neo-classical worldview of the emerging élite. Blinded, by the separation of good faith and reason, to any paradox in their own literary methods of making history they could hardly be expected to consider a further paradox.

The ballads, by association with this new model of tradition, had undergone a complete transformation from a communally arbitrated traditional product into the individual products of a community historian – the bard. As such they were confirmed as empirical units of history albeit of a different kind to the military and political histories that were already available to the literary culture. The vital history of a contemporary oral culture was distilled into virtual history at the convenience of a literary culture undergoing an identity crisis.

This virtual history of customs and manners provided a framework for Walter Scott's *Minstrelsy of the Scottish Border*, which was held together by the editor's sense of identification with the central authenticating device – the bard Scott, perhaps the ultimate educated reader of his day, not only authenticated the text instinctively but, as a modern day bard, he assumed control of that text moving through interpolation, as a means of improving existing texts, to imitation as exemplifications of what ballads might become when sifted through the literary process. Scott's sense of literary identity depended on fixing the materials of tradition, and the evanescent nature of the oral tradition terrified him.

The ballads had to be originally the work of bards – a special class of artist because, as Scott claims in his *Introductory Remarks on Popular Poetry*: 'the qualities necessary for composing such poems are not the portion of every man in the tribe'.[21] He goes on to describe those bardic qualities in highly individualistic terms and the typical ballad maker he describes is essentially himself. That these ballads were the work of the bards is evidenced, for Scott, by their corruption:

> The more popular the composition of an ancient poet ... the
> greater chance there was of its being corrupted; for a poem
> transmitted through a number of reciters, like a book

reprinted in a multitude of editions, incurs the risk of impertinent interpolations from the conceit of one rehearser, unintelligible blunders from the stupidity of another, and omissions equally to be regretted, from the want of memory in a third.[22]

This catalogue of incremental decay was absolutely vital to Scott's sense of identity because it allowed him, as educated reader, to intervene and redeem those texts not as an oral blunderer but as the true literary heir of the bard – the self-appointed, skilful critic whose ingenuity could revive and restore the original meaning, so re-constructing the original history.

The adoption of this stance confirmed the autocratic sensibility of the literary culture and denied outright the role of the popular oral culture in mediating its own historical materials. Tradition had to be fixed to make it comprehensible to a literary culture that was in the process of dreaming up its own history. It could not be allowed to compete because the natural democracy implied by the oral aesthetic had no place in that dream.

NOTES

1 J. Vansina, *Oral Tradition as History* (Wisconsin 1985), 3.
2 E. Muir, *Scott and Scotland* (London 1936), 87–90. Central to Muir's critique of Scottish Literature is his notion that, '... there can be no dramatic poetry except in a language where the poet can both think and feel, and the ballads bear out this contention; for they are almost the only Scottish dialect poetry extant in which the poet both thinks and feels in the dialect he uses. Scottish folk-song is pure feeling.' He argues, elsewhere, that the absence of a critical response in that same language or dialect is symptomatic of a national literature's failure to cohere. It is worth pointing out here that the critical role of the ballad audience contributes as much to the coherence of the ballad as 'the pure feeling' of the poet upon which Muir's argument depends here.
3 M. Parry, *The Making of Homeric Verse* (Oxford 1971), 421. Parry demonstrates further his support of the notion of creative individualism of the oral poets with the tradition at their disposal through his comment that, '... it required a great poet to turn it into great poetry'. This is only realised when 'the genius of the artist has blended with that of his race so inextricably that the two are hard to distinguish: they can only be realised in the perfection of the result', 431.
4 S. Wittig, *Stylistic and Narrative Structures in the Middle English Romance* (Austin 1978), 43. Wittig, perhaps, carries this argument one stage too far by claiming that formulaic structure results in an audience's ability to accurately predict the next formulaic phrase. This is unfortunate because it detracts from the essential part of her case that formulaic phrases, in orally conceived poetry and song, are the building blocks of a predictable world. That world is predictable not because the audience forecasts the next formulaic phrase but because it is familiar with all the materials of construction and it knows not what comes next so much as how each succeeding phrase relates to the construction. Just as a layman is familiar enough with building materials to know that glass is, generally, an inappropriate material

for a floor, the traditional audience will expect and admire creative disposition of formulas but only as they are appropriate to the overall architecture of the work.

5 A. B. Lord, *The Singer of Tales* (London 1960), 98. Lord's phrase, 'tension of essences', although it focuses more directly on the internal relationships of formulaic language, can be seen as a development of the creative equation that Parry describes when he discusses the fusing of consciousness between the artist and his audience. Together they describe the process through which a communal agreement is reached on the relationship between the historical events described in the narrative and the contemporary situation as it relates to those events.

6 D. Buchan, *The Ballad and the Folk* (London 1972), 171–3.

7 It is worth noting the possibility that Watson himself may have had relatively little to do with the choice of materials, and there is some evidence to suggest that the advocate James Spottiswoode and the Jacobite antiquarian Archibald Pitcairne may have influenced the content. The first volume of Watson's collection consisted largely of older poems in Scots by literary authors such as Dunbar and Henryson which had already been circulating in broadside editions in the intervening period, as well as popular works like *Christ's Kirk*. Volumes 2 and 3 relied more heavily on 17th-century poems which reflected a trend towards anglicisation in the wake of the Union of the Crowns, and he included works in almost standard English. There were also some popular works gleaned from commonplace books and family albums. For a full analysis of content and sources, see *James Watson's Choice Collection of Comic and Serious Scots Poems*, ed. H. H. Wood (2 vols., Scottish Text Soc., 1977, 1991), ii, pp. xviii–xix.

8 *The Works of Allan Ramsay*, ed. A. M. Kinghorn and A. Law (4 vols., Edinburgh 1961–74), iv, 128.

9 Ibid., 138.

10 Allan Ramsay, *Evergreen* (Edinburgh 1723): title page, and 211.

11 R. Crawford, *Devolving English Literature* (Oxford 1992), 32.

12 Adam Smith, *Lectures on Rhetoric and Belles Lettres*, ed. J. C. Bryce and A. S. Skinner (Oxford 1983), 137, lecture 23.

13 *Works of Allan Ramsay*, iv, 140.

14 David Herd, 'Preface' to *Ancient and Modern Scottish Songs* (Edinburgh, 1769).

15 I. Haywood, *The Making of History* (London 1986), ch. 4.

16 Herd, 'Preface' to *Ancient and Modern Scottish Songs*.

17 J. L. Greenway, 'Macpherson's Ossian and the Nordic Bard as Myth', in H. Bloom (ed.), *Poets of Sensibility and the Sublime* (New York 1986), 251–2. Greenway, in noting Herder's remarks on Kretschmann's 'bardic' creativity, to the effect that his works were not *Volkspoesie* but *about Volkspoesie*, touches upon an interpretation of sentimental primitivism which illustrates the inherent flaw in the creative strategy: 'Even though myth's truths are not primarily validated by reason, a modern myth must maintain a factual superstructure to complement that part of it which operates extra-rationally. This requirement implies a separation of Faith and Reason which, in fact, worked to render the bardic myth inexpressive.' When this is taken in context with his observation that 'the mythic world given symbolic form by Ossian ... was for a time more real to the general perception of the age than historical fact'. We can perhaps begin to understand the cultural climate in terms of that temporary separation of 'Faith and Reason' – a manifestation of the cultural capacity for self-delusion which made the Ossianic deception possible. This is particularly the case where, as will be argued below, the cultural authorities are largely responsible for the creative strategy.

18 Greenway, 'Macpherson's Ossian', 251–2.

19 David Hume, Letter to Hugh Blair, 19 Sep. 1763 in *Report of the Committee of the Highland Society of Scotland* (Edinburgh 1805), 5.

20 F. J. Stafford, *The Sublime Savage* (Edinburgh 1991), 97. Stafford widens the list of subscribers to this notion where she notes that, 'The men who had first encouraged Macpherson to translate his Gaelic verse were in the forefront of a general drive to improve Scottish arts. John Home's controversial tragedy, *Douglas* (1757) proclaimed the importance of Athenian "learning and the love of every art", and drew a direct parallel between Greece and Scotland. This admiration for the multi-faceted genius of Athens was shared by David Hume and other members of the Select Society who were all keen to promote improvements, both practical and cultural' (p. 114). The literati were, it seems, intellectually and politically drunk on the idea of a Scottish Homer who could reinforce the neo-classical civic and martial virtues which lay behind the cultural agenda. See J. Dwyer, 'The melancholy savage', in H. Gaskill (ed.), *Ossian Revisited* (Edinburgh 1991), 176–7; see also R. Sher, '"Those Scotch Impostors and Their Cabal": Ossian and the Scottish Enlightenment', in R. L. Emerson and others (eds.), *Man and Nature: Proceedings of the Canadian Society for Eighteenth Century Studies*, 1 (London, Ontario, 1982), 55–63.

21 Walter Scott, *Minstrelsy of the Scottish Border*, rev. and ed. T. F. Henderson (Edinburgh 1902), 3.

22 Ibid., 9–10.

3

Just How Was the Bonny Earl of Moray Killed?
[Child 181 A and B]

IAN A. OLSON

Although this paper will consider the Child ballad 'The Bonny Earl of Murray' [181] *in* Scottish History, it is perhaps also pertinent to consider the question of this 'famous and misleading ballad'[1] (or, indeed, any other ballad) *as* Scottish History.

Child himself was cheerfully dismissive of any attempt to use his ballad corpus as reliable historical evidence: 'To tell the truth I like to have the ballads quite in the air. It is the next best thing to their flying in the face of all history.'[2] This view – that the ballads, *especially* the historical ballads are not to be taken seriously – was vigorously challenged by the late David Buchan in his analysis of 'The Battle of Harlaw'[163]:

> The historical ballads, we would all agree, are no 'documents', but the evidence just presented would indicate that they can be nearer to the truth than is normally realised. They can contain factual truths that are not found in the often scanty records, and they can contain emotional truths, the attitudes and reactions of the ballad-singing folk to the world around them.[3]

Buchan also emphasised that although a ballad account might not always be *true* in the strictest sense of the word, it was capable of presenting a far wider picture:

> ... the researcher has to be sensitive to the existence of traditional motifs, episodic incidents, characters, and in general the pull of traditional narrative patterns and their possible utilisation in any fictional heightening. The ballads are not written documents; they are instruments within culture, and a major cultural function, especially in a non-literate society, as the North East was essentially until the late eighteenth century, was to educate. These ballads educated their listeners by portraying the political history of the region through

stories involving representation of the regional group (and their adversaries from extra-regional groups) and of various subgroups within the region.

With regard to this present paper it is interesting to note that Buchan also prefaced these comments with a statement that, in the case of 'The Bonny Earl of Murray', the documentary sources were 'reliable in this instance'.[4]

The ballad

'The Bonny Earl of Murray' [Child 181] is one of the most poignant of Scottish ballads, still sung throughout the land in classroom and concert-hall, and still on the lips of the general population. To be honest, this popular ballad, beloved by both concert performer and revival folk-singer, is a 'sawn-off' version set to a 'dramatic', if rather lugubrious, 1885 Victorian arrangement,[5] for as Goldstein noted, the ballad as such has 'not been reported from tradition in England and Scotland since Child'.[6] The words were collected by Child (and called his 'A' version) from Ramsay's 1750 *Tea-Table Miscellany*[7] (although he did not notice that William Thomson had in fact published both words and music in the second edition of his collection of Scottish Songs, *Orpheus Caledonius*, published in 1733).[8] This 'A' version, which appears to have gained an eighteenth-century opening verse along the way, runs as follows:[9]

1.   Ye Highlands, and ye Lawlands,
        Oh where have you been?
     They have slain the Earl of Murray,
        And they layd him on the green.

2.   'Now wae be to thee, Huntly!
        And wherefore did you sae?
     I bade you bring him wi you,
        But forbade you him to slay.'

3.   He was a braw gallant,
        And he rid at the ring;
     And the bonny Earl of Murray,
        Oh he might have been a king!

4.   He was a braw gallant,
        And he playd at the ba;
     And the bonny Earl of Murray
        Was the flower amang them a'.

5.   He was a braw gallant,
        And he played at the glove;
    And the bonny Earl of Murray,
        Oh he was the Queen's love!

6.   Oh lang will his lady
        Look oer the castle Down,
    Eer she see the Earl of Murray
        Come sounding thro the town!
    Eer she, etc.[10]

The details of the murder, other than that the body was 'laid on the green', are not given, but the ballad appears otherwise to encapsulate the event as recorded by a number of chroniclers, for James Stewart, the second earl of Moray, was indeed killed on the late afternoon of 7 February 1592 at his mother's house at Donnibristle, which lies near the north shore of the Firth of Forth opposite Edinburgh, during an attack by a party of men led by George Gordon, sixth earl of Huntly.[11]

It was the inevitable end to a feud which Moray, the then young Lord Doune, had inherited as a lethal dowry when he not only married into a House with a long-standing feud with the neighbouring earldom of Huntly, but proceeded to escalate it:

> This was a local dispute which, because of the people involved, had a far wider national impact than most; it was begun by Moray, and was fought out on traditional lines by both sides, relying on that most traditional and conservative feature of society, the ties of loyalty and allegiance and, in this case, the breaking of them. The loser was Moray, and the loser paid what was, again, almost the inevitable price.[12]

Child also published a 'B' version of the ballad as though it were completely separate from his 'A' version, and this is something of a puzzle, for John Finlay, from whose *Scottish Historical and Romantic Ballads* (1808) Child had copied this 'B' version, had come to the conclusion that it was *not* a separate version, but part of a single ballad. Finlay's publication was in two volumes: volume one includes a version of 'The Bonny Earl of Murray' virtually identical to the 'A' version Child had taken from Ramsay's 1750 edition; volume two contained the text that Child was later to call his 'B' version. In his notes on this volume two ballad version [later to be called 'B' by Child], Finlay wrote:

> The present ballad, which, as well as the other [in his volume one – later Child's 'A' version], I suspect to be coeval with

the event it celebrates, was taken down from recitation. Owing to the same peculiarities of measure of both, a suspicion arises that they may at one period have been united. It is singular, that they are likewise both of them dramatic in their structure.[13]

William Motherwell, in his 1827 *Minstrelsy*, agreed that Finlay's 'conjectures' were 'not at all unlikely',[14] and Child himself, in an earlier publication of his ballad researches entitled *English and Scottish Ballads* (1859), had indeed taken on board Finlay's comments on 'The Bonny Earl O Murray', for his own note states:

> the second [version he later called his 'B' version], which may perhaps be a part of the same ballad [version he was to call 'A'], was first printed in Finlay's collection.[15]

But when Child finally published his definitive *The English and Scottish Popular Ballads* between 1882 and 1898, his extensive commentary on 'The Bonny Earl of Murray' dealt almost entirely with his 'A' version; in the couple of lines referring to the 'B' version, he either deliberately omitted, or forgot about, Finlay's hypothesis.[16]

The additional verses of the 'B' version had apparently been lost from the repertoires of both popular and traditional singers. Neither Peter Buchan (1790–1854),[17] nor William Christie (c.1778–1849),[18] have other than the shortened ('A') version in their collections and there are no versions of any sort in the early twentieth-century John Ord[19] and Greig-Duncan collections.[20]

In 1931, however, James Madison Carpenter from Harvard collected an almost complete version of 'The Bonny Earl o' Murry' from a Mrs Watson Gray of Fochabers in Aberdeenshire.[21] From this evidence it would seem that the original 'complete' version was as follows (major Gray variations italicised):

1. 'Open the gates,   [Finlay (Child 'B') v1]
        and let him come in;
    He is my brother Huntly,
        he'll do him nae harm.'

2. The gates they were opent, [Finlay (Child 'B') v2]
        they let him come in,
    But fause traitor Huntly,
        he did him great harm.

3. He's ben an' ben,   [Finlay (Child 'B') v3; Gray v1]
        an ben to his bed,
    An with a shairp rapier,
        he stabbed him dead.

4. The lady came down the stair, [Finlay (Child 'B') v4; Gray v2]
        wringing her hands:
    'He has slain the Earl o Murray,
        the flower o Scotland.'

5. But Huntly lap on his horse   [Finlay (Child 'B') v5; Gray v3]
        rade to the king:
    'Ye're welcome hame, Huntly
        and whare hae ye been?

6. Whare hae ye been?   [Finlay (Child B) v6; Gray v4]
        and how hae ye sped?'
    'I've killed the Earl o Murray,
        dead in his bed.'

7. 'Foul fa you, Huntly!   [Finlay (Child 'B') v7; Gray v5]
        An why did ye so?
    You might have taen the Earl o Murray / *I bad ye bring him wie ye,*
        and saved his life too / *but forbad ye him tae slay.*'

8. He was a braw gallant,   [Ramsay (Child 'A') v3; Gray v6]
        And he rid at the ring,
    An the bonny Earl of Murray,
        Oh he might hae been a king!

9. He was a braw gallant, [Ramsay (Child 'A') v5; Gray v8]
        And he played at the ba;
    And the bonny Earl of Murray,
        Was the flower amang them a'.

10. He was a braw gallant, [Ramsay (Child 'A') v5; Gray v7]
        And he played at the glove,
    And the bonny Earl of Murray,
        Oh he was the Queen's love!

11. 'Her bread it's to bake,   [Finlay (Child 'B') v8]
        her yill is to brew;
    My sister's a widow,
        and sair do I rue.'

12. 'Her corn grows ripe,   [Finlay (Child 'B') v9]
     her meadows grow green,
  But in bonny Dinnibristle
    I darena be seen.'

13. O lang will his lady   [Ramsay (Child 'A') v6; Gray v9]
    Look owre the castle Down,
  Ere she see the Earl of Murray
    Come sounding through the town!

The complete ballad as historical evidence

The complete ballad paints the following picture of Moray's murder:

1. Moray is married to Huntly's sister.
2. Huntly's sister, in response to Huntly's arrival and/or his presumed request for admission, admits Huntly to the house (of Donnibristle).
3. Her grounds are that he will commit no treachery, being her brother.
4. Huntly, however, goes to Moray's bed (although no time of day is indicated), and
5. Huntly stabs Moray to death with a sharp rapier.
6. Huntly then rides to the King.
7. The King welcomes Huntly and asks him where he has been and how he has fared.
8. Huntly admits to the killing of Moray in his bed.
9. The King remonstrates with Huntly and
10. The King states he wanted Moray only to be brought in and not killed.
11. Moray is lamented as a 'braw gallant' who 'rade at the ring'.
12. Moray is lamented as one who 'might have been a king'.
13. Moray is lamented as a 'braw gallant' who 'played at the ba'.
14. Moray is described as 'floor o' them a''.
15. Moray is lamented as a 'braw gallant' who 'played at the glove'.
16. Moray is described as 'the Queen's love'.
17. Huntly laments that he has made his sister a widow.
18. Huntly laments that even though his sister's household and lands are neglected he cannot return to Donnibristle.
19. Moray's lady will look long over the walls of Doune Castle for his return.

The following historical facts are inconsistent with the complete ballad:

(a) Moray's wife, Elizabeth, was no relation of George Gordon, sixth earl of Huntly.[22]

(b) Moray's wife had died three months before the murder.[23]

(c) Huntly did not take the news of the murder to the King in person.[24]

(d) Numerous reports agree that Huntly attacked Donnibristle with a large body of men and forced Moray out by setting fire to it; Moray was killed after having run out of the house.[25]

(e) Perhaps even Moray's mother, Margaret Campbell, could not have been 'his lady' who looked 'owre the castle Down', as she is reported as having died soon afterwards of smoke inhalation.[26]

The following historical facts and reports are, however, consistent with the complete ballad:

i) Huntly gained a commission to arrest Bothwell and his co-conspirators, of whom Moray was one.[27]

(ii) Moray was big, powerful, handsome and capable of manly pursuits.[28]

(iii) Moray attended the Court of King James.[29]

(iv) Moray's death was generally lamented.[30]

(v) Margaret, Moray's mother, was Lady Doune, and grieved for his non-return.[31]

(vi) Queen Anne had favoured Moray.[32]

(viii) King James denied publicly than he had ordered Moray to be killed by, or even arrested by, Huntly.[33]

(ix) Huntly left from the scene of the murder and could not return.[34]

(x) *Moray's death portrait shows the body of a man with stab and slash and gunshot wounds who had been wearing no body armour (see illustration).*

(xi) *Moray's portrayed wounds are consistent with a naked or lightly clad man killed while lying on his back/left side, quite possibly in bed.*

The evidence of the death portrait

'The Erle of Murray's Mother caused draw her son's picture as he was demaimed, and presented it to the King on a fine layne cloth with lamentations and earnest sute for Justice.'[35] The portrait is very carefully painted in great and close detail. Three types of wound are present: there are multiple puncture wounds, mainly of the chest; there are three pistol ball entry holes, two in the right side of the chest and one in the upper right abdomen; there are multiple right-sided slash wounds of the head, neck and leg. These slash wounds, furthermore, are so angled as to have been inflicted from behind, on a victim who was lying on his left side and partially curled up, by an assailant standing on the victim's right, attacking from the lower (feet) end of the victim's body. *All these forensic details are quite consistent with an assault upon a man in bed, lightly clad or naked, and certainly not wearing armour.*

The usual armour of the time had probably started life as a common soldier's cheap substitute for mail or plate armour, and was simply plates or scales of metal sewn between two layers of cloth, and known as a jack[36] (a superior version in which the metal plates were riveted together for added strength was called a brigantine).[37] Scots of all ranks (including the King) wore them in the fifteenth and sixteenth centuries, and they could be obtained from Scottish craftsmen.[38] They were capable of stopping a sword or dagger, but probably not a pistol ball, especially if fired at close range; on the other hand the entry wound caused by a lead ball splaying through a metal plate would have been 'pretty messy' – certainly quite unlike the three neat entry holes in the Bonny Earl's body.[39] These firearm injuries are mentioned in two sources (and one of these suggests that at least one ball was so undistorted as to have been reusable):

> The Erle of Murray's Mother caused draw her son's picture as he was demaimed, and presented it to the King on a fine layne cloth with lamentations and earnest sute for Justice ... of the three bullets she found in the bowelling of the Body of her Son she presented one to the King, another to Maitland [the Chancellor], the third she reserved to herself and said 'I sall not part with this till it be bestowed on him that hindreth justice.'[40]

If the many accounts of the attack on Donnibristle are accurate, it clearly lasted some time and Moray seems to have been forced out last of all.[41] There would have been ample time for Moray to have donned such a simple piece of armour as the jack or brigantine – even if he were not already wearing it – yet the death portrait shows a man with stab wounds and clean ball entry points in the chest. These wounds are inflicted from the front, and are consistent with an attack by discharge of pistols and by rapier thrust on an unarmoured man lying on his back, who then turns, curled up to diminish the force of the attack, on to his left side, receiving thereafter multiple slash wounds to his exposed neck and right thigh. The slash and puncture wounds are indeed in keeping with those caused by 'a sharp rapier', for the rapier of the period was capable of cutting along its length.[42] In other words, the forensic details of the death portrait fit the apparently historically inaccurate ballad very well indeed.

Although, as already noted, Child himself professed to enjoy the apparent historical inaccuracy of the ballads, David Buchan demonstrated that the ballad singer was concerned to show a truth (or truths) concerning a situation,[43] and that might involve conflating historical events – as in a similar Gordon family feud ballad, 'The Baron of Brackley' [203], which combined two events at the same venue fifty-four years apart. In fact, it was Moray's son who was to be married to a Gordon, Huntly's daughter Anne, in 1607[44] (in a royal attempt to end the feud, further to the king having immediately ordered the ten-year-old boy not to take action against his father's murderer).[45] This would suggest either that the singer fabricated the sister-in-law business simply to blacken Huntly, or confused the marriages of second and third earls of Moray.

The documentary evidence

But surely, the lurid and detailed descriptions of Huntly's murderous attack on Moray in Donnibristle are, as David Buchan states, confirmed by 'documentary sources (reliable in this instance)'?[46] Certainly by the time Walter Scott, busy as ever inventing Scottish history, recounted the event in 1827 it had lost nothing in the telling:

> [Huntly] beset the house of Dunnibristle ... and summoned Moray to surrender. In reply, a gun was fired which mortally wounded one of the Gordons. The assailants proceeded to set fire to the house; when Dunbar, sheriff of the county of Moray, said to the earl, 'Let us not stay to be burned in the flaming house; I will go out foremost, and the Gordons, taking me for your lordship, will kill me, while you escape in the confusion.' They rushed out among their enemies accordingly, and Dunbar was slain. But his death did not save his friend, as he had generously intended. Murray indeed escaped for the moment, but as he fled to the rocks by the sea-shore, he was traced by the silken tassels attached to his headpiece, which had taken fire as he broke out from among the flames. By this means the pursuers followed him down amongst the cliffs near the sea, and Gordon of Buckie, who is said to have been the first that overtook him, wounded him mortally.

Scott's confabulation ends with one of the most famous 'romantic' speeches in Scottish history:

> As Murray was gasping in his last agony, Huntly came up; it is alleged by tradition, that Gordon pointed his dirk against the person of his chief, saying, 'By Heaven, my lord, you shall be as deep in as I,' and so compelled him to wound Murray as he was dying. Huntly, with a wavering hand, struck the expiring earl on the face. Thinking of his superior beauty, even in that moment of parting life, Murray stammered out the dying words, 'You have spoiled a better face than your own.'[47]

Some of the core details of the above do appear in contemporary or near-contemporary accounts,[48] but their elaboration is an excellent example of how a legend develops, indeed, probably as it rapidly developed in the days after the murder. Gordon of Buckie was, moreover, in no fit state to participate in Scott's famous drama for he had been so seriously wounded during the attack that he was to be left for dead by Huntly and his dispersing raiders[49] (although only after they had solicitously removed 'his hatt, his purse, his gold, his weapons ... [and] his shankes were pulled off'). Gordon was resuscitated by Moray's mother and taken across to Leith, along with Moray's corpse, where he was rapidly arrested and incarcerated. Gordon appears to have been hastily and summarily executed and perhaps as a result there appear to be no recorded eye-witness accounts of the murder.[50]

The ballad as indictment

Some of the romantic details (the self-sacrifice of the sheriff, Moray's give-away burning head-piece) appear in a contemporary diary,[51] but Huntly being forced to incriminate himself first appears in Spottiswood's *The History of the Church of Scotland*, published posthumously, sixty-three years after the event:

> they supposed he was escaped; yet searching him among the rocks, he was discovered by the tip of his Head-piece, which had taken fire before he left the House, and unmercifully slain. The report went that Huntly's friends, fearing he should disclaim the fact (for he desired rather to have taken him alive), made him light from his horse, and give some strokes to the dead corps ...[52]

Is it possible or even likely that Huntly gained entry to the house under trust and stabbed Moray in his bed, as the ballad firmly maintains? Admittedly even the contemporary accounts vary in detail, especially regarding whether Moray was killed in the daytime, or at night[53] (although this may only reflect a prolonged incident at a time of year when dark fell early).

Most accounts state that Moray was resting at Donnibristle with a false sense of security, not knowing or even suspecting that Huntly had managed to gain a commission which could be interpreted as allowing him to arrest Moray. It is possible that Huntly could have gained access by pretext, especially as Donnibristle appears to have been constructed more as farm buildings with protection against animals and casual marauders rather than as a fortified house, despite its surrounding walls.[54] The burning of the house could have followed the killing, and the body could thereafter have been dumped on the shore to give credence to a claim that Moray was killed while fleeing and resisting legal arrest.

But it must be admitted that against such a scenario even the bare accounts tend to tell of a sequence of fire followed by the escaping Moray being cut down by the Firth, and the death portrait has a small supine figure top right, on the shore, which is presumably the corpse *in situ* – although admittedly it could merely indicate where the body was finally laid. (Interestingly enough the body is painted as being fully clothed, and, with the accounts that Moray had donned a 'Head-piece' or 'Knapscal',[55] it would still seem strange that he had not also had time to don simple body-armour which would have prevented the chest wounds shown on the naked corpse itself.)

Perhaps the clue comes from the extract from the diary of another clergyman, Rev. James Melville, where he describes the crime as 'murdour ... with forthought, fellon hamsukin, and treason under tryst, maist crewalie with fyre and sworde'.[56] These words have been very carefully chosen, and not merely for maximum dramatic effect. The earl of Huntly is accused of premeditated acts of:

1. Murder
2. Hamesucken
3. Treason under trust
4. Arson
5. Armed assault.

In any legal system these crimes are heinous and deserving of severe punishment, but 2 and 3 have even more significance. Murder 'under trust', especially in relation to a feud, referred to a recent Act of 1587 which classified such a crime as treason, with forfeiture of life, lands and property. If that were not enough, Melville accuses Huntly of the Scots Law crime of 'hamesucken' – the premeditated felonious seeking (that is with corrupt and evil intention) and invasion of a person in his dwelling-place or house with intention to assault. This crime carried an automatic death sentence.[57]

But why were these members of the reformed church so keen to have Huntly executed, and why was there such a popular revulsion against the incident? Admittedly it took place close to Edinburgh, from whose outskirts the smoking house was visible,[58] but it was hardly an unusual episode for those turbulent times (there were no ballads concerning the murder of Queen Mary's secretary, Rizzio, in 1566 and *he* was reputed to have suffered fifty-six stab wounds).[59] Furthermore, Huntly had the excuses that (a) he was acting under royal orders in an attempt to neutral-ise the activities and agents of the frightening earl of Bothwell (who really was a Public Enemy Number One with his terrifying invasions of the capital), and (b) Moray got himself killed by mistake while resisting arrest.[60]

Moray's murder, although not particularly unique for the times, appears to have been the last straw for a nation in a politically turbulent condition – and an opportunity for the Kirk to gain the upper hand. The king's chancellor saw the precipitous situation all too clearly:

> The body of the slaughtered Earl of Moray was lying still unburied in Leith, and the cry for revenge for that and other acts of murder and lawlessness was growing louder and louder; attacks on the King and his mis-government were incessant, not only in sermons, but also in rhymes, songs and popular pasquils; the rebel Earl Bothwell was zig-zagging in arms over the country as he chose, not only defying capture, and meditating no one knew what wild new demonstration of his own, but drawing to him the sympathies of many who thought his revolutionary leadership better than nothing; how could the King save himself and recover popularity?[61]

When Parliament rose on 5 June 1592, four months after Moray's death, the presbyterian clergy were delighted to see that amongst one hundred and eighty-one Acts passed that day, the vaguely titled 'Act for abolisheing of the Actis contrair the trew Religion' was the most compre-hensive and sweeping that had yet been passed by a Scottish Parliament in favour of the presbyterian system. It became known as the 'Golden Act', for it ratified all previous Acts in favour of that system, abrogated any anti-presbyterian Acts, rescinded and repealed all Acts of a popish tinge or capable of popish construction still remaining in the statute-book, and guaranteed the future government of the Kirk forever by strict democratic presbyterian method, with annual general assemblies, together with presbyteries and synods.[62]

This astute piece of statesmanship seems to have been successful, for the 'publict threatning of God's judgements thairupon from pulpites'[63] appears largely to have ceased. Bothwell was to disappear from Scotland to die in poverty in Naples but Huntly's enemies attacked and wasted his lands. The Gordon retaliation was terrible and the whole country north of the Tay entered a state of internal feud and warfare.[64]

It was not until five years after, at the General Assembly of May 1597, that Huntly declared his penitence for the murder of the earl of Moray, and was received into the Kirk, along with the other catholic earls, to great public celebration.[65] His estates and titles were restored in December of that year, and two years later he was created marquis.[66] Most significantly, in February 1597, the privy council ordered the immediate burial of Moray's corpse in response to complaints by '... certane of the ministerie'. As the murder had been first and foremost among the charges pressed fiercely by the clergy against Huntly, this signalled their willingness to bury also their constant pursuit of his crime.[67]

It is perhaps unsurprising, therefore, that the full version of the ballad disappeared from oral tradition, for Huntly was not only back in favour, he was back in town. Reciting, singing or hawking 'The Bonny Earl of Murray' would have been a decidedly unhealthy pursuit in Edinburgh, or indeed in any of the Gordon lands, where, on the other hand, similar ballads recounting heinous crimes *against* the Gordons have survived until the present day; murder, hamesucken, arson and treachery are also the themes of 'Edom O Gordon' [178] relating to 1571, 'The Baron of Brackley' [203], relating to events in 1592, and 'The Fire of Frendraught' [196], relating to events in 1630.

* * *

The weight of historical evidence would suggest that the 'famous and misleading'[68] ballad, 'The Bonny Earl of Murray' (now known to be a combination of Child's versions 'A' and 'B')[69] is not correct in suggesting a family relationship between the countess of Moray and the earl of Huntly which might have facilitated the latter's entry into the house of Donnibristle and enabled him to kill the 'Bonny Earl' of Moray treacherously in his bed.

On the other hand the forensic evidence of the death portrait is highly compatible with the murder of a man surprised in his bed, wearing no armour. Furthermore, none of the accounts of the murder is by an eye-witness, many are highly biased, and the most lurid versions appear to have been written years after the event.

Why was the only captured raider executed so hurriedly? Might he have witnessed that Huntly or members of his party had not only been given authorisation to enter the House of Donnibristle but had also been given to understand, explicitly or implicitly, that it would be highly convenient if Moray were not to survive arrest? At the time the finger of accusation was pointed firmly at the king and his chancellor, and since then few historians have disagreed.[70] Is the ballad really misleading? Can we be *completely* sure we know just how the Bonny Earl of Moray was killed?

NOTES

I am grateful to the Earl and Countess of Moray, and Lord Doune, for their family knowledge, permission to photograph the death portrait in Darnaway Castle, access to and help with family papers, and for their kind hospitality; also to the ever-helpful staff of the Archives and Special Collections, University of Aberdeen, and of the Reference and Local Collections of Aberdeen Central Library. I am indebted to the following: for specialist advice on weaponry and armour to David Caldwell, Assistant Keeper, Scottish Mediaeval Collection, National Museums of Scotland, and Phillip Lankester, Curator, Royal Armouries; concerning Scots Law to Hugh Olson, Faculty of Advocates, Edinburgh; for transcription of Moray Muniment documentation and for reading the manuscript to Grant Simpson; to the late David Buchan, Ted Cowan, Alexander Fenton, James Kirk, the late Iain Moncreiffe of that Ilk, Leslie Macfarlane, and Donald Withrington. The paper was written with the aid of a generous grant from the Forbes Family, New York.

1 J. Wormald, *Lords and Men in Scotland: Bonds of Manrent 1442–1603* (Edinburgh 1985), 437, note 15. Michael Lynch in *Scotland: A New History* (London 1991), 233, states: 'The only relationship which the well-known ballad [presumably he is referring to the Child A version] bears to reality is that the Earl was indeed bonnie.'

2 *Letters on Scottish Ballads from Professor Francis J. Child to W. W., Aberdeen*, ed. W. Walker (Aberdeen 1930), F. J. C. to W. W., 17 Mar. 1891, 4.

3 D. Buchan, 'History and Harlaw', *Journal of the Folklore Institute*, v (1968), 58–67.

4 D. Buchan, 'The historical balladry of the North-East', *Aberdeen University Review*, lv (1994), 377–87 (at 380) [expanded version of *Ballata e Storia*, special issue of *Lares*, li (4) (1985), 443–51].

5 A. C. MacLeod and H. Boulton, *Songs of the North. Music arranged by Malcolm Lawson* (London 1885), 142–6.

6 *The English and Scottish Popular Ballads*, ed. K. S. Goldstein, 8 LP records. Riverside RLP 12-621-628 (1965).

7 Allan Ramsay, *The Tea-Table Miscellany* (11th edn, London 1750), iv, 356.

8 William Thomson, *Orpheus Caledonius* (2nd edn, London 1733), ii, 8.

9 See, e.g., W. Muir, *Living With Ballads* (London 1965), 202–3 in which she shrewdly comments: 'At that time [1592] no one in the Northern marches would have coupled Highlands and Lowlands together as a whole ... I incline to think that these lines came into the song nearer the time of printing it (1763) when public opinion about Highlanders was beginning to change.' For a history of that change, see W. Donaldson, 'Bonnie Highland Laddie: the making of a myth', in *Scottish Literary Journal*, iii, no. 2 (1976), 30–50; and W. Donaldson, *The Jacobite Song: Political Myth and National Identity* (Aberdeen 1988).

10 *The English and Scottish Popular Ballads*, ed. F. J. Child (5 vols., Boston and London, 1882–98), iii, pt. 6, 447–9.

11 See, e.g., David Moysie, *Memoirs of the Affairs of Scotland* (Bannatyne Club, 1830), 87–92.

12 Wormald, *Lords and Men*, 121. For more details of the wider historical background, see also K. M. Brown, *Bloodfeud in Scotland 1573–1625* (Edinburgh 1986), ch. 6. Even worse, treachery amongst the Campbells during the 1590s left Moray dangerously vulnerable; his ally, John Campbell of Cawdor, was also killed [by Huntly?] three days beforehand. See E. J. Cowan, 'Clanship, kinship and the Campbell acquisition of Islay', *Scot. Hist. Rev.*, lviii (1979), 132–57; and his 'Calvinism and the survival of Folk', in E. J. Cowan (ed.), *The People's Past* (Edinburgh 1980), 46–8.

13 J. Finlay, *Scottish Historical and Romantic Ballads, Chiefly Ancient* (2 vols., Edinburgh 1808), i, 77–84 (at 81–2); and ii, 11–23 (at 21–3).

14 W. Motherwell, *Minstrelsy: Ancient and Modern with an Historical Introduction and Notes* (Glasgow 1827), 78–82.

15 Child, *Ballads*, vii, 119–21 (at 120).

16 Ibid., iii, pt. 6, 447–9.

17 P. Buchan, *Gleanings of Scarce Old Ballads Chiefly Tragical and Historical, Many of them connected with the localities of Aberdeenshire and to be found in no other place* (Peterhead 1825; repr. Aberdeen 1891), 91–2, 195.

18 W. Christie and Wm. Christie, *Traditional Ballad Airs arranged and harmonised for the pianoforte and harmonium, from copies procured in the counties of Aberdeen, Banff and Moray* (2 vols., Edinburgh 1876, 1881), i, 202–3. Apart from *Orpheus Caledonius* this is the only other known tune to the ballad (discounting the 1885 arrangement), 'sung ... by the Editor's maternal grandmother. Through her and her mother it can be traced in this form as far back as the year 1760.' Although the Christies admitted to extensive editing and combining of texts and music, in this case their version would appear to be untampered with.

19 J. Ord, *Bothy Songs and Ballads of Aberdeen, Banff & Moray, Angus and the Mearns* (Paisley 1930).

20 *The Greig-Duncan Folk-Song Collection*, ed. P. Shuldham-Shaw and E. Lyle (7 vols., Aberdeen and Edinburgh, 1981–95).

21 'A Guide To The James Madison Carpenter Manuscripts. Microfilm of the Library of Congress Manuscript written by James Carpenter of the University of Harvard 1979/80', Library of Congress Music 3109, Reel 4 [titles in rough alphabetical order]. The typed transcript has handwritten alterations as in v3, line 1. There seems to be no more information on Mrs Gray on the microfilm. Remote and isolated Glenlivet, which lies on the eastern edge of the principal Gordon territory in the North-East, is famous for its whisky and as a staunch redoubt of indigenous Catholicism in Scotland. See I. A. Olson, 'Scottish Song in the James Madison Carpenter Collection', *Folk Music Journal*, vii (4) (1998), 421–33.

22 *Burke's Peerage and Baronetage*, ed. P. Townsend (105th edn, London 1970), 1399, 1880.

23 G. E. C[okayne], *The Complete Peerage*, rev. V. Gibbs and others (13 vols. in 14, London 1910–59), x, 185.

24 Moysie, *Memoirs*, 89.

25 John Spottiswood, *The History of the Church of Scotland, Beginning the Year of our Lord 203 and continued to the end of the Reign of King James the VI of ever blessed Memory* (Edinburgh 1655; 3rd edn corrected and amended, London 1666), 387; David Calderwood, *The true history of the Church of Scotland from the beginning of the Reformation, unto the end of the reigne of King James VI* (Edinburgh 1678), 267.

26 *Burke's Peerage*, 1877, states that she died in February 1571/2 (presumably this is a misprint for 1591/2) of injuries from the fire. A draft petition to Parliament on behalf of Moray's son stated that she 'wes sa suffocat, that be occasione thairof she deceissit schortlie thaireftir': Moray Muniments, TD81/3/4/58.

27 Moysie, *Memoirs*, 88; Spottiswood, *History*, 387.

28 *The Bannatyne Miscellany*, ed. Walter Scott and D. Laing (3 vols. in 4, Bannatyne Club, 1827–55), i, 57; Sir James Melville of Halhill, *Memoirs of his own life 1549–1593*, ed. T. Thomson (Bannatyne Club, 1827), 407; *The Historie and Life of King James the Sext*, ed. T. Thomson (Bannatyne Club, 1825), 246; P. F. Tytler, *History of Scotland* (10 vols., Edinburgh 1841–50), ix, 65.

29 Melville, *Memoirs*, 406.

30 E.g. *Calendar of the State Papers relating to Scotland and Mary Queen of Scots, 1547–1603*, ed. J. Bain and others (Edinburgh 1898–) [*CSP Scot.*], vol. X: *1589–93*, 637.

31 E.g. Spottiswood, *History*, 387.

32 *The Historical Works of Sir James Balfour*, ed. J. Haig (4 vols., Edinburgh 1824–5), i, 390. See also E. C. Williams, *Anne of Denmark* (London 1970), where she states that Anne remarked on 'his good looks and lovely golden hair', 41–2.

33 David Calderwood, *The History of the Kirk of Scotland*, ed. T. Thomson (8 vols., Wodrow Soc., 1842–9), v, 145. *Register of the Privy Council of Scotland*, ed. J. H. Burton and others (1st ser., 14 vols., Edinburgh 1877–98) [*RPC*], iv, 725; Melville, *Memoirs*, 407; Moysie, *Memoirs*, 89.

34 Moysie, *Memoirs*, 92.

35 Calderwood, *History of the Kirk*, v, 145.

36 T. Gabra-Sanders, 'Part of a 16th century Quilted Jack of Plate found at Craigievar castle, Aberdeenshire', in *The Journal of the Arms and Armour Society*, xiv (3) (1993), 147–52. Huntly's attacking force are described as wearing 'jakkis': Moray Muniments, TD/81/3/4/59.

37 D. H. Caldwell, 'Royal patronage of arms and armour making' in D. H. Caldwell (ed.), *Scottish Weapons and Fortifications 1100–1800* (Edinburgh 1981), 88–9.

38 Gabra-Sanders, 'Quilted Jack', 151.

39 D. Caldwell, National Museums of Scotland, personal communication, 29 Oct. 1995.

40 Calderwood, *History of the Kirk*, v, 145; *CSP Scot.* x, 641. The English Ambassador reported that Moray's mother handed them to friends who were willing to 'hazard themselves and lives' firing them into bodies of 'the principal executioners'.

41 Such as Spottiswood, *History*, 387; Calderwood, *History of the Kirk*, v, 144; *CSP. Scot.* x, 633, 635.

42 D. Caldwell, personal communication, 6 Nov. 1995. Swords with rapier-type hilts and long blades are shown in contemporary portraits of Scotsmen such as the 1592 portrait of Sir Thomas Kennedy of Culzean, or the 1601 portrait of Sir Duncan Campbell of Glenorchy, in D. Thomson, *Painting in Scotland 1570–1650* (Edinburgh 1975), 27, 35.

43 D. Buchan, 'History and Harlaw', 66–7; D. Buchan, 'The Ballad and the Folk. Studies in the Balladry and the Society of the North-east of Scotland', Appendix

'The Historical Ballads of the North-East' (Aberdeen University, Ph.D thesis, 1965), 388.

44 *Burke's Peerage*, 1880, where the date of the marriage contract is given as 1607. See also Morton, seventeenth Earl of Moray, *Painting of James, 2nd earl of Moray*, a pamphlet concerning the death portrait in Darnaway Castle (Kinfauns, 19 Dec. 1912), which gives the date as 1601. The numbers '7' and '1' are, however, easily confused in these early documents.

45 Balfour, *Historical Works*, i, 390.

46 Buchan, 'Historical balladry', 380.

47 Walter Scott, *Tales of a Grandfather*, ed. R. Cadell (3 vols., London 1836), ii, 191–2. A novelist who could, e.g., transform a sadistic, perverted, absentee Angevin monarch into 'Good King Richard the Lionheart' (see I. Olson, 'Legend Debunked', *The Times*, 3 Jul. 1996) clearly found no problem with romanticising this sordid feud between the Morays and the Huntlys.

48 Robert Birrel, 'The Diarey [sic] of Robert Birrel', in *Fragments of Scottish History*, ed. J. G. Dalyell (Edinburgh 1798), 26–7. The contemporary English reports (*CSP Scot.* 633, 635) state only that a badly burned Moray almost escaped when he shot out of the house like 'a gon' but went slap into a group watching out for such an eventuality.

49 It appears to have been Buckie's enraged brother, Gordon of Gight, who cut Moray down with the aid of Gordon of Cluny, as recounted by the courtier Sir Robert Gordon (b. 1580), in *A Genealogical History of the Earldom of Sutherland* (Edinburgh 1813), 216–17.

50 Calderwood, *History of the Kirk*, v, 145–6.

51 Birrel, 'Diarey', 26–7.

52 Spottiswood, *History*, 387.

53 *The Autobiography and Diary of Mr James Melvill, Minister of Kilrenny in Fife and Professor of Theology in the University of St Andrews*, ed. R. Pitcairn (Wodrow Soc., 1842), 294, says 'in fear [broad] day-light'; Spottiswood, *History*, gives '... the night falling down ...', 387; Calderwood's *True History* states '... that night set the House of Dinnibristle on fire', 267.

54 A. Fenton, personal communication, 4 Dec. 1995. Also Donnibristle is described as 'Nocht being ane fenceable nor strenthe houss': Moray Muniments, TD81/3/4/59.

55 Calderwood, *True History*, 267; Spottiswood, *History*, 387.

56 Melvill, *Autobiography and Diary*, 294.

57 David Hume, *Commentaries on the Law of Scotland respecting Crimes* (2 vols., Edinburgh 1797; repr. with a Foreword by Lord Cameron, Edinburgh 1986), 286–8 (murder under trust) and 312–23. Hume derives hamesucken from the German 'heimsuchen' – to seek at home, but modern authorities derive it from ME *hamesok(e)ne*, ON *heimsókn*: *The Concise Scots Dictionary*, ed. M. Robinson (Aberdeen 1985).

58 Calderwood, *History of the Kirk*, v, 144.

59 Scott, *Tales of a Grandfather*, ii, 109.

60 Moysie, *Memoirs*, 89; Spottiswood, *History*, attributes Huntly, 'for he desired rather to have taken him alive', 387; in Balfour, *Historical Works*, i, 390, Huntly protested 'naither airt nor pairt of the murther'; *CSP Scot.* iv, 637, 'Murray so far disobeyed him [Huntly] that he was driven thus to assault him in his house'.

61 *RPC* iv, 725: editor's footnote.

62 *RPC* iv, 749; Calderwood, *True History*, 268–70. The king preferred an episcopalian system, with bishops appointed by the crown; accepting the crown of England, with her flattering Anglican church gave him the opportunity to fight back. He had ignored the articles and spirit of the Golden Act, and exiled Knox's successor

Andrew Melville with many other protesting kirkmen by the time he restored crown-nominated bishops in 1607.

63 Melvill, *Autobiography and Diary*, 294.

64 Tytler, *History of Scotland*, ix, 67–9.

65 J. Mackintosh, *Historic Earls and Earldoms of Scotland* (Aberdeen 1898), 173–5.

66 *Burke's Peerage*, 1399.

67 *RPC* v, 444–5, and 445 note.

68 Wormald, *Lords and Men*, 437, note 15.

69 The evidence for the combined ballad is given in I. A. Olson, 'The dreadful death of the Bonny Earl of Moray: clues from the Carpenter Song Collection, *Folk Music Journal*, vii (3) (1997), 281–310. North American combined versions are given in the excellent E. D. Ives, *The Bonny Earl of Murray* (East Linton 1997), 134–8).

70 E.g. A. G. Stuart, *A Genealogical & Historical Sketch of the Stuarts of Castlestuart in Ireland* (Edinburgh 1854), 174–7; Tytler, *History of Scotland*, ix, 68.

4

The Road to Elfland: Fairy Belief and the Child Ballads

LIZANNE HENDERSON

And see not ye that bonny road,
Which winds about the fernie brae?
That is the road to fair Elfland,
Where you and I this night maun gae. [37A:13][1]

During the period from roughly 1500 to 1700, the majority of Scottish people believed in the existence of fairies. It is important to keep in mind, however, that the fairies of folk tradition bore little or no resemblance to modern day images of fairies. Rather, the preconceptions that have been inherited in the twentieth century find their source in the butterfly winged, diaphanously clad, frolicking nymphs of writers and artists such as Shakespeare, Blake and Fuseli.[2] The romantic Cottingley Fairies, the materialistic Tooth Fairy,[3] and Walt Disney's version of the mischievous Tinkerbell are the pervasive iconographic forms in the popular culture of today. If it were possible to ask ordinary people from sixteenth or seventeenth-century Scotland what they thought of these creations of artistry, they would probably have replied that, in their experience, there was nothing very merry, or coy, or playfully mischievous about the fairy folk. The fairies were dangerous, capable of inflicting terrible harm upon people and their property, and every precaution had to be taken to keep them at bay, or at least, placated. Though it was possible for them to do good, their proclivity to cruelty and general malevolence meant that it was best to avoid them at all costs. While ideas about fairies constituted only a fragment of a much larger complex of beliefs, the study of the fairy tradition is potentially illuminating. Through consideration of folk beliefs we can hopefully begin to understand something of the mindset of the people who lived in these centuries.

Fundamentally, there are two major questions that must be considered. Are the ballads a valuable historical source in the investigation of fairy belief? Can ballads tell us anything about the mental world of the ordinary person living in early modern Scotland? The supernatural is a fairly prominent feature in the classical ballads: for example, fourteen of the 305 Child ballads are concerned with ghosts or 'revenants', and a further four include a magical corpse; eleven refer to fairies; there are seven witch ballads; 'Billie Blin', a type of brownie, is encountered in at least four Scottish ballads;[4] mermaids play a role in five ballads; and there is one selchie ballad. The world of the ballads is a place of magic and enchantment, populated by talking animals and singing bones, by fairies who seduce and abduct human beings on land, by mermaids who lure the unsuspecting to a watery grave, by witches that curse, and by ghosts that return from the grave craving either to comfort the living or to seek revenge upon them. It is also a world of metamorphosis, of people transformed into animals, plants, or birds, where everything is not necessarily as it seems. And yet there is rarely a clear distinction between supernatural creatures and humans; fairies and revenants are like mortals in appearance, and supernatural occurrences are handled in a mundane and matter-of-fact way. This, one could argue, is because at the time these ballads were composed the supernatural was natural, was part of the everyday and an accepted explanation for a variety of events and happenings.

David Buchan opined that ballads which take the Otherworld as their central theme are preponderantly Scottish, reflecting the strong ties Scottish balladry shares with Scandinavian, rather than English, ballad tradition.[5] On the surface this would indeed appear to be the case; for instance, 'The Great Silkie of Sule Skerry' [113] and 'King Orfeo' [19] have only been recorded from Orkney and Shetland, and all the witch ballads were recorded from the north-east of Scotland. However, perhaps it may be the way in which ballads have been collected,[6] categorised, and their motifs interpreted, that has led to this kind of assumption.

There has existed, in some quarters, an idea that Scotland was more 'superstitious' than England, which has in turn led to comments about Scottish balladry, such as M. J. C. Hodgart's, that 'Scottish versions generally have a richer content of folk-beliefs and pagan survivals.'[7] 'Thomas Rymer' [37], a well-known Scottish supernatural ballad, is based upon an actual historical figure for whom there exists written evidence. On the other hand the Robin Hood ballads, of which Child collected thirty-eight [117–54], are usually classified as English 'outlaw ballads' or 'yeoman minstrelsy'[8]. There is, as yet, no concrete evidence to prove that the outlaw of Sherwood Forest was a historical personage and he thus remains caught in a shady realm, more legend than history. He was appropriated by folk tradition and custom, such as the adoption of Robin Hood into May Day festivities from the fifteenth century onwards, and there are numerous locations associated with his deeds. There is much resistance to the idea that Robin Hood was in any way connected to a belief in nature spirits, fairies or the like. There is, after all, no particular reason to ascribe supernatural features to Robin; he is portrayed as a mortal man (as is Thomas Rymer) who dresses in green, calls his comrades with a horn, lives undetectably in the forest, helps the poor and the oppressed, shoots his enemies with arrows, and generally fights against evil forces. But most significantly, he receives help and guidance from God through prayer, and from the assistance and supernatural intervention of the Virgin Mary. Though it is not my intention to suggest a connection between Robin Hood and Thomas Rymer – as none exists – I *am* interested in what constitutes 'supernatural'.

The following ballads can be identified as containing fairy material: 'The Elfin Knight' [2], 'Lady Isobel and the Elf-Knight' [4], 'King Orfeo' [19], 'Allison Gross' [35], 'Thomas Rymer' [37], 'The Wee Wee Man' [38], 'Tam Lin' [39], 'The Queen of Elfan's Nourice' [40], 'Hind Etin' [41], 'Young Beichan' [53], and 'Sir Cawline' [61].[9] Though fairies cannot be said to feature prominently in the classical ballads, arguably what presence they do have is worthy of investigation. Contrary to Gordon Gerould's view that the ballads 'present no coherent record of either historical event or of popular belief and custom at any one particular period',[10] this paper will illuminate the importance of the Child ballads as a gateway to the folk beliefs of the early modern period. When we study the ballads we are studying not only the 'poetry of the folk'[11] but stylistic representations of belief as well.

Perhaps unexpectedly, Child was sceptical about the historical value of the ballads he collected. His introduction to 'The Battle of Harlaw' [163] stated, 'a ballad taken down some four hundred years after the event will be apt to retain very little of sober history'. David Buchan was to refute this claim, and the general attitude of so many others who have professed that ballads cannot be taken seriously as history, in his article, 'History and Harlaw'.[12] He found that 'Harlaw' was 'historical in a rather extraordinary way'. It reflected, he said, the kind of 'historical truth' that rarely finds its way into the documents, 'the ways in which the folk imagination reacted to, moulded, and used for its own emotional purposes, the raw material of historical event'.[13] It is to these emotional truths that we now turn.

Outwith ballads, accounts of sixteenth and seventeenth-century fairy belief are found in other contemporary sources, for instance, church records, literature, travellers' memoirs, and the writings of investigators such as the pioneer folklorist, Rev. Robert Kirk. Of crucial importance to any study of fairy belief in this period of Scotland's history are transcripts from witch trials. There is substantial mention of interludes with fairies in the trial evidence, and in many cases the fairy association was the sole reason that accusations of witchcraft were made against the victim. Aside from the fact that the Scottish witch hunt is an understudied phenomenon in its own right, the reluctance to use the depositions of those accused of witchcraft has sprung from the prevailing attitude that the confessions are no more than a consequence of torture and leading questions by the judges. The confessions are thus denied any element of spontaneity,[14] and the accused are reduced to the role of puppets. The fact that witch trial depositions are not an 'objective' source does not, one could argue, render them useless or unusable,[15] but rather involves looking at the trial evidence in a different way. As Carlo Ginzburg points out, it is the importance of 'the anomalies, the cracks that occasionally (albeit very rarely) appear in the documentation, undermining its coherence'[16] that we must look for. The anomalous material in the Scottish witch trials with which this paper is concerned involves alleged encounters with the fairy folk. Another problem, according to Ginzburg, is that academics have been concerned to study and focus upon persecution, 'giving little or no attention to the attitudes and behaviour of the persecuted'.[17] Rather, attempts should be made to uncover the beliefs of the women and men accused of witchcraft as opposed to beliefs 'about' witches. Through comparison with such sources the relationship between the ballad fairy and fairy beliefs as elsewhere recorded, will hopefully reveal whether or not the ballads can be said to shed light upon this long-standing supernatural belief tradition. The works of later antiquarians need not be dismissed outright, but they must be used with the utmost critical care.

Quite possibly, the most remarkable depiction of the journey to Elfland known to exist, in the ballads or any other source, is that made by Thomas Rymer. It is the most elaborately described journey of its kind, and is alluring in its attention to detail and phantasmal atmosphere. Seduced by the Queen of Elfland, Thomas is taken, part way on horseback, on an incredible journey to her country. He travels through subterranean caverns and luscious orchards, in a land of perpetual twilight, from where he can hear the roaring of the sea. The crossing of some sort of water barrier is a common requirement for many travellers to the Otherworld, found time and again in myths, legends, sagas and medieval romances. Thomas is by no means free from this preternatural obstacle and, in [37C:15], must wade across water. In most versions of this ballad, however, Thomas is faced with a more horrific task than many of his fellow adventurers to the Otherworld in that he must wade through rivers of blood, the very essence of life itself.

> For forty days and forty nights
> He wade thro red blude to the knee,
> And he saw neither sun nor moon,
> But heard the roaring of the sea. [37A:7]

Thomas Rymer's sanguinary adventure conjures a vivid depiction, if not an alarming portrayal, of this significant stage of the journey. Another notable incident in Thomas's journey is the point at which he is invited to rest his head on the Queen's knee while she shows him 'ferlies three',[18] namely a choice of three roads, leading to very different destinations. In [37B:10] the Queen explains that the first road leads straight to the gates of Hell, though bafflingly, in [37A:12] and [37C:11], the same route is described as the path of righteousness. The second track, in [37A:13], [37B:11] and [37C:12], leads to Heaven. The third trail, and the one which Thomas is to follow in [37A:14] and [37C:13], will lead them to Elfland.[19] The cosmography, confusing though it is, represents an interesting blend of folk and Christian motifs.

In the ballad of 'Tam Lin' no details are given of his journey to Fairyland other than the assumption that he too is led there by the Queen of Elfland. In 'The Wee Wee Man' there is a similarly sparse account. Again, all that seems clear is that the mortal is accompanied by a fairy guide and they travel on horseback. Interestingly enough, not much is made of the actual excursion to Elfland in the witch confessions either. Generally speaking, the accused reported that they were escorted to the abode of the fairies, or else they accidentally stumbled across the homes or favourite haunts of the 'guid neighbours'. Little mention is made of the journey or mode of transportation, though some people reported that the fairies conveyed them by means of a whirlwind or some other form of levitation. Bessie Flinkar of Edinburgh, tried in 1661, said she was taken 'upon the hills by a whirle of wind & masked herselfe, & [th]e[r] danced with the rest'.[20] There are several accounts of people claiming to have been carried quite significant distances, often finding themselves in places totally unknown to them.

With regard to the location of Elfland there is wider scope of information though the details are confusing and often fragmentary. Lowry Wimberly discovered through his study of folklore in the classical ballads that the dwelling places of the fairies were remarkably diverse:

> Is the abode of the departed, or the land of the elves and demons, associated with the forest; is it on a hill or mountain; is it

subterranean, submarine, over the sea, or on an island; is it far away; is it terrestrial or celestial?[21]

The answer, potentially, is yes to all of the above for visitors to Fairyland found it in a variety of locations. Thomas Rymer and Tam Lin's Elfland existed in a subterranean locale, having neither sun nor moon. 'The Elfin Knight' [2A], 'Tam Lin' [39A], 'The Wee Wee Man' [38A], 'The Queen of Elfan's Nourice', and 'Sir Cawline' mention hills or glens. 'Hind Etin' and 'Lady Isabel and The Elf-Knight' [4A] highlight forests, while version [4B] refers to a well. 'Tam Lin' merges both of these locations, appearing to Janet in a forest by a well. The fairy lover in 'Hind Etin' [41A] takes his mortal wife to 'Elmond's wood' and in [41B:7], whilst still within the forest, the mortal bride is kept more or less a prisoner inside a very deep cave.

Considerable mention is made of the location of fairy homes in the witch trials. Virtually every example places the fairies beside, or inside, hills. The trial of Lady Foulis or Katherine Ross in 1590, reported that she 'wald gang in hillis to speik [to] the elf folk'.[22] In 1615, Jonet Drever was convicted for the 'fostering of ane bairne in the hill of Westray (Orkney) to the fary folk, callit of hir our guid nichbouris'.[23] In Shetland Katherine Jonesdochter, tried in 1616, saw trows – the Shetland term for fairies – on a hill called 'Greinfaill'.[24] John Stewart, tried in Irvine in 1618, regularly met with the fairies on top of 'Lanark Hill' and 'Kilmaurs Hill'.[25] When asked if she had any 'conversatioun with the ffarye-folk' Isobel Haldane, tried in Perth in 1623, said that she had been taken out of her bed by the fairies one night and was carried 'to ane hill-syde: the hill oppynit, and scho enterit in'.[26] Nowhere in the trials does anyone specifically refer to the forest as a location for Elfland, though a hawthorn tree is mentioned by Bessie Dunlop, from Ayrshire, as a place to meet with fairies. Bessie, whose trial occurred in 1576, also witnessed a fairy host on horseback gallop straight into 'Restalrig-loch', near Edinburgh, and Elspeth Reoch, tried in Orkney in 1616, first met the fairies at a loch side in the district of Lochaber.[27]

Rev. Robert Kirk, an episcopalian minister successively in the parishes of Balquhidder and Aberfoyle, and author of *The Secret Common-Wealth* (1691), an invaluable source of fairy belief in the seventeenth century, was aware that 'there be manie places called fayrie hills, which the mountain-people think impious and dangerous to peel or discover'.[28] Walter Scott also preserved the tradition that mountain lochs, wells, or cavities on top of high hills were thought to lead to Fairyland.[29] What emerges from the ballads and our other sources is that there are specific places connected with fairies – a supernatural landscape coinciding with the natural landscape. Sean Kane described it as an 'oral narrative map of a landscape touched everywhere by footprints of the supernatural'.[30]

Not exclusive to, but nonetheless of great significance to, the supernatural landscape is the concept of boundaries. Boundaries exist at the junctures between the world of the natural and the supernatural. Like a membranous film they separate and delineate one place or one state from another. When Janet went to 'Carterhaugh' in the ballad of 'Tam Lin,' she was on the threshold of a boundary, tenuously separating her from the Otherworld. Though she was able to communicate, and indeed have sexual relations with Tam Lin, she herself did not cross the boundary that so fatefully ensnared her lover. Whilst Janet presumably recognised the markers delineating this boundary, Tam Lin evidently did not or could not.

Once travellers, reluctant or otherwise, have reached Elfland they invariably find it to be a land of stunning beauty and compelling mystique: a sort of subterranean Elysium. 'King Orfeo' describes a hall where fine music is appreciated. 'Thomas Rymer' evokes images of a Celtic overseas paradise, abundant in fruit trees, flowers and fine clothes. 'Tam Lin' [39D] refers to a 'fairy court' that is 'a pretty place, / In which I love to dwell'. In 'The Wee Wee Man' the 'bonny hall' has a ceiling of gold and a crystal floor.

Descriptions of Fairyland in the witch trials are also remarkably favourable. At her trial in 1588 Alison Peirson of Byrehill said, though she found the fairies often cruel to her, the 'Court of Elfane' is a place of 'pypeing and mirrynes and gude cheir'.[31] The 1662 confession of Isobel Gowdie of Auldearn records:

> We went in to the Downie-hillis; the hill opened, and we
> cam to an fair and lairge braw rowme, in the day tym. Thair
> ar great bullis rowtting and skoylling ther, at the entrie ...[32]

Fairyland's propensity to vanish into thin air occurs in the ballad 'The Wee Wee Man' 'in the twinkling of an eye', despite the fact that only moments before there stood a great hall filled with activity. Analogous sudden disappearance is noted in the 1597–8 trial of Andrew Man:

> Thow grantis the elphis will mak thee appeir to be in a fair
> chalmer, and yit thow will find thy selff in a moss on the
> morne; and that thay will appeir to have candlis, and licht,
> and swordis, quhilk wilbe nothing els bot deed gress and
> strayes.[33]

Physical and material descriptions of fairies and their property are relatively consistent. However, there is one area where contentions arise and that is with the stature of the fairy folk. While, on the whole, Scottish fairies were reportedly of human size, some discrepancies exist. There were occasional references to pygmies or little people – enough, perhaps, to warrant speculation as to whether these smaller creatures were a regional variant, the remnants of an even older tradition, a distinct class of fairy, or, what seems most probable, a competing tradition. In 1549, Donald Monro's *Description of the Western Isles of Scotland* makes reference to the Pygmy Isle, in Lewis.[34] Martin Martin also heard of it during his travels in 1695, adding that the islanders called it 'The Island of Little Men'.[35]

The closest account so far found in the witch trials to the Wee Wee Man of the ballads occurs in the confession of Isobel Gowdie. She described the 'elf-boys' she saw inside a fairy hill as 'little ones, hollow, and boss-baked'; they spoke 'gowstie lyk'.[36] Since 'boss-baked' seems to mean diminutive and hump-backed, while 'gowstie' means roughly or gruffly, comparisons between Isobel's brownie or trow-like creatures and the Wee Wee Man could be made. The latter furnishes the only example in the Child corpus of small fairies. In every other case the ballad fairy is of human size. The Wee Wee Man is different in other ways also:

> His legs were scare a shathmont's [6 inches] length,
> And thick and thimber was his thigh;
> Between his brows there was a span,
> And between his shoulders there was three. [38A:2]

Perhaps what is depicted is a creature similar to the *duergar* or dwarf, gnome or kobold found in Germanic and Scandinavian traditions.

The answer to the confusing question of variable size may lie in the fairies' ability to alter their height at will. In Scott's version of 'Tam Lin' some stanzas referred to the ability of fairies to alter their shape: 'Our shapes and size we can convert / To either large or small;' [39I:34]. However, Child was suspicious of these stanzas, putting them in an appendix, in spite of the fact that a central motif in this ballad is shape-shifting.

The ballad fairies are repeatedly portrayed as lavishly adorned and accoutred beings. They live in opulent courts, eat the most delectable foods, and dress in sumptuous clothes. They own, or guard, treasures rich beyond the imagination of most mortals, outfitting even their horses in golden bridles and silver bells. The horses themselves are of the finest stock, are traditionally milk-white, and run swifter than the wind. The fairies are almost always clad in the colour green. In 'Thomas Rymer' [37A; 37C] the Queen of Elfland wears a 'grass-green silk' skirt and a mantle of green velvet. The 'Four and twenty' little fairy women in 'The

Wee Wee Man' are similarly 'clad out in green'. The woman who makes an impromptu appearance in 'Young Beichan' [53M] is identifiable as a fairy due to her choice of attire: 'Up starts a woman, clad in green'.

In the witch testimonies the fairies are fairly consistently attributed with the appearance and clothing of the human population at large. Green, black, brown, and white were all popular colours. Isobel Gowdie remembered the Fairy Queen as 'brawlie clothed in whyt linens, and in whyt and browne cloathes', and the Fairy King as 'a braw man, weill favoured, and broad faced'.[37] Robert Kirk described fairy apparel as native Scots garb. He said 'their apparel and speech is like that of the people and countrey under which they live: so are they seen to wear plaids'.[38]

The ballads relate the fairy love of hunting, of music and dancing. Beaten by the knight in 'Sir Cawline' [61:25] the Elf King promises nevermore to 'sport, gamon, or play' on Eldrige Hill. The fairy rade, or procession, as mentioned in 'King Orfeo', 'Allison Gross', and 'Tam Lin', is probably their favoured and best-known activity. From the witch trials, Andrew Man and Donald McIlmichall both said they witnessed fairies dancing and playing music. Donald, tried in Inveraray in 1677, claimed he 'playd on trumps to them quhen they danced'.[39] In Shetland, the trows were notoriously odd dancers. They were said to 'henk' or 'lunk' which seemed to infer a limping motion.[40] Another recreational activity, as the experiences of Tam Lin and Thomas Rymer testify, was abduction.

The fairies were emphatically aristocratic. In many cases their home was described as a hall or court. The very title of Queen and King, so prevalent in the descriptions, is a pretty good indicator of their political structure. The power yielded by this unearthly monarchy was awesome and, according to the protagonist in 'The Wee Wee Man', the Queen of Fairy was a match for even the most powerful of earthly mortals: 'Though the King of Scotland had been there, / The warst o them might hae been his queen.' [38A:6] Kirk found the social and political infrastructure of Fairyland parallel to that of the human world. They were organised into 'tribes and orders' and had 'children, nurses, marriages, deaths and burials'. They also had 'aristocratical rulers and laws, but no discernible religion', nor 'love or devotion towards God', and would disappear on hearing his name. They were subject to the same conflicts and controversies that humans experienced, having 'doubts, disputes, feuds, and syding of parties'.[41]

The ways used by fairies to cast their glamour over mortals were many and varied. At times it would seem that there was very little that one could do, or not do, to avoid these capricious creatures. Activities such as eating, drinking, speaking, or sleeping in a tabooed place were all common mistakes made by human captives. Physical contact with an Otherworld being through gifts, music, riddles or charms were equally common traps. Sometimes entrapment was procured through the use of fairy darts (that is spears, lances, or javelins), arrows, or blasts. Attacks from fairies were prone to occur beneath apple trees, or close to wells, hills or woods, invariably known to be frequented by the elves. The reasons behind enchantment, if fairies could be said to have a motive, were often to obtain an earthly nurse or midwife, and so childbirth was a particularly vulnerable time. Fairies would steal a human baby and replace it with one of their own changelings, attract a mortal lover, or pay a 'teind' to hell.[42] The payment of a teind to hell was one of the most frightening prospects that a captured mortal could face. In some cases it was believed that the Queen of Fairies was pledged to the devil to submit the teind, but in order to save members of her own population from this fate human adults and children were stolen and proffered as the obligatory stipend instead.

Glamoury is also routinely employed in the ballads. Thomas Rymer is warned not to eat the fruit he sees in the garden nor speak to anyone when he arrives in Elfland. Janet in 'Tam Lin' outwits the Queen by refusing the offer of fairy gifts. The very name 'Tamlin' may have been given to him by the fairies to keep him trapped in the Otherworld – a sort of naming magic.[43] The Motherwell text does seem to suggest the possibility:

> 'First they did call me Jack,' he said,
> 'And then they called me John,
> But since I lived in the fairy court
> Tomlin has always been my name. [39D:9][44]

'The Elfin Knight', 'Lady Isabel and the Elfin-Knight', and 'Sir Cawline' speak of a fairy horn or harp. 'King Orfeo' loses his wife to the fairies when she is struck by a fairy dart. Tam Lin [39G and K] was asleep under an apple tree at the time of his capture, while Thomas was taken from under the Eildon tree [37C]. Lady Isabel [4B] escapes death at the hands of the Elf-Knight at 'Wearie's Well'. Magical woods are featured in 'Tam Lin' and 'Hind Etin'. Payment of the teind to hell is exemplified best in 'Thomas Rymer' and 'Tam Lin'. And 'The Queen of Elfan's Nourice' provides an excellent example of the fairy need for human midwives and nurses.

The dangers of eating fairy contaminated food, such as expressed in 'Thomas Rymer', were known to Kirk who said men with second sight had seen fairies eat at funeral banquets, 'hence many of the Scotish-Irish will not tast meat at those meetings, least they have communion with, or be poysoned by them'.[45]

In the trial of Bessie Dunlop she said she was forbidden to speak during
a visit to a fairy tryst, even when asked direct questions. Likewise she is
warned not to speak to her fairy contact if ever she sees him in public
unless he has first addressed her, echoes once more of Thomas Rymer.
Also, Bessie had just given birth when she first encountered the fairies.
Isobel Gowdie could identify elf-shot victims and even claimed she saw elf
darts being made: first, the Devil would 'shape them with his awin hand',
then elf-boys would 'whyttis and dightis' them, or shape and trim the
arrows.[46] Alison Peirson said her uncle told her to sain, or bless, herself so
'that scho be nocht tane away with thame agane; for the teynd of thame
gais everie yeir to hell'.[47]

A curious omission from the ballads is the concept of the changeling.[48]
The belief in changelings, or human babies stolen by fairies and fairy
children left in their place, is among the most commonly held and
widespread fairy tradition, found not only throughout most of western
Europe but all over the world. There are references to changelings in
witch trials, generally regarding cures to be rid of the unfortunate creatures.
An attempt, regrettably unsuccessful, to cure a changeling, or 'sharg,' with
a potion is described in the trial of Isobel Haldane:

> David Moreise wyff com to hir [Isobel], and thryse for
> Goddis saik askit help to hir bairne that wes ane scharge:
> And scho send furth hir sone to gether sochsterrie leaweis,
> quhairof scho directit the bairnes mother to mak a drink. –
> Bot the bairneis mother deponit, that the said Issobell Haldane,
> on-requirit, cam to her house and saw the bairne; said, 'it wes
> ane scharge taikin away;' tuke on hand to cure it; and to that
> effect, gaiff the barne a drink; efter the ressait quhairof the
> bairne died.[49]

A slightly different, though related experience, was spoken of in the 1616
Shetland trial of Barbara Thomasdochter. Among her alleged crimes was
witnessing a visit from a changeling, though it is not mentioned whether
Barbara lost any of her own children in the process: 'she saw ane litle
creatour in hir awin hous amongis hir awin bairnes quhom she callit the
bowmanes [fairy man's] bairne'.[50] Robert Kirk was also familiar with the
changelings and told of women 'taken away when in child-bed to nurse
ffayrie children, a lingring voracious image of theirs being left in their
place'.[51]

In almost every case, the time of day or year when fairies appear is
specified in the ballads. In 'Lady Isobel and the Elf-Knight' [4A] the fairy
appears on the 'first morning in May', or Beltane. The Queen of Fairies in

'Allison Gross' breaks the witch's spell on Hallowe'en, and Tam Lin is rescued on Hallowe'en. The Elf King arrives, heralded by a bugle, at midnight in 'Sir Cawline'.

In the witch trials, Bessie Dunlop's fairy contact usually appeared to her on the twelfth hour of the day. Katherine Ross highlighted Hallowe'en and Midsummer,[52] while Ewfame Makcalzane (1591) pointed to Lammas as a fairy time.[53] In Shetland Katherine Jonesdochter, tried in 1616, claimed to have met a fairy man every year for forty years on Hallowe'en and Holy Cross day (14 September) and mentioned that the trows would come to any house where there was 'feasting, or great mirrines and speciallie at Yule'.[54] Katherine Caray, also tried in 1616, said that when she went to the hills 'at the doun going of the sun, ane great number of fairie men mett her'.[55] Even the fairies themselves, according to Kirk, recognised special days. He says, 'they remove to other lodgings at the beginning of each quarter of the year', and at such times, 'seers or men of the second sight' have frightening experiences with them. Not surprisingly, Kirk commented that church attendance on the Sundays closest to the four quarter days went up as people came to bless themselves and their property against fairy attacks.[56]

The relationship of fairy activity with specific temporal and spatial locations is a close one. It is no accident that particular times and places are denoted, or that fairies would appear to have a fondness for special occasions. Frequently the time and place specified are significant in a broader supernatural or customary context, and are not necessarily only conditional to fairies. As was mentioned above, in discussing the landscape of the supernatural, place and periodicity operate conjointly with the concept of boundaries – 'the magic points where worlds impinge'.[57]

The numbers three and seven[58] are repeatedly encountered in the ballads. The most frequent lapse of time in Elfland is seven years. Thomas Rymer was enchanted for seven years and Hind Etin lived with a mortal wife for seven years during which time she managed to produce one son a year. Tam Lin was the third rider in the Hallowe'en procession. He also warned Janet that if she failed to rescue him he would be confined in Elfland seven more years, barring the possibility that he might be used to pay the teind to hell. In 'Lady Isabel and the Elf-Knight' [4A:9] the elfin assassin had murdered seven times, 'Seven king's-daughters here hae I slain'. In 'Allison Gross' the Queen of Fairy cured the metamorphosed man by stroking him three times over her knee. Though repetition of particular numbers in the witch trials is not as standardised as in the ballads, it is not altogether absent. In 1598–9 Thomas Lorn was brought before the provost of Aberdeen, on charges of communication with, and repeated abductions by, fairies for seven weeks at a time.[59] Isobel Haldane's first visit inside a fairy hill lasted three days, from Thursday till Sunday at noon.[60]

Interludes or relationships with fairy folk could be, on occasion, of some benefit to a mortal. Encounters might leave the human with special gifts or qualities, such as second-sight (like Thomas Rymer) or an ability to heal (like Bessie Dunlop or Alison Peirson). Usually, however, there was a price to pay for these gifts and what initially may have seemed a profitable venture turned out to be a dangerous liaison. For example, Alison Peirson was taught medicinal cures. However, for refusing to join the fairy league and for failing to remain silent about the wonders she witnessed in their world, she was paralysed. Two fairy men taught Elspeth Reoch a ritual which enabled her to gain the power of second sight. Ominously, one of them arrived at her bedside in the night and would not let her rest, relentlessly blackmailing her with threats until she slept with him. After three nights of this abuse she succumbed but when she awoke the next morning she had 'no power of hir toung nor could nocht speik'.[61]

For most people avoidance, or at least appeasement, was the best policy when dealing with fairies. There were various precautions and placations undertaken to avoid enchantment. Amulets were employed to protect against supernatural attacks.[62] Specially chosen pebbles and stones could hold apotropaic qualities or be utilised as part of a larger ritual to ward off evil influences. Elf arrows (or flints) were worn around the neck as protection from elf shot. While some trees, such as apple and hawthorn, were known to be favoured haunts of the fairies, holly and rowan (or mountain ash) were a potent protection against fairies. Evoking the power of God, whether through prayer, using a cross, a bible, or holy water, could also be tried. In the ballad 'Sir Cawline' the mortal knight overcame the Elf King because he disabled the latter's supernatural powers at the outset of battle by calling on the name of Christ. When Alison Peirson was visited by a large group of fairy folk, she attempted to ward them off by saining and praying for herself,[63] and as already mentioned Robert Kirk enjoyed particularly large congregations on quarter days. Kirk also noted that the Highlanders 'put bread, the Bible, or a piece of iron, in womens beds' to protect either mother or baby from being stolen from childbed. The protective power of iron was, of course, not limited to post-natal mothers. Kirk had spoken to a man who had cut a fairy in two with his 'iron weapon' to avert enchantment.[64]

The modes of disenchantment from fairy power are curiously similar to the modes of enchantment. In other words, what in one case may act as a spell may in another case act as a counter-spell. In 'King Orfeo' the music that the fairies love so much is used as a way to win back Lady Isabel. In 'Allison Gross' and 'Tam Lin' physical contact produces both enchantment and disenchantment. The fact that Janet, in 'Tam Lin,' wears a green dress, garb traditionally worn by fairies themselves, is probably no accident and has 'countermagical significance'.[65] The lady of 'Lady Isabel and the Elf-Knight' [4A] lulls the elf-knight to sleep with a 'sma charm' before stabbing and killing him with his own dagger. She thus has employed two countermagical methods, the charm and the dagger, to overcome the supernatural knight. Significant dates, such as May Day in 'Lady Isabel and the Elfin-Knight,' can be dangerous times for mortals to fall under the power of the fairies. Conversely, such times often provide relief to those suffering Otherworld confinement, as with Tam Lin and Allison Gross's unnamed protagonist, both of whom are rescued on Hallowe'en.

If 'Thomas Rymer' can be said to provide the best description of the journey to Fairyland, then 'Tam Lin' surely presents the most memorable account of a rescue from Elfland, which has no equivalent in the witch trials. Janet, the real protagonist in this story, decides to win back the father of her child. In order to do so she must observe a series of rites, leading to an incredible sequence of shape-shifting, and the eventual metamorphosis of Tam Lin into a mortal man once more. Firstly, Janet must know when and where the rescue can take place:

> The night it is good Halloween,
> When fairy folk will ride,
> And they that wad their true-love win,
> At Miles Cross they maun bide. [39I: 34]

Tam Lin tells Janet that when the procession arrives she will be able to identify him, as he will be the third rider to pass and will be mounted on a milk-white steed. She must pull him down from his horse and hold on to him – seemingly straightforward if daunting instructions, except that Tam Lin undergoes a succession of frightening shape changes, such as those of a snake, a lion, or a red-hot bar of iron, before the enchantment is broken. Finally, Janet immerses him in water or milk and then wraps him in her mantle.

A useful tool in considering these accounts of fairy activity and enchantment is the late David Buchan's talerole method of analysis developed from Vladimir Propp's work on the wonder tale or folk tale. Basically, it distinguishes the primary function of the characters. Buchan applied talerole analysis to the Otherworld ballads and found three main taleroles (Bespeller, Bespelled, and Unspeller), existing within two main subgroups: land-based Otherworld beings and water creatures.[66] He found that witch ballads also followed this pattern of Bespeller, Bespelled, and Unspeller. When applied to the revenant or ghost ballads he discovered two main roles (Visitor, and Visited).

Of most relevance to this paper, with regard to the talerole findings, is that the types of the first subgroup, the land-based beings, all result in a happy ending. The types of the second subgroup (not detailed in this paper), the water creatures, end unhappily. In other words, when we read a ballad concerning an Otherworldly land-based creature, such as a fairy, the listener will always hear of a way of escape for the mortal involved. If the mortal has encountered a mermaid or a selchie, one can be sure of forthcoming doom. Such ballads function, contends Buchan, as conveyors of useful cultural knowledge: 'the portrayal of both the personnel and the environment of the Otherworld conveys important cultural information about not only the world around, but the world around that'.[67] This knowledge can only be communicated if the audience of the ballad perfor-mances is aware of the figurative language employed. Barre Toelken points out that the usage of green, or particular plants and trees, the combing of hair or plucking of fruits, is only significant if the connotative meaning is understood as well as the denotative meaning. The majority of the audience must recognise the figurative language or the meanings are lost.[68]

The talerole findings, when applied to witch ballads, reveal that the main concern with this group is not really about witchcraft *per se*. In this they are different from the fairy ballads which convey information about the Otherworld and its folk. The cultural function of the witch ballads and their major focus lie in human relationships, and particularly, though not exclusively, those concerning women. In every one the Bespeller role is played by a woman. When the taleroles are examined in the revenant ballads, the cultural function appears to be designed around helping people, particularly women, cope with grieving and the dislocations of death.[69]

Though by and large the disclosures revealed by talerole analysis are convincing, additionally it could be said that the fairy ballads do not exclusively relate only information about the supernatural world but also, to some degree, express the tensions and concerns within ordinary human relationships. For instance, though 'Tam Lin' is unquestionably a story, the major theme of which is 'supernatural', it is also about the relation-ship between a father and daughter, and between male and female lovers. The daughter defies the paternalism of her father by venturing outside his lands and thus outside his control; thereafter she is immediately engaged in a battle to win the father of her child from the control of another woman.

The fairy ballad shares with folk tale the eucatastrophe, the reversal of catastrophe, or a happy ending. If a happy ending is a sure bet for mortals encountering fairies in the ballads, this can certainly be said to be untrue of human experiences with them via the information given in most other sources. It would seem that, in the lived world, though much of the same figurative language is used, babies are taken by the fairies for evermore, or are left as changelings. People and livestock are maimed, paralysed, killed, or just generally harassed by their fairy neighbours. Some of the witch confessions report seeing dead friends or people known to them in the fairy courts, but one wonders how they ended up there in the first place. Were they abducted, seduced, or simply accidental wanderers into these preternatural havens? Though it is possible to find parallels for almost every fairy motif mentioned in the ballads in other sources, it is noteworthy that the image of the fairy differs significantly when the outcome of dealings with them is considered.

The relative optimism of the fairy ballads as opposed to the gloomier conclusion of the sea-creature ballads may hold further implications. Perhaps the lighter tone of the fairy ballads is indicative of shifting attitudes towards the belief in the power of fairies. By the eighteenth century fairy belief, though by no means absent, was in a process of decline, or at least transformation. On the other hand, a fear of the power of the sea and its multitude of dangers, both natural and supernatural, may have persisted longer. These suggestions must, however, remain speculative.

So are the ballads a valuable historical source in the investigation of fairy belief, despite the fact that the earliest dating of the ballads is to the eighteenth century? It is possible to reconstruct a picture of this once very vital folk belief without looking at the ballads at all. As already stated, an abundance of corroborative evidence for the ballad fairy belief in the sixteenth and seventeenth centuries can be found. Ballad scholars generally have manifested a tendency to concentrate on the differences between ballad versions. However, if we allow ourselves to be drawn to the similarities, we begin to see the forging of specific relationships and patterns of a kind that exist within other mediums of folk articulation. The ballads, I would suggest, are a heavily figurative and motifemic expression of the fairy beliefs of the folk. In the words of David Buchan:

> [ballads] can contain factual truths that are not found in the often scanty records, and they can contain emotional truths, the attitudes and reactions of the ballad-singing folk to the world around them.[70]

Whether the guid neighbours would agree is another matter.

NOTES

1 *The English and Scottish Popular Ballads*, ed. F. J. Child (5 vols., Boston and London, 1882–98).

2 E. C. Mason, *The Mind of Henry Fuseli* (London 1951), points out that the fairies of Blake and Fuseli were inventions of their own sexual fantasy and have a 'peculiar way of employing, and charging with supernatural intensity, nude figures with wide-flung arms and remarkably long legs in fantastic straddling and crouching attitudes, in abandoned embraces, or swaying, hovering, soaring, flying at every possible angle ...'

3 For an excellent appraisal of these topics, see P. Smith, 'The Cottingley fairies: the end of a legend'; T. Tuleja, 'The tooth fairy: perspectives on money and magic'; and R. Wells, 'The making of an icon: the tooth fairy in North American folklore and popular culture', all in P. Narváez (ed.), *The Good People: New Fairylore Essays* (New York 1991).

4 'Billie Blin' is perhaps a tutelary being, such as a brownie, which F. J. Child called 'a serviceable household demon': Child, *Ballads*, 1, 67. 'Billie Blin' is found in 'Gil Brenton' [5], 'Willie's Lady' [6], 'Young Beichan' [53], and 'The Knight and the Shepherd's Daughter' [110]. He also appears in the English ballad 'King Arthur and the King of Cornwall' [30].

5 D. Buchan, 'Taleroles and the Otherworld Ballads', in W. Puchner (ed.), *Tod und Jenseits im Europäischen Volkslied* (Ioannina 1986 [1989]), 247–61.

6 It may be significant that Child was inspired by Svend Gruntvig's edition of Danish ballads and that Gruntvig was influenced by William Motherwell, the Scottish collector. See S. B. Hustvedt, *Ballad Books and Ballad Men* (Cambridge 1930), 205–304.

7 M. J. C. Hodgart, *The Ballads* (New York 1962), 18.

8 'Yeoman minstrelsy' is a term used by E. K. Chambers, *English Literature at the Close of the Middle Ages* (*The Oxford History of Literature*, vol. II, pt. 2) (Oxford 1945), 136.

9 There are a few ballads, though not considered to be supernatural in nature, which have been suggested to contain possible traces of fairy-lore, e.g. 'Fair Annie' [62], 'Child Waters' [63], 'The Lass of Roch Royal' [76], 'Child Maurice' [83], 'Jellon Grame' [90], and 'The Knight and the Shepherd's Daughter' [110]. See Child, *Ballads*, i, 112–13; W. M. Hart, *Ballad and Epic* (Boston 1907), 29; and L. C. Wimberly, *Folklore in the English and Scottish Ballads* (Chicago 1928), 124, 144–5.

10 G. H. Gerould, *The Ballad of Tradition* (Oxford 1932), 161.

11 H. Child Sargent and G. L. Kittredge (eds.), *The English and Scottish Popular Ballads* (London n.d.), p. xii.

12 D. Buchan, 'History and Harlaw', in E. B. Lyle (ed.), *Ballad Studies* (London 1976), 29–40.

13 Buchan, 'History and Harlaw', 37.

14 C. Ginzburg, *The Night Battles: Witchcraft and Agrarian Cults in the Sixteenth and Seventeenth Centuries*, trans. J. and A. Tedeschi (Italian edn, 1966; Baltimore 1992), xvii.

15 C. Ginzburg, *The Cheese and the Worms: The Cosmos of a Sixteenth-Century Miller*, trans. J. and A. Tedeschi (Italian edn, 1976; Harmondsworth 1982), xvii.

16 C. Ginzburg, *Ecstasies*, 10.

17 Ibid., 2.

18 [37C:10]. 'Ferlie' means 'an unusual or strange sight; a wonder, marvel'. It can also signify 'to pry into what does not concern one': *Scottish National Dictionary* [*SND*], s.v.

19 Wimberly, *Folklore in the English and Scottish Ballads*, 116–19.

20 Trial of Bessie Flinkar, 1661 (case 396): C. Larner, C. H. Lee and H. V. McLachlan, *A Source-Book of Scottish Witchcraft* (Glasgow 1977), 258.

21 Wimberly, *Folklore in the English and Scottish Ballads*, 121.

22 Trial of Katherine Ross Lady Fowlis, 22 Jul. 1590: *Criminal Trials in Scotland from 1488 to 1624*, ed. R. Pitcairn (4 vols., Edinburgh 1833; also Bannatyne and Maitland Clubs), i, 196.

23 Trial of Jonet Drever, 1615: *The Court Books of Orkney and Shetland, 1614–1615*, ed. R. S. Barclay (Scot. Hist. Soc., 1967), 18–20.

24 Trial of Katherine Jonesdochter, 2 Oct. 1616: *Court Book of Shetland 1615–1629*, ed. G. Donaldson (Lerwick 1991), 38–43.

25 Trial of John Stewart, 1618, Irvine. Trial, Confession, and Execution of Isobel Inch, John Stewart, Margaret Barclay and Isobel Crawford, for Witchcraft, at Irvine, Anno 1618. From the Original Manuscript (Ardrossan and Saltcoats c.1855).

26 Trial of Isobell Haldane, 15 May 1623: Pitcairn, *Criminal Trials*, ii, 537.

27 Trial of Bessie Dunlop, 8 Nov. 1576: Pitcairn, *Criminal Trials*, i, 52–8. Trial of Elspeth Reoch, 1616: *Miscellany of the Maitland Club* (Maitland Club, 1833), i (1), 187–91. Elspeth was born in Caithness.

28 Robert Kirk, *The Secret Common-Wealth 1691*, ed. S. Sanderson (Cambridge 1976), 61.

29 Walter Scott, *Minstrelsy of the Scottish Border 1802–3* (London 1839), 195.

30 S. Kane, *Wisdom of the Mythtellers* (Peterborough, Ontario, 1994), 75.

31 Trial of Alison Peirson, 28 May 1588: Pitcairn, *Criminal Trials*, i, 163.

32 Trial of Isobel Gowdie, 13 Apr., 3 and 15 May 1662: Pitcairn, *Criminal Trials*, iii, 611. 'Rowtting' – a roar; bellowing of cattle; 'Skoylling' – a yell, a high-pitched roar or bellow, esp. of a cow, *SND*, s.v.

33 Trial of Andrew Man, 1597–8: *Miscellany of the Spalding Club* (Spalding Club, 1841–52), i (1), 121–2.

34 R. W. Munro (ed.), *Monro's Western Isles of Scotland 1549* (Edinburgh 1961).

35 Martin Martin, *A Description of the Western Isles of Scotland 1703, 1716* (Edinburgh 1976). It was written c.1695. For more on the Pygmy Isle, see L. Henderson, 'Martin Martin and the Little People', article forthcoming in M. Bennett (ed.), *The Proceedings of the Martin Martin Conference*.

36 Pitcairn, *Criminal Trials*, iii, 604.

37 Ibid.

38 Kirk, *Secret Common-Wealth*, 55.

39 Trial of Donald McIlmichall, 27 Oct. 1677: J. N. R. MacPhail, *Highland Papers* 2nd ser., vol. 20: 3 (Edinburgh 1928), 38. By 'Trumps' is generally understood a Jew's harp.

40 J. Nicolson, *Shetland Folklore* (London 1981), 77; J. Saxby, *Shetland Traditional Lore* (Edinburgh 1932), 116–17; J. Spence, *Shetland Folklore* (Lerwick 1899), 39.

41 Kirk, *Secret Common-Wealth*, 51, 56, 62.

42 Wimberly, *Folklore in the English and Scottish Ballads*, 275. See also E. B. Lyle 'The Teind to Hell in Tam Lin', *Folklore*, lxxxi (1970) 177–81. A teind is a tithe, or the tenth part. In Scotland, 'that portion of the estates of the laity which is liable to be assessed for the stipend of the clergy of the established church'.

43 Lewis Spence did not approve of this suggestion and said he 'cannot recall any kidnapped hero in fairy legend whose name underwent a change once he became a denizen in the land of the fays': *The Magic Arts in Celtic Britain* (London 1945), 65.

44 To name is to control in folk belief; however, this stanza is a formulaic commonplace of ballad so is not necessarily proof, in this instance, of a direct reflection of belief in naming magic. See 'The Knight and the Shepherd's Daughter' [110A:6].

45 Kirk, *Secret Common-Wealth*, 52.

46 Pitcairn, *Criminal Trials*, iii, 604.

47 Pitcairn, *Criminal Trials*, i, 163.
48 The closest hint of a changeling tradition in the Child ballads is found in 'Tam Lin'. In versions A:22 and B:21, Tam was out hunting with his grandfather when he was taken by the fairies, and in G:25 he was three years old, while in I:29 he was a boy of nine.
49 Pitcairn, *Criminal Trials*, ii, 538. Pitcairn suggests 'sochsterrie leaweis' are the leaves of a herb, perhaps star-grass, bog-star-grass. The *SND* gives Sharg as 'a tiny mischievous creature; a puny, stunted or weakly creature, an ill-thriving child'.
50 Trial of Barbara Thomasdochter or Scord, 2 Oct. 1616: Donaldson, *Court Book of Shetland*, 40.
51 Kirk, *Secret Common-Wealth*, 54.
52 Trial of Katherine Ross Lady Fowlis, 22 Jul. 1590: Pitcairn, *Criminal Trials*, i, 196.
53 Trial of Ewfame (Euphemia) Makcalzane, 9 Jun. 1591: Pitcairn, *Criminal Trials*, i, 252.
54 Trial of Katherine Jonesdochter, 2 Oct. 1616: Donaldson, *Court Book of Shetland* 38–9.
55 Trial of Katherine Caray, Jun. 1616, in J. G. Dalyell, *The Darker Superstitions of Scotland* (Glasgow 1835), 536.
56 Kirk, *Secret Common-Wealth*, 51.
57 Kane, *Wisdom of the Mythtellers*, 103.
58 See Axel Olrik on the 'law of three': A. Olrik, 'Epic Laws of Folk Narrative', in A. Dundes (ed.), *The Study of Folklore* (New Jersey 1965), 129–41.
59 Trial of Thomas Lorn, 19 Jan. 1598–9. *Extracts From the Council Register of the Burgh of Aberdeen*, ed. J. Stuart (Spalding Club, 1844–8).
60 Pitcairn, *Criminal Trials*, ii, 537.
61 *Maitland Club Misc.*, vol. I, pt. 1, 112–13.
62 For more on amulets and charms, see W. MacKenzie, 'Gaelic incantations, charms, and blessings of the Hebrides', *Trans. Gaelic Soc. of Inverness*, xviii (1892), 97–182; G. F. Black, 'Scottish charms and amulets', *Proc. Soc. Antiquaries of Scotland*, xxvii (1892–3), 433–526; F. Marian McNeill, *The Silver Bough* (4 vols., Glasgow 1959), i, 90–6; and J. G. Dent, 'The holed stone amulet and its uses', *Folk Life*, iii (1965), 68–78.
63 Pitcairn, *Criminal Trials*, i, 163.
64 Kirk, *Secret Common-Wealth*, 54, 59.
65 Wimberly, *Folklore in the English and Scottish Ballads*, 391.
66 See D. Buchan, 'Propp's Tale Role and a Ballad Repertoire', *Journal of American Folklore*, xcv (1982), 159–72; and Buchan, 'Taleroles and the Otherworld Ballads'. In the fairy ballads he distinguished the Bespeller–King or Queen of Elfland, or an Elfin being; the Bespelled–mortal, mostly of the opposite sex from the Bespeller; Unspeller–spouse, lover, son. Sometimes Queen of Elfland is both the Bespeller and the Unspeller.
67 Buchan, 'Taleroles and the Otherworld Ballads', 252, 254.
68 B. Toelken, 'Figurative language and cultural contexts in the traditional ballads', *Western Folklore*, xlv (1986), 128–42.
69 D. Buchan, 'Taleroles and the Witch Ballads', in Z. Raj Kovic (ed.), *Ballads and Other Genres* (Zagreb 1988), 133–9; and 'Tale roles and revenants: a morphology of ghosts', *Western Folklore*, xlv (1986), 143–60.
70 Buchan, 'History and Harlaw', 39.

5

Proude Armstrongs and Border Rogues: History in 'Kinmont Willie', 'Jock o the Side' and 'Archie o Cawfield'

KAYE MCALPINE

Historic content and context sit more easily on some ballads than others. If groups of ballads are considered, with an eye to historic content, then those concerning the Border reivers have some of the strongest links with recorded incidents and people, both in terms of the ballad tales themselves and also the singers of the ballads. Bishop Leslie noted that the Borderers 'delyt mekle in thair awin musick and Harmonie in singing, quile of the acts of thair foirbears thay have leired, or quhat thame selfes have inuented of ane ingenious policie to dryue a pray',[1] and around two hundred years or so on, the ministers of Wamphray and Castleton confirmed the Bishop's words, if confirmation were needed. The minister of Wamphray noted that 'songs are still sung, descriptive of the barbarous deeds and bloody feuds of some former age, of which this parish was the scene',[2] and his colleague at Castleton remarked 'as it [Castleton Parish] lies directly along the English Border, it must have been, for a long period, the scene of action, of fierce contention, of barbarous feuds, and marauding expeditions ... exploits have been recorded in the poetry of the times, which are still sung by the aged, and listened to with eagerness by the young'.[3] Such remarks are the foundation of the seductive aspects of the riding and reiving ballads in particular. The families which are glorified in them are actual Border clans, many of the characters are named after individuals who lived the kind of lives which these ballads describe, and even more tellingly, the places mentioned in the ballad tales are actual places. The strong sense of locality which exists in the ballads can add credence to the tales: the argument being that the story must be true because the places where the action occurred exist. For instance, the muster-call in 'Jamie Telfer of the Fair Dodhead' gives geographic to-names – those names which were given to members of the Border clans in order that individuals could be identified among many who bore the same

name. These identification 'tags' are still names of farms and localities in
what was the West Border March and Liddesdale:

> Warn Wat o' Harden and his sons,
> Wi' them will Borthwick Water ride;
> Warn Gaudilands and Allanhaugh
> And Gilmancleugh and Commonside;
>
> Ride by the gate at Priesthaughswire
> And Warn the Currors o the Lea
> And as ye cum doon the Hermitage Slack
> Warn doughty Willie o' Gorrinberry [190]

The ballads with which this paper is concerned, 'Kinmont Willie', 'Jock
o the Side' and 'Archie o Cawfield', are part of this tradition and they take
us into the undeniably attractive, but rather dangerous territory of
historicity: what is historically accurate regarding documentation, what is
accurate regarding what can be gleaned about the character types inhabit-
ing the ballads, and what is fiction – and whose fiction is it? – are all
questions which are very relevant to the following discussion. These
ballads share the same story line, the rescue of a condemned reiver on the
night before his execution from within a town (Carlisle, Newcastle or
Dumfries)[4] by friends and family.

'Jock o the Side' [187] exists in various versions in Child. In addition to
the Child versions, 'Archie o Cawfield' [188] exists in broadsheet forms,[5]
was recorded by Gavin Greig from Bell Robertson under the title 'Johnnie
Ha',[6] and survived trans-Atlantic transportation.[7] However, there is only
one text of 'Kinmont Willie' [186] – from Scott's *Minstrelsy* – which Scott
claimed was 'much mangled by reciters, so that some conjectural emenda-
tions have been absolutely necessary to render it intelligible'.[8] It may be
that Kinmont Willie is Scott's reworking of an existing 'rescued prisoner'
ballad tale (perhaps one with an Armstrong victim-hero), incorporating
the historically recorded rescue of Kinmont Willie Armstrong from Carlisle
into an existing tale. I suggest this because a version of 'Jock o the Side'
was known before the end of the sixteenth century. Bronson records:

> That there was a song on this subject known familiarly
> before the end of the sixteenth century is proved, as has been
> noted by Hyder Rollins, by a ballad in Bodleian Rawlinson
> MS. Poet. 185, fols 9–10, the date of which is not later than
> 1592. It is to be sung to the tune of 'Hobbinoble and Iohn A
> Side'.[9]

In addition, although Archie is identified as a Hall in various versions of 'Archie o Cawfield', Child recorded that at the end of the Glenriddel MS., from which this [188B] version comes, it was noted that 'Tradition says that his [Archie's] name was Archibald Armstrong',[10] something Scott also remarked upon, noting that 'Ca'field, or Calfield, is a place in Wauchopedale belonging of old to the Armstrongs.'[11]

Alternatively, it may well be that various versions of the ballad tale, containing heroes and victims of different names, were already in existence in the period of the events to which they relate. Whatever the origin of the three tales (the rescues of Jock of the Side, Archie of Ca'field and Kinmont Willie), the ballad of 'Kinmont Willie' is the most historic, with its roots set firmly in a known event – an escape from the apparently impregnable Carlisle Castle.[12]

However, the facts as they are presented in the ballad and those contained within the records of the time do not always agree, and the ballad of 'Kinmont Willie' stands as a good example of a sequence of events worked into popular narrative, whether or not Scott had a major hand in the final product.

To bring drama and excitement to a tale, the teller must at times embellish the telling, with gestures, with facial expression, or, as in this case, with an exaggeration of the facts. For example, 'Kinmont Willie' presents the rescue as a last-minute attempt to free the reiver from death: historically, there is no evidence of this. However, a rescue from imprisonment without impending doom does not make for the same dramatic tale, even when the rescue is an audacious one. To appreciate fully the political and cultural implications of these ballads, the relevant laws of the Border Marches have to be considered, and note will be made of their effect on the actual ballad tale.

The rescue of William Armstrong of Kynmonth – Kinmont Willie – from Carlisle Castle was an audacious act and remains impressive. However, the daring nature of the rescue should not blind us to the fact that Kinmont Willie was no innocent man. He was a notorious reiver and the raids in which he was involved were not small-scale reiving. A document dated 24 February 1587/8, written by the clerk of John Forster, the English West March Warden, complained against:

> Davye Ellot called 'the Carlinge', Cleme Crozer called 'Nebles Cleme', Thome Armstrone called Syme's Thom, Will Armstrong, called Kynmothe, Ecktor of the Hilhouse, and other 300 aryen, who ran a day foray and took away forty score kye and oxen, three score horses and meares, 500

sheep, burned houses and spoiling the same to the value of
2000L sterling and slaying 10 men at Michaelmas 1584.[13]

Indeed, Kinmont Willie's name was used as a byword for reif and disorder.
James Melvine used the reiver's name in his speech against subscribing to
the Act of Supremacy in 1584, demanding 'who shall take order with vice
and wickedness? The court and bishops? As well as Martine Ellot and Will
of Kinmonthe, with stealing upon the Borders.'[14] No mention of this or
any similar affair is contained in the ballad of 'Kinmont Willie' and, while
inclusion of the reiver's name may suggest the raids and reif in which the
man was involved to a knowledgeable listener, what the ballad is intent on
portraying is the duplicitous nature of the deputy Salkeld, and so
Kinmont Willie is presented as an innocent party in the events depicted.

   The portrayal of the condemned man as guiltless is not paralleled in
'Jock o the Side'. In three of the four known versions, a raid is mentioned
in the opening verse:

> Now Liddesdale has ridden raid,
>   But I wat they had better staid at hame,
> For Mitchel o Winfield he is dead
>   And my son Johnie is prisner tane. [187B:1]

> Now Liddesdale has ridden a rade,
>   But I wat they had a better staid at home,
> For Michel o Windfield he is slain
>   And my son Johnny they have him tane. [C:1]

> Liddisdaill has ridden a raid,
>   But they had better ha staid at hame;
> For Michael a Wingfield he is slain
>   And Jock o the Side they hae taen. [D:1]

This concentrates the necessary information referring to action prior to
the ballad tale into four lines, which are notable for their dramatic tone
and insistent, driving narrative, interplaying active and passive phrases and
effectively identifying the character types, through the placement of the
word 'Liddesdale', for as James Reed noted, Liddesdale 'would be heavy
with significance for its [the ballad's] original audience, place names to
them being often a matter of life and death'.[15] The [A] version omits the
raid, but offers information regarding the location and prisoner status of
Jock:

> Peeter a Whifield he hath slaine,
> And Iohn a Side, he is tane,

> And Iohn is bound both hand and foote,
> And to the New-castle he is gone. [187A:1]

In [188B], the victim is 'condemned to death / die', which suggests a judicial process, but it is only the [A] version of 'Archie o Cawfield', which provides any insight into what the character's crime has been. In [188A] the character of Archie tells the audience / reader:

> 'Today has been a justice court,
>
>   ...
>
> And a' Liddesdale were here the night,
> The morn's the day at I'se to die.'

> 'What is thy crime, Archie, my billie?
> What is the crime they lay to thee?'
> 'I brake a spear i the warden's breast,
> For saving my master's land,' said he. [188A:19,20]

Where this differs from the other rescue ballads is that Archie is a Scot, held in Scotland, for an act committed there. However, we may assume that Jock o the Side was also involved in a fray with Border officials, if we take the evidence presented to us in 'Hobie Noble' [189]. Hobie states that 'The land-sergeant has me at feid ... For Peter of Whitfield his brother's dead' [189:9]. Peter of Whitfield is mentioned in 'Jock o the Side' [187A] as being a victim of the Liddesdale raid.[16]

Although Bronson states that the Bodleian ballad which was to be sung to the tune of 'Hobbinoble and Iohn A Side' could be dated 'no later than 1592', we do not know the precise story content of 'Hobbinoble and John A Side', the song or ballad from which the tune was derived. I would therefore suggest that the repetitive inclusion of the name of a Whitfield along with a reference to Liddesdale riders – and Armstrongs in particular – may connect the initial scenes of the extant versions of 'Jock o the Side' with either an official plot 'to break the force of Liddesdale'[17] by William Bowes in 1598 or an incident of 1599, which occurred after a football match.

In his letter of February 1598, Bowes explained that there had been unrest on the Scottish side of the Border, for 'some of the principal Ellots and Armstrongs, breaking their faith to Buccleuch formerly to enter as pledges, have stirred up in him an earnest desire for revenge',[18] and that 'these wretches' were responsible for the 'killinge of Mr Whitfield, and then instantly foure within my brother's office of Tyndale'.[19] The Bowes brothers and Buccleuch had therefore hatched a plot 'to tame these outlawes, that Baclughe should restrayne all his freinds, and suffer our men to scourge the rest'. Even though 'this purpose was discovered by some Scottish thieves', the plan worked, for:

> the Ellots and Armstrangs were 'so proude, and contemninge poore decayed Tyndale', that though they rose to the fray, they removed not their goods, and my brother took 200 of their cattle, and slew three, whereof the principall killer of Mr Whitfield was one.[20]

If we take the information as it is presented, William Bowes refers to two confrontations, one in which a Nicolas Whitfield was killed by Liddesdale Elliots and Armstrongs and another in which revenge was taken.

The second incident also involved Liddesdale men, but it took place in Eskdale, at Bewcastle. Two letters exist which refer to the incident:

> Upon Sunday 13th May Mr Ridley and his friends hearing that Scotsmen to the number of 12 were to come to a tryst in the West March of England, he having had friends 'murdered downe bye the sayd Scotes men' took his friends and men to the number of 40, and thought to apprehend them on English ground. But the Scots having intelligence of his design, came 200 strong or more into England, 'and ther did most crewelly murder Mr William Rydley of Willimonstwyk, with two other of his frendes, and wounding John Whitfield hir Majesties officer soe grevously, which we think it is impossable he should leave.[21]

Henry Woodrington, writing to Robert Carey, was more vivid in his description of the incident, specifying that the skirmish took place after 'a footbal playing and after that a drynkyng hard at Bewcastle house',[22] and that the perpetrators were 'the great thieves and arch murderers ... especially them of Whythaugh',[23] noting that the Scots had 'cut Mr Rydley and Mr Nicol Welton's throats, slain one Robson tenant of her Majesties and taken 30 prisoners, mostly her tenants except Francis Whytfield', and left 'many sore hurt, especially John Whytfield, whose bowells came out, but they are sowed upp agayne, and is thought shall hardly escape, but as yet lyveth'.[24]

I wonder, then, if, through historical 'layering' where one tale or historical event is connected with another,[25] the tale of 'Jock o the Side' recalls part of the repercussions of one or both of these incidents, for the Whitfields were West March officials – John was described as 'hir Majesties officer' in the letter signed by the Whitfields and the Ridleys – something which is mentioned in 'Hobie Noble'. The statement, in both 'Hobie

Noble' and 'Jock o the Side', that Hobbie was 'a banished man' may relate to the facts that while the Bewcastle Nobles – including a Hobbe Noble – were English subjects in 1583, according to Musgrave's list,[26] by March 1596, in an Award by John Forster, the Nobles were Scottish.[27] There are some indications, then, either in the texts or in historical records, that all three prisoners may have committed offences which led to their capture. However, in 'Kinmont Willie', the nature of the capture is presented as questionable and the ballad includes an attack on the character of the captor, Salkeld.

Despite Kinmont Willie's repute, his capture could not have legally progressed to a hanging due to a legal loophole, although I use the word 'legally' with some caution, since the law could be variously interpreted on the Borders, both by the 'notorious' reivers and by the Wardens and other supposed law-keepers. It was the timing of his capture which rendered the taking of the reiver questionable. Kinmont Willie was taken on 17 March 1596, after attending a Warden Meeting, and therefore was under the protection of the terms set for Truce Days. An Assurance of Truce was meant to be enacted, by both sides, until sunrise of the next day, in the event of a single Truce-Day:

> On the day of the meeting, both sides attended 'in peaceable wise without harness' and each side proclaimed an 'assurance' that no man would harm other 'by word or deed or look'.[28]

This meant that no reiving, no theft and no kidnap should have been practised during these hours by the parties attending the Truce; this seems to have been something which was adhered to, and it meant that everyone concerned could ride home with the knowledge that riders from the other side would make no attempt upon them.

According to some reports of the incident, Kinmont Willie had attended the Truce near the Kershopefoot, between Scott of Haining of Liddesdale and the deputy Warden of the English West March, Salkeld. The English party, ostensibly riding home, was on the south side of the Liddel Water; Kinmont was riding home on the north. The English host seems to have then made a play for Kinmont Willie for, 'the great cumpany of Ingland ... dang him to the ground, perforce wittinglie and willinglie, notwithstanding of any crying or showting that he might mak for his saftie'.[29]

The dubious nature of the capture was something which haunted Scrope, the March Warden. He never stated that the capture was rightful, amongst all his excuses for the subsequent rescue, and other March

Wardens were acutely aware of the debate surrounding the capture. Ralph
Eure wrote to Burghley, acknowledging the fact that 'when they [men at a
truce meeting] remain but one day, they take assurance from the sunrise
of the one day till sunrise of the next, that every man may likely be
returned safe to his dwelling as he came to the place of meeting'.[30]
However, Eure did not support the argument in the ballad – that Scrope's
man acted unlawfully – and politically recommended that the ambiguities
surrounding truce days which had been revealed through the taking of
Kinmont Willie had better be examined and refined, for the same problem
'may arise with any other warden and your lordship may now take
occasion to prevent future harmes'.[31]

Scrope would have been an imprudent man to have had an Armstrong
hanged after he had been taken in such a way, especially a man of such
note. As it was, Scrope was not even present in the town of Carlisle when
Salkeld brought his prize home. As deputy, Salkeld probably would not
have dared to execute a summary hanging, due to the possibility of
retaliation from his superiors as well as from Liddesdale and the threat of
hanging never really materialised. Thus, the opening verses of 'Kinmont
Willie' contain a mix of fact and fancy:

> O have ye na heard o the fause Sakelde?
> O have ye na heard o the keen Lord Scroop?
> How they hae taen bauld Kinmont Willie
> On Hairibee to hang him up?

> Had Willie had but twenty men
> But twenty men as guid as he,
> Fause Sakelde had never the Kinmont taen,
> Wi eight score in his companie. [186:1,2]

Salkeld is 'fause' because of the breaking of the truce, a fact which is
emphasised later on in the ballad, not only by Buccleuch's statement, 'O
have they taen him Kinmont Willie, / Against the truce of Border side',
but also by the presentation of the news of the capture to Buccleuch,
'Lord Scroop has taen the Kinmont Willie, / Between the hours of night
and day' [186:5], which emphasises the nature of the one-day truce, as
explained by Eure (see above). In addition Willie did only have a few
riders with him, but the eightscore of Salkeld's men mentioned in the
ballad perhaps sells Kinmont Willie short, since the records show that
around two hundred men went after him. However, Scrope was not
present and Kinmont Willie was not taken to be hanged.

The invective within the ballad, attributed to Buccleuch, bears some
relation to the real reason for the rescue of Kinmont Willie. Buccleuch

engineered the rescue not for love of Kinmont Willie, but as a way of satisfying his outraged honour, honour which was severely dented, if Moysie's account is to be believed, in that Kinmont Willie had been 'takin ... be the Inglischmen, at a meiting: at a day of trew of the opposit warden with Balcleuch (being lord and keipar of Liddisdeall) and [to] his dishonour as he comptit':[32]

> He has taen the table in his hand
> He gard the red wine spring on hie;
> 'Now Christ's curse on my head,' he said
> 'But avenged of Lord Scroop I'll be!' [186:9]

Buccleuch and Scrope cultivated a mutual mistrust and dislike, and Buccleuch viewed Scrope's lack of intervention in the whole affair as an affront. Indeed, letters had been written, first to Salkeld, then to Scrope, who 'behaved himself so straitly in this matter that he would do no kind of reason',[33] then to Bowes, the English Ambassador, and even to King James, but Buccleuch had gained no satisfaction from any man. This process reveals the insistent nature of the ballad's opening lines, where it seems that Kinmont Willie is to be hanged almost immediately, as purely fictional.

In the ballad, Buccleuch wishes that there was war between Scotland and England, for then he would 'slight Carlisle castell high, / Tho it were builded of marble-stane' [186:13] and continues:

> I would set that castell in a low
> And sloken it with English blood,
> There's nevir a man in Cumberland
> Should ken where Carlisle castell stood [186:14]

However, he nobly notes 'But since nae war's between the lands, / And there is peace, as peace should be.' [186:15], and vows not to harm an English subject. These lines suggest a 'fierce-but-fair' attitude, which perhaps owes little to Buccleuch's actual intentions. The rescue was a point of honour. The intent was to recover Kinmont Willie from right within Scrope's mighty Carlisle Castle, not to ride a retaliation-raid into the West March. Buccleuch of the ballad, honour outraged ('Have they taen him Kinmont Willie ... and forgotten that the bauld Buccleuch / Is keeper here on the Scottish side?' [186:11]), musters 'forty marchmen bauld' [186:16], all of the name of Scott, save 'Sir Gilbert Elliot, calld, / The Laird of Stobs' [186:18]. This turns the ballad into a glorification of the Scott clan, but in reality the interfamilial, cross-Border intrigues which were rife, played an integral part in the rescue. If Salkeld's taking of

Kinmont Willie was technically illegal, so was Buccleuch's rescue, for as
chapter 35 of Balfour's *Practicks* noted:

> Gif ony person of ather realme sall cum within the uther
> realme, to mak sturt, raise fire, bear armour, or with force
> mak ony impediment to the Wardane of that realme ... the
> persoun swa doand sall be reputit publick offendar aganis the
> treatie of peace.[34]

The roll-call of the principal riders recorded in the *Calendar* letters
allows us to see the Anglo-Scottish nature of the venture. The following
list is a compilation of the names given in Scrope's letter to Burghley,
dated 14 April 1596, and another, unsigned, which was sent to Scrope
around 24 April 1596, and which may have come from Richie's Will:[35]

Walter Scott of Buccleuch

his lieutentants:
>   Gib Eliot
>   'Auld' Wat [Scott] of Harden

Grahams:
>   Richey of Brackenhill
>   Geordie's Sandey
>   Will's Jocke
>   Andrew
>   Hutcheon [also known as Richie's Hutcheon]
>   Willie of the Rose Trees
>   Willie of the Mote
>   Richie's Will
>   Rob of the Faulde
>   Walter of Netherby

Two Carletons, the brothers:
>   Lancelot
>   Thomas[36]
>   [Both brothers had been English West march officials]

Irvines:
>   Willie Kang and 'his bretheren'
>   four other Kangs

Bells:
>   Will 'Redcloak' and his brother John
>   Rob from Annerdale

Armstrongs, including:
>   Kinmont's Jock
>   Kinmont's Francie
>   Kinmont's Geordy
>   Kinmont's Sandy
>   the Laird of Mangerton
>   the young Laird of Whithaugh and his son
>   three of the Calfhills, Jocke Bighames and 'one Ally, a bastard'
>   Ebes [Hobbye's] Sandy
>
>   Young John of Langholm and his brother Kirste
>   Kirste of Barngleish and his brother Rob
>   three 'bretheren of Tweda'
>   young John of the Hollace and 'one of his bretheren'
>   the 'Chingles' [possibly Archie of the Gingles, Jock of Gingles, George of Gingles]

24 assorted Elliots and Scotts, including:
>   Will Elliot, 'goodman of Gorrombye'[37]
>   John Elliot, 'called of the Copshawe'
>   Walter Scott of Goldelands another Scott, 'named Todrigges'

Buccleuch put his force at eighty: the ballad has forty riders, the same number as Ralph Eure, the English Middle March Warden, gave; the aggrieved Scrope estimated a greater force: 'five hundred horse "armed and appointed with gavlockes and crowes of iron, handpeckes, axes and skailinge lathers"'.[38] The involvement of the Grahams of Eske[39] and the Carletons suggests that the crime of March Treason, 'trysting with a Scot and bringing him into England to slaughter, burn, rob, steal &c.',[40] could certainly have been levelled at some of the rescuers. Information regarding the intended rescue, such as Kinmont Willie's actual location and the nature of the defences of Carlisle Castle, seems to have been bought or given freely. What aided the actual rescue was that Kinmont Willie was not weighed down with 'airn' in 'the inner prison' [186:34], as the ballad presents him.

   The receipt of news that a man is condemned to die is less elaborate in 'Jock o the Side'. The news is relayed to Mangerton, by way of the 'what news, what news' formula. He responds, in formulaic fashion, with the 'I'd gie them a' formula, which indicates Mangerton's resolve to save Jock.[41] This is very different from the seven-verse invective of Buccleuch in 'Kinmont Willie'. Mangerton begins to organise the rescue immediately, taking (with three or five men) the road to Newcastle. Disguises are effected in [187A] and [C] ('Wee will ryde like noe men of warr; / But like

poore badgers wee wilbe' [187A:8], 'Like gentlemen ye must not seem /
But look like corn-gaugers ae road' [187C:8]),[42] but whether the riders are
disguised or not, all ballad versions present them riding to Newcastle by
way of the Chollerton ford, called Culerton ford in [A] and [D] and
Cholerford in [B] and [C].

In 'Archie o Cawfield', once the number of men to ride has been
decided ('They mounted ten well-wight men, / Ten o the best in Christenty'
[188A:7], 'Ye's hae six true men an yoursel, / And me to bear ye
company'),[43] the ride also begins, once the horses have had their shoes
turned backwards, in order to leave false trails:

> He has shod them a their horse,
> He's shod them siccar and honestly,
> And as he turned the cakers backwards oer
> Where foremost they were want to be [188A:9]
>
> Turn back the cakers of our horses' feet!
> For it is forward we would be. [188B:7]

This measure is also taken in the [B] version of 'Jock o the Side', while in
the [A] version, the horses are to be unshod, presumably for the same
purpose. In 'Kinmont Willie', however, the rescuers rely on stealth ('we
crept on knees, and held our breath' [186:29]), and are aided by a storm.

In all three ballads, the rescuers must cross a river before reaching the
town, but, before this crossing is effected in 'Kinmont Willie', a form of
summary justice is executed, which is entirely fictitious. During this scene
and in those that follow, the voice of the ballad changes, from being a
third person narrative to a first person plural account, drawing the singer
and the listener into the tale.

The riders meet with Salkeld, who questions the various appearances of
the men: the 'five and five ... Wi hunting horns and bugles bright', Salkeld
identifies as hunters; the 'five and five ... Like Warden's men, arrayed for
fight [186:18], he calls marshal men' [186:22]; and the 'five and five like a
mason gang' [186:19], he calls mason-lads:

> 'Where be ye gaun, ye hunters keen?'
> Quo false Sakelde; 'come tell tae me!'
> 'We go to hunt an English stag,
> Has trespassed on the Scots countrie'
>
> 'Where be ye gaun, ye marshal men?'
> Quo fause Sakelde; 'come tell me true!'
> 'We go to catch a rank reiver,
> Has broken faith wi the bauld Buccleuch.'

> 'Where be you gaun, ye mason-lads,
> Wi a your ladders lang and hie?'
> 'We gang to herry a corbie's nest
> That wens not far from Woodhouselee.' [186:21,22,23]

In verse 21, as in 'Hobie Noble' and 'Hughie Graham', a man is symbolised by a deer; in this case, I would suggest that Salkeld himself is the cipher, for his trespass was to take a man outwith his warden jurisdiction, with no form of trod. The 'rank reiver' is most probably an elaboration of the first metaphor directed at Salkeld, this time including an insult, due to the application of the derogatory adjective 'rank'. Elsewhere, Salkeld is 'fause', but Scrope is described in no other terms but 'keen'. The 'corbie's nest' is, of course, Carlisle Castle.

The fourth group of 'broken-men' do not respond to Salkeld's questioning. Instead, their leader, Dickie of Dryhope, exacts a revenge on Salkeld, who seems well aware of the rider's intentions:

> 'Why trespass on the English-side?
> Row footed outlaws, stand!' quo he;
> The neer a word had Dickie to say,
> Sae he thrust the lance thro his fause bodie. [186:25]

Although Dick Armstrong of Dryhope does not appear in the lists of riders on the Kinmont Willie rescue sent to Burghley by Scrope, the violent action of the character of that name in the ballad has precedents in known raids. John Forster complained against Dickie Armstrange of Driauppe in 1584, along with many others, including Nebles Clemy; for 'running an open foray at the Slymefoote on the Middle Marches, stealing 300 kie and oxen, 40 horses and meires, spoiling 30 'sheles' to the value of 100*l* and taking 20 prisoners'.[44] In Scrope's 'breviat of complainte', sent to Burghley, Hecky Noble is stated as making a complaint against 'Dick [of Driupp] and other 100 Scots for burning to dede his sonne John, and his wief great with child, nine houses and taking 200 nolt'.[45] Dickie of Dryhope is last mentioned in 1594, which makes him contemporary with the men listed in Scrope's letter to Burghley, dated 14 April 1596, so although there is no written record of his participation in the raid, his inclusion in the ballad is not entirely out of place. However, the death of Salkeld on the point of Dickie of Dryhope's lance, is fabrication, although it settles well into the ballad sense of retributive justice.

'Kinmont Willie' and the [A] version of 'Jock o the Side' share a rescue-entry method. The way Kinmont Willie was rescued has previously been mentioned. The rescuers of Jock of the Side also effect entry by scaling walls:

> And some did climbe up by the walls
> And some climbe up by the tree,
> Untill they came upp to the top of the castle,
> Where Iohn made his mone trulye. [187A:19]

In the other versions of 'Jock o the Side' the ladder, which has been made out of a tree, is too short to effect entry and the town gate has to be forced. This act is reminiscent of the entry made by Adam Bell and Clim of the Clough into Carlisle in 'Adam Bell, Clim of the Clough and William of Cloudesly' [116].

The murder of the porter in 'Jock o the Side', in order to gain entry to Newcastle ('I wat they were obliged to wring his neck in twa' [187C:10], 'His neck in twa I wat they hae wrung ... His life and his keys at anes they hae taen' [187B:14]), also bears a strong resemblance to the way in which Adam Bell and Clim of the Clough enter Carlisle in order to rescue William of Cloudesly in Child [116]. Adam and Clim first try to enter Carlisle by sleight:

> Adam sayd, I haue a lettre wryten wele,
> Now let us wysely werke;
> We wyll say we haue the kynges seale,
> I hold the porter no clerke. [116:55]

This piece of ingenuity almost fails ('Here cometh no man ... Tyll a false thefe be hanged, / Called Wyllyam of Clowdysle.' [116:59]), but the porter believes their tale that '[here] we haue the kynges seale' [116:61] and admits entry, whereupon the two men kill him:

> [They] called the porter to a councell,
> [And] wrunge his neck in two
> [And] kest him in a depe dongeon,
> [And] toke the keyes hym fro. [116:65]

The vocabulary used to describe the act remains the same in 'Adam Bell, Clim of the Clough and William of Cloudesly' and the later 'Jock o the Side' versions – the porter's neck is 'wrung in two / twa' – perhaps suggesting that the one influenced the other.

With reference to the Kinmont Willie rescue, entry into Carlisle was aided either by someone leaving the postern open, or by the rescuers battering the gate down. In the ballad, however, the rescuers scale the walls and enter over the rooftops of the castle and, in keeping with Buccleuch's previous declaration that there will be no random killing ('I'll neither harm English lad or lass' [186:15], the watchman does not have his neck wrung:

He has taen the watchman by the throat,
He flung him down upon the lead;
'Had there not been peace between our lands,
Upon the other side thou hadst gaed.' [186:30]

This is all very gallant, but Moysie's account of the affair does not present quite so gracious a picture of Buccleuch:

[He] cause blaw his trumpet on the hicht of the castell wall,
and then brocht the said William away hailscart, slaying and
hurting in the meanetyme thrie of the watches of the castell.[46]

Scrope, in his report, gave a slightly different account, stating that two watchmen were killed.

The noise and confusion which the raid was believed to have caused, such as Moysie's account of a trumpet call, and Birrel's statement that there was shouting, general noise and, once again, a trumpet, is certainly recorded in Kinmont Willie. The description of the rescue includes Buccleuch calling 'Now sound out, trumpets!' [186:31] and a reference to the type of tools used to break out Kinmont Willie ('Wi coulters and wi forehammers, / We garrd the bars ring merrilie' [186:34]). Scrope's letter to Burghley of 14 April includes the report that Buccleuch shouted out, in the midst of the action, 'Stand to yt, for I have vowed to God and to my prince that I will featch out of England Kinmont dead or quicke.'[47]

The noise recorded in 'Kinmont Willie' is also present in 'Jock of the Side' – doors are broken ('four did breake one dore without, / Then Iohn brake fiue himsell' [187A:29], 'The nest chaind dore that they cam at, / They gard it a in flinders flee.' [187B:21], 'And the nest they brak in flinders three' [187C:7]), and locks are filed off ('And hee fyled downe that iron dore' [187A:32]). Similarly, in 'Archie o Cawfield', the door is battered down ('he's taen the door aye with his foot, / And fast he followed it with his knee' [188A:23]; 'And doors of deal, and bands of steel, / He got them all in flinders flee' [C:12]; 'With plough-coulters and gavellocks / They made the jail-house door to flee' [D:10]):

O Jockie Hall stept to the door,
And he bended it back upon his knee,
And he made the bolts that the door hang on
Jump to the wa right wantonlie. [188B:14]

Bold Dickie broke lock, Bold Dickie broke key,
Bold Dickie broke everything that he could see; [188F:10][48]

The tools mentioned in the [D] version of 'Archie o Cawfield' are reminiscent of the reports made by Scrope about Buccleuch's raid on Carlisle: Scrope claimed they were 'armed and appointed with gavlockes and crowes of iron, handpeckes, axes and skailinge lathers'.[49]

The rescue is effected by one member of the rescue party physically carrying the chained prisoner to his horse: in [187A], it is Hobie Noble, who says 'This night I am comen for to loose thee' [187A:26]; [187:B] has 'The Laird's Jock's gotten up fu hie; / And down the stair him, irons and a' [187B:22]; in [187C], 'Jack has got the prisoner on his back' [187C:18]; while in [188A:25], the hero is Dickie ('he's got the prisoner on o his back, / He's gotten him irons and aw'), as it is in [Bb], [D] and [F]; and in [B] and [C], it is Jocky Ha ('he took the prisoner on his back' [188B:15], 'He's taen the prisoner on his back / And a' his heavy irons tee.' [188C:14]). In 'Kinmont Willie', the rescuer is Red Rowan.

Irrespective of which ballad is considered, the presentation of the prisoner is the same. All three men, Kinmont Willie, Jock o the Side and Archie o Cawfield are resigned to death and can foresee no escape. Kinmont Willie is asked, 'Sleep ye, wake ye, Kinmont Willie / Upon the morn that thou's to die?', to which he replies:

> 'O I sleep saft, and I wake aft,
> It's lang since sleeping was fleyed frae me;
> Gie my service back to my wyfe and bairns,
> And a gude fellows that speer for me. [186:36]

Jock o the Side and Archie o Cawfield are even more pessimistic. They lament that their cause is lost, with striking parallels in the language, which suggests that they have a common origin: 'if a' Liddisdale were here the (this) night, / The morn is (morn's) the day that I maun (must) die' [187B:18; C:14]; 'the morn's the day that I man die' [188B:11]; and 'I sleep not aft, I lie not saft' [188C:8]. In [188C] and [188D], the prisoner also expresses concern over the safety of his rescuers, insisting that 'if you be found at jail-house door / I fear like dogs they'll gar ye die.' / 'If the lord Lieutenant come on you / Like unto dogs he'll cause you die.' This is a direct warning that, if caught, they will also hang. Blind Harry's *Wallace* refers to the fate of dogs, 'As bestiall houndis hangit our a tre', and Montgomerie, in his flyting against Polwart, talks of a suitable death for the 'fowmard face', that is the ferret, or weasel-faced, Polwart, 'by throwing of the throate / Like a tyke over a tree'.[50]

The prisoners' distress is compounded by the fact that they are all restrained with fetters. In 'Jock o the Side' and 'Archie o Cawfield' the restraints are made from 'Spanish airn', of various weights, but all of which are excessive:

> Full fifteen stane o Spanish iron
> They hae laid a' right sair on me; [187B:19]
>
> For there is fifty stone of Spanish iron
> Laid on me fast wee lock and key. [187C:15]
>
> There's fifteen stone of Spanish iron
> Lyes fast to me with lock and key [188A:22][51]

Kinmont Willie is also fettered, for, like the other prisoners, he has to be carried to freedom and 'At every stride Red Rowan made, I wot the Kinmont's airns played clang' [186:39]. The specific reference to Spanish iron in the above quotations may be two-fold: Spanish iron and steel – especially that from Toledo – was famous for its durability and using 'Spanish' as an adjective may suggest the extent of the cruel nature of the incarceration. The *Oxford English Dictionary* notes that in 1584 Walsingham used 'Spanish', to mean 'deceitful, perfidious, treacherous', and at the time there was political comment on Spanish practices in the New World of the Americas.[52]

Once the prisoner has been liberated from the jail, all three ballads have references to crossing wild running water: the Eden Water in 'Kinmont Willie'; Chollerton Ford on the Tyne in 'Jock o the Side' [187A,B,C,D]; and the Annan in 'Archie o Cawfield' [188A,B,C]. In all cases, the pursuers refuse to cross the river and risk their lives for the sake of a prisoner and it is this which ensures that the rescuers ride free. A link between 'Jock o the Side' and 'Archie o Cawfield' is the request by the pursuing land sergeant or lieutenant for his fetters, which is refused by the man who has carried the prisoner. However, there is no exact parallel of statement within the ballads. All three 'Archie o Cawfield' versions, which include the incident, use the word 'throw' ('throw me thro my irons' [188A:43], 'Throw me my irons' [188B:27], 'Throw ower the fetters' [188:29]), while 'Jock o the Side' has 'leave' and 'cast' in [B] and [C] ('leave me my irons, I pray to me' [187B:33], 'cast me my irons' 187C:24]). In every case, the request is refused and the reply comes, most usually from the character who has carried the prisoner, that he will use the iron to shoe his faithful horse.[53] For example, Dickie says of his 'little black mare': 'while a bit o your iron hauds thegither / Barefit sall she never be' [188Bb:23].

The aftermath of the Kinmont Willie rescue affected Scrope more than any other. He had to explain, again and again, how a prisoner in his stronghold could be rescued so efficiently. Scrope blamed the weather, the laxity of the guard, the 'awfull Grahams', and had to defend himself from the wrath of his superiors. Buccleuch had succeeded in returning the insult. Scrope's pride and honour were outraged: 'yt shall cost me both life and lyvinge, rather than such an indignitie to her highnes [Elizabeth], and contempt to me selfe, shalbe tolerated'.[54]

The ballad presents Scrope as suffering from shocked incredulity, as well as from crippled honour:

> All sore abashed stood Lord Scrope
> He stood as still as rock of stane;
> He scarcely dared to trew his eyes
> When thro the water they had gane.
>
> 'He is either himself a devil frae hell
> Or else his mother a witch maun be;
> I wad na have ridden that wan water
> For a' the gowd in Christentie' [186:45,46]

'Kinmont Willie', 'Jock o the Side' and 'Archie o Cawfield' all contain several parallels, which suggests a common ancestry. However, we may also have a transposition from 'Adam Bell, Clim of the Clough and William of Cloudesly' in the murder of the porter, since this ballad predates all the others in extant copies. A diagrammatical representation of the parallels between the four rescue ballads mentioned above may help to elucidate the comparable aspects of the tales (See Table 1).

With reference to all three ballads discussed in this essay, the most notable difference is the geographic one. The rescue attempts are made in different towns, which are in different Marches: Buccleuch rescues Kinmont Willie from Carlisle, in the English West March; Hobie Noble rescues Jock o the Side from Newcastle, in the English East March; and Jockie/Dickie Ha rescues Archie o Cawfield from Dumfries town, in the Scottish West March. In addition to this, the method of effecting entry into the town varies: Buccleuch and his men use their ladders to climb up the walls, then they make a hole through the stone into the prison; Hobie Noble and the two Armstrongs try to climb the walls, but, finding their means of scaling the walls too short, they have to force an entry through the gates, killing the porter in the process; the Halls have no such trouble, apparently riding to a tolbooth-style prison, which is not within a castle compound.

It would seem that William of Kynmont was never in any real danger of being hanged while he was being held in Carlisle Castle, due to the debatable nature of his capture and, although we do not know how he finally met his end, we know that he was back in Carlisle in 1600, this time on a raid, and that he was still alive in 1604 – another Border rogue who rode wild and who seems to have evaded the gallows. However, the inclusion of a hanging within the ballad heightens the necessity for a rescue: saving a man's life is more noble than retaliation for wounded pride and a rescue of a paroled individual. It must be noted also, that the mention of a hanging is not outwith the historical parameters which the riding ballads reflect. With reference to the Kinmont Willie rescue, the main features of the historical episode are all recalled in the ballad: the English betrayal of the truce assurance; Salkeld and Scrope's refusal to comply with Buccleuch's demands; the entering of Carlisle and her seemingly impregnable castle; the rescue of Kinmont Willie; and the English inability to prevent the reivers' escape.

Like other ballads, such as 'Johnie Armstrong' or 'Hughie Graham', all three ballads are unashamedly pro-reiver, presenting the representatives of law and order as the criminals, and Kinmont Willie is perhaps the most nationalistic, omitting the essential help of the English Carletons and Grahams, recalling the English 'villains' Salkeld and Scrope, and giving the glory to Scott of Buccleuch. History, as it exists in records, has been altered and manipulated. However, the emotional content of the Kinmont Willie affair – the injured pride of Buccleuch, the audacity of the raid, the appalled incredulity of Scrope – are all still present: we may consider, then, that the emotional history has been retained. If we consider the other two ballads discussed above, it follows that we cannot dismiss them entirely as fiction, since they contain much which can be substantiated by the warden's letters and reports. I do not suggest that everything in them is historically accurate as far as records, times and evidential facts are concerned. What I do propose is that they contain much which is reminiscent of recorded actions – be that the audacity of the rescuers, reflections of 'proude' Armstrongs complained of by Bowes perhaps, or the reason for Jock of the Side's capture. We cannot be sure. Recorded evidence does not provide us with the answers in these cases. It is not enough. What we are left with may be a case of layering one event upon the other, or it may be merely a celebration of the reivers through artistic invention. What is perhaps most important in this case is that the audience and singer believe in the truth that the ballads present, and that they are drawn by the tales. It is not a matter of good against evil or right against wrong; it is the urgent, reckless and intrepid nature of these ballad stories. Reed calls it 'heroic villainy', and villains they certainly may well have been, but it was the peers and contemporaries and families of the reivers who kept the tales in the years prior to antiquarian and academic interest. 'If the people had

not loved the songs, many of the best would have vanished', remarked
G. M. Trevelyan.[55] So, perhaps we should not let too much history get in
the way of a damn good story.

TABLE 1

Points of Comparison Between Reiver-rescue
Ballads as Named

Locations	Kinmont Willie	Jock o the Side	Archie o Cawfield	Adam Bell, etc.
Carlisle	√			√
Newcastle		√		
Dumfries			√	
Walls climbed	√	√		
Porter killed		√		√
Prison break-in	√	√	√	
Prisoner laments	√	√	√	
Prisoner defiant	√			√
Prisoner carried	√	√	√	
Water crossed	√	√	√	
One coward		√	√	
Carrier's rebuke		√	√	
Pursuers will not cross	√	√	√	
Pursuer curses rescuers	√	√	√	

NOTES

1　John Leslie, *The Historie of Scotland*, ed. E. G. Cody (2 vols., Edinburgh 1888), i.
　　102.
2　*The Statistical Account of Scotland 1791–1799*, ed. J. Sinclair (20 vols., Wakefield
　　1983), iii, 522.
3　*Statistical Account*, iv, 400.
4　In Child's [188C] version of Archie o Cawfield the town is identified as Annan.
5　In broadsheets, the ballad is commonly found under the title 'The Bold Prisoner'.
6　*The Greig-Duncan Folk-Song Collection*, ed. P. Shuldham-Shaw and E. Lyle (7 vols.,
　　Aberdeen and Edinburgh, 1981–95), ii, 207, no. 244.
7　See T. P. Coffin, *The British Traditional Ballad in North America* (Philadelphia
　　1963), 117–18. Some American versions have altered the nature of the plot to fit
　　'the affair of John Webster, who appears to have been rescued from jail in a fash-
　　ion sufficiently similar to suggest the adaptation': B. H. Bronson, *The Traditional
　　Tunes of the Child Ballads* (4 vols., Princeton 1962), ii, 175.
8　Walter Scott, *Minstrelsy of the Scottish Border*, ed. T. Henderson (London, 1931),
　　185.

9   Bronson, *Traditional Tunes of the Child Ballads*, ii, 171.
10 *The English and Scottish Popular Ballads*, ed. F. J. Child (5 vols., Boston and London, 1882–98), iii, 485.
11 Scott, *Minstrelsy*, 119.
12 However, Kinmont Willie was not the first man to be involved in a daring escape. In 1528, Richie Graham, an Englishman, escaped from the castle, while being held for March treason by Lord Dacre. Reference to this is in Thomas Musgrave's list of Border riders, under the Grahams of Esk, in *The Calendar of Border Papers*, ed. J. Bain (2 vols., Edinburgh 1894) [*CBP*], i, 595.
13 Ibid., i, 595.
14 David Calderwood, *The History of the Kirk of Scotland*, ed. T. Thomson (8 vols., Wodrow Soc., 1843), iv, 230.
15 J. Reed, *The Border Ballads* (Stocksfield 1991), 58.
16 The victim's name is given as Mitchel in [B], Michel in [C] and Michael in [D].
17 *CBP* ii, 907: Sir William Bowes (brother to Henry) to Henry Cecil, 15 Feb. 1598.
18 Ibid., ii, 907.
19 This victim was Nicolas Whitfield, who was killed in January of 1597–8. See ibid., ii, 514.
20 Ibid., ii, 907.
21 Ibid., ii, 1065: letter signed by John Whitfield, Frauncis Whitfield, 9 members of the Ridley family and Nicholas Snawdon of Plenmeller.
22 Ibid., ii, 1066: 18 May 1599.
23 Whithaugh was Armstrong territory.
24 *CBP* ii, 1066. John Whytfield was still at Bewcastle on 26 May, too ill to be moved (see ibid., ii, 1068). No further reference is made to him in the letters.
25 For an example of this 'layering', see D. Buchan, 'History and Harlaw', in E. B. Lyle (ed.), *Ballad Studies* (Totowa, New Jersey, 1976), 29–40.
26 *CBP* ii, 197.
27 Of course, the suggestion that 'Jock o the Side' is connected to any of these incidents must remain just that, as not enough facts have been recorded, either in historical reports or ballad tradition, to make an irrefutable statement, but I believe that the facts, as we have them, do have links with the ballad tale and I feel that they should be considered.
28 W. C. Dickinson, 'Courts of Special Jurisdiction', in G. C. H. Paton (ed.), *An Introduction to Scottish Legal History* (Stair Soc., 1958), 398.
29 *The Historie and Life of King James the Sext* (Bannatyne Club, 1825), 363.
30 *CBP* ii, 283.
31 Ibid., ii, 283.
32 D. Moysie, *Memoirs of the Affairs of Scotland* (Bannatyne Club, 1830), 126.
33 D. L. W. Tough, *Last Years of Frontier* (Oxford 1928; repr. Alnwick 1987), 261.
34 James Balfour, 'Bordour Matteris', in *The Practicks of James Balfour of Pittendreich*, ed. P. G. B. McNeill (2 vols., Stair Soc., 1962–3), ii, xxii, 610.
35 Although unsigned, the letter ends with the request that Scrope should 'read this and ryve it, or els I thinke your lordship farce to me' (see *CBP* ii, 257). Editorial notes referring to this letter state that the writer was considered to be Ritchie's Will, who was one of the Grahams who rode with Buccleuch.
36 Thomas Carleton had been Scrope's deputy and the Constable of Carlisle, but various factors, perhaps including his stake in a blackmail venture with Richard Graham of Brackenhill, caused Scrope to dismiss him, doubting his trustworthiness.
37 This is most probably the 'doughty Willie o' Gorrinberry' mentioned in 'Jamie Telfer of the Fair Dodhead'.
38 *CBP* ii, 252, Scrope to Burghley, 24 Apr. 1596; Tough, *Last Years of a Frontier*, 261.

39 Buccleuch himself admitted that he 'could not have done in that matter without the great friendship of the Grahams of Eske' in a letter intercepted by Scrope: *CBP* ii, 699, Scrope to Burghley, enclosing 'a coppe of the lettre the Lard of Baclughe wrote unto a great man in Scotland'.

40 Balfour, *Practicks*, 157.

41 Both of these formulas indicate bad news. See F. G. Anderson, *Commonplace and Creativity* (Odense 1985), 201–7; and K. McAlpine, '"I'd Gie Them A"': the formula in "Geordie" and other ballads', *Folklore*, cvii (1996), 71–6.

42 The corn-gaugers disguise is also effected in 'Archie o Cawfield' [C6] and [D4].

43 Shuldam-Shaw and Lyle, *Greig-Duncan Folk-Song Collection*, ii, 244.

44 *CBP* ii, 229: complaints by Forster, written by his clerk, 2–19 May 1584.

45 Ibid., i, 677, Scrope to Burghley, 24 Sep. 1588.

46 Moysie, *Memoirs*, 126.

47 *CBP* ii, 252, Scrope to Burghley, 14 Apr. 1596.

48 I wonder, if Archie was an Armstrong, should Jock and Dickie not be associated with those Armstrongs previously mentioned, such as The Laird's Jock and Dickie of Dryhope.

49 *CBP* ii, 252; Tough, *Last Years of a Frontier*, 261.

50 *The Actis and Deidis of the Illustere and Vailyeand Campioun Schir William Wallace Knicht of Elderslie*, ed. J. Moir (Scottish Text Soc., 1889), 148: 'Polwart and Montgomeries Flyting', in *The Poems of Alexander Montgomerie*, ed. J. Cranstoun (Scottish Text Soc., 1887), 72.

51 See also [188B:13, C11, D9, E4 and F9].

52 Further information regarding anti-Spanish propaganda can be found in D. Kunzle, *The Early Modern Comic Strip 1450–1825* (Berkeley 1973), 60–3. This includes an illustration showing the excesses and cruelty of the Spanish in Europe and the New World.

53 It should perhaps be noted that another point of similarity between ballad tales lies in the description of Hobie Noble's horse. In 'Hobie Noble', he rides a 'fringed gray', while in 'Jock o the Side', he rides a 'freckled Gray', never any other colour.

54 *CBP* ii, 252.

55 Reed, *Border Ballads*, 17, quoting G. M. Trevelyan, *The Middle Marches* (Newcastle 1935), 25.

6

Sex and Violence in the Scottish Ballads

EDWARD J. COWAN

> Few countries have such a store of ballads, country rhymes,
> and sources of like kind to disclose what the commonalty
> thought and felt. No historian worth his salt would neglect
> them. If State papers reveal the designs of politicians, the ballads
> tell what the people thought about things – a matter quite as
> important if not more so.
>
> T. M. Lindsay[1]

Despite the contrary claims of certain historians,[2] Scotland in the six-
teenth and seventeenth centuries was undoubtedly a violent place and as it
happens many, but not all, of our finest ballads – the so called 'big ballads'
– date from that era, particularly from the reign of James VI (1567–1625)
who self-consciously introduced a policy of 'pacification' to his kingdom.
The verses positively reek of smoke and blood, the rhythms echoing the
thump of horses' hooves on raids across the border, while the use of direct
speech lends the stories an immediacy reminiscent of the cinema, a
close-up of panting warriors and blood-soaked heather. As with modern
film, violence is not essential to narrative but it is frequently associated
with sex and sexual relations, broadly defined.

By way of introduction it may be useful to jettison a few widely
cherished misconceptions about the Child ballad corpus. Child printed
305 ballads with their numerous variants. A rough estimate – and it must
be stressed that due to problems of classification and plurality of motifs
the following figures are not precise[3] – suggests that over 30% (some 100+
ballads) of the corpus is centrally concerned with women. By way of
contrast only some 20–25 items could be described as 'Riding Ballads' or
'Feuding Ballads' and from these women are by no means excluded.
Despite the comparatively small number in this category it contains some
of the best known or most familiar of all the ballads, possibly because
they are most frequently anthologised, critically discussed, or sung. By
way of comparison Child printed 37 Robin Hood ballads. In
approximately one third of ballads which are here distinguished as having

females as their main subjects, women are betrayed or outsmarted but in the rest they are triumphant, outwitting their men or supernatural creatures and emphatically placing themselves on top.[4] Yet, victorious or otherwise, both women and men inhabited a cruel and unforgiving world in which violence was ever-present.

Douglas at the battle of Otterburn has a vision of his own doom:

> But I have seen a dreary dream,
> Beyond the isle o Sky;
> I saw a dead man won the fight,
> And I think that man was I. [161C][5]

The tone, while obviously prophetic, is almost elegiac but the harsh bloody reality of hand-to-hand combat is swiftly introduced:

> When Piercy wi the Douglas met,
> I wat he was right keen;
> They swakked their swords till sair they swat,
> And the blood ran them between. [161C]

Violence dominates ballad after ballad; it is omnipresent, ever threatening to erupt. Johnie Cock's mother informs him that the seven foresters of Pickeram have targeted him for vengeance: 'for a drop of thy heart's bluid / They wad ride the fords of hell' [114A]. The ballad of 'Johnie Armstrong' perhaps betrays a touch of social criticism because Johnie, leader of a bunch of border reivers, had been treacherously betrayed by his king under safe conduct.

> To seik het water beneth cauld yce,
> Surely it is a great folie;
> I haif asked grace at a graceless face,
> But there is nane for my men and me. [169C]

Rather than be hanged Johnie and his men try to fight their way out until Johnie is struck down by a cowardly stab in the back. The older, seventeenth-century version of the ballad, 'John Armstrong's last Good-Night', continues in its matter of fact style,

> Said John, Fight on, my merry men all,
> I am a little hurt, but I am not slain;
> I will lay me down for to bleed a while,
> Then I'le rise and fight with you again. [169B]

Johnie's demise was a historical event more accurately commemorated perhaps in 'Ihonne Ermistrangis dance', mentioned, as were a number of ballads, in *The Complaynt of Scotland* of 1550, only nineteen years after the episode took place. Lindsay of Pitscottie who completed his *Historie and Cronicles of Scotland* in the 1570s strongly implied that at least part of Border bloodshed and mayhem was to be attributed to the Crown. He related that after a massive deer hunt in the Meggat Water region James V, in 1530, hanged Johnie and thirty-six accomplices, traditionally, across the hills from Meggat, at Carlinrig, in Liddesdale. The idea that the victims thought they were present to parley was strongly insinuated, while Lindsay's account carried echoes of the ballad with reference to Johnie's gorgeous apparel and his reported statement, 'It is folly to to seek grace at a graceless face', though he makes no mention of a fight. Whether the ballad influenced Lindsay or he the latter is now impossible to ascertain but the chronicler's namesake, David, inserted a reference to Johnie's hanging into his *Satyre of the Thrie Estatis* (1540). The problem was that since medieval times it had suited Scottish kings to maintain marcher lords on the frontier as a defence against English incursion but changing political considerations had rendered the arrangement redundant. The *Historie* was probably accurate in reflecting that many Scots lamented Johnie's treatment 'for he was a doubtit man and as good a chieftain as ever was upon the borders' and he 'never molested no Scotsman'.[6] Whatever the rights or wrongs of the matter it is remarkable how many historians appear to sanction state terrorism and conspire in the condemnation of the accused, unquestioned and unheard, while the folk tradition tends to empathise with the point of view of the victims.

All ballads, however, do not derive from the Scottish Borders; as the late David Buchan never tired of pointing out, there was an equally important frontier, in terms of ballad production, extending along the Highland line, particularly in the north-east – the Mearns, Aberdeenshire, Moray and Nairn – an area enmeshed in a complex weave of feuds, mostly involving Clan Chattan and the Gordons. One such was that between the families of Gordon and Forbes 'of long rooted between them' and compounded by issues of politics and religion which absorbed the entire country. According to the ballad 'Edom O Gordon' its eponym, Adam Gordon of Auchindoun, brother of the Earl of Huntly, sent Captain Thomas Ker in 1571 to reduce the Forbes stronghold of Towie in Aberdeenshire. The Forbes castellan was absent, but as is usual in these stories, stout resistance was offered by his wife, who, having just set the supper table and said grace, mistook the hostile riders approaching her castle for her husband and his followers. When Ker demanded possession of her person as well as the castle she defiantly shot three of his men despite the entreaties of her eldest son that she surrender. To her request that her son be allowed to go free, Ker urged her to lower the boy over the wall in a sheet but on taking receipt of the victim he revealed his sadistic treachery:

> Wyth sped, before the rest,
> He cut his tonge out of his head,
> His hart out of his brest,

wrapping them in a cloth and tossing them back over the castle wall to the distraught mother, who, with her other children was burned to death when the castle was subsequently torched [178A]. In various versions of the ballad the pathos is enhanced by the youngest son complaining that he was being smothered by the reek or smoke. It is fairly common in such ballads that the event is rendered the more horrific because a third party is employed – in this case Ker – who operates counter to convention and to the detriment of his master's otherwise favourable reputation; historically Adam Gordon was regarded as a somewhat gallant and attractive individual whose name was sullied by this deplorable episode.

In another historical Aberdeenshire burning, 'The Fire of Frendraught', Rothiemay's servant begs him to jump to escape the flames, an impossible request since the fire has already reached him. Melting lead from the window is pouring over his head and his feet are on fire.

> My eyes are seething in my head,
> My flesh roasting also,
> My bowels are boiling with my blood;
> Is not that a woeful woe? [196A]

The understatement of the last line may appear faintly comic to modern audiences but it represents convincing ballad-speak and the entire stanza, brief and laconic though it is, may rank as one of the most horrifying descriptions of a human burning in literature.

The contention is not that such ballads represent historical fact; rather they voice a sense of contemporary outrage while at the same time they have a propaganda function for they were intended to actually advance and foment the very feuds which they described. Another ballad combining the essential themes of heroically defiant female, lustful assailant and a burning, 'The Bonnie House o Airlie', which seems to originate in an episode that took place in 1591, was dusted down and recycled with reference to events in 1640 and 1746.[7]

Horrific though such ballads are their historicity has been further obscured by the alarming eagerness of later antiquaries to claim them for their own localities. 'Edom O Gordon', for example, has been situated at Corgarff Castle in Strathdon, at the House o' Rhodes near Gordon in

Berwickshire and at Loudoun Castle in Ayrshire.[8] Ballad migration is a
valid and worthwhile subject but many errors and misconceptions are due
to the misplaced enthusiasm of later generations, who seem to have
derived a perverse pride from past atrocities.

In yet another song, 'Jamie Telfer of the Fair Dodhead', we are given
the gratuitous, and exact, information that while fighting a man was shot
through his left testicle.

> The Captain was shot through the head,
> And also through the left ba-stane;
> Tho he had lived this hundred years,
> He'd never been looed by woman again.[9]

The stunningly superfluous observation is absolutely typical of the folk
tradition which seldom hesitates to state the obvious. Scott, on the other
hand, cleaned up the incident, by having the victim 'run thro the thick of
the thigh / And broken was his right leg bane' [190A], an injury which,
incomprehensibly, also ensured the end of his love-life.

When we turn to the question of sex and sexual relations in the ballads
we do not, unfortunately, turn our backs upon violence. To judge from
the evidence pre-marital sex might almost be regarded as the norm. Indeed
so frequently does it occur that it is tempting to hypothesise that sex leads
to courtship rather than the other way about and the women, as often as
not, though not invariably, are willing partners. To judge from 'The
Knight and Shepherd's Daughter' it would appear that the relationship is
consummated before formal introductions are made. In the third verse the
shepherdess makes a modest request of her seducer:

> I syne ye've got your will o me,
> Your will o me ye've taen,
> Tis all I ask o you, kind sir,
> Is to tell to me your name. [110B]

Pregnancy almost always results. One father tells his son about how he
got together with his mother:

> Just at that fatal time,
> I catchd her on a misty night,
> Whan summer was in prime. [41A]

Less happy are the consequences in 'The Bonny Hind',

> Perhaps there may be bairns, kind sir
> Perhaps there may be nane;

> But if you be a courtier,
> You'll tell to me your name, [50]

for the lovers turn out to be siblings, with predictably fatal consequences. It is impossible to recover any kind of satisfactory statistical information on illegitimacy rates for Scotland in the early modern period but figures from 1711–80 indicate a noticeably higher level of irregular marriages in the Scottish border and south-western counties compared to the rest of Scotland.[10] It is also quite well attested that women, especially servants, were likely to be preyed upon by socially superior males.[11] The point of such ballads as 'Shepherd's Daughter' is that the spirited and tenacious heroine ultimately outwits her would-be predator.

Modern prejudice must always be placed to one side in approaching texts from the past, particularly in the case of such an example as 'Leesome Brand'.

> This ladye was scarce eleven years auld,
> When on her love she was right bauld;
> She was scarce up to my right knee,
> When oft in bed wi men I'm tauld.
>
> But when nine months were come and gane,
> This ladye's face turnd pale and wane. [15A]

Bishop Hay's *Lectures on Marriage* (1534) indicate that twelve was the minimum age for marriage of females though he cited various respected authorities who reported cases of girls of eight or nine who became pregnant – 'sometimes malice makes up for the lack of age, in the sense that in some cases the natural vigour and capacity for intercourse, as well as the use of reason, develops before puberty'.[12] There is much in Hay on such topics as impotence, consanguinity and prior vows to corroborate the testimony of the ballads.

It is clear that society at large, and especially parents, often disapproved of pre-marital adventures and they frequently led to tragedy. Fathers and brothers of females were particularly prone to object – sometimes with incestuous overtones – and the male lover either triumphed over them (with his partner's assistance) or else he was killed and as often as not the woman died with him. Although 'The Douglas Tragedy' shares certain features with Scandinavian ballads and with the Old Icelandic poem 'Helgaqviða Hundingsbana' (the Second Lay),[13] it enjoys a peculiarly Scottish, and fittingly non-sentimental, if brutal, conclusion. The doomed lovers are buried at St Mary's churchyard: 'out o the lady's grave grew a bonny red rose, / And out o the knight's a briar', both entwining above their graves as a symbol of their love.[14] The ballad, however does not end on this touching note for,

> ... bye and rade the Black Douglas,
> And wow but he was rough!
> For he pulld up the bonny brier,
> And flang't in St Mary's Loch. [7B]

The irate father kills Clerk Saunders while the two lovers sleep together.

> She thought it had been a loathsome sweat,
> A wat it had fallen this twa between;
> But it was the blood of his fair body. [69A]

In the horrific 'Edward' the eponym has been urged to patricide by his mother. [25B]

It has been suggested, controversially, that an absence of affective relationships between parents and children in this period may have driven the latter towards incest.[15] Comparatively few ballads, however, deal with this sad topic, which is often linked with infanticide.[16] The 'Cruel Brother' stabs his sister's newly wed husband apparently out of sheer jealousy [11A]. In the suggestively titled 'Sheath and Knife', which survives in a commonplace book of about 1630 now in the National Library of Scotland, the brother kills his sister and their incestuous child but he cannot extinguish his love for her [16A]. In both 'The Bonny Hind' [50] and 'The King's Dochter Lady Jean' [52] the brother returns from afar to father a child upon his sister, neither being aware of the other's identity, with predictably tragic but non-judgemental consequences. In the rather strange but complex 'Lizie Wan' [51] the eponym tells her father she is pregnant by her brother who, on receiving the news, decapitates her and goes off to visit their mother. When she asks what ails her son, 'For I see by thy ill colour / Some fallow's deed thou hast done' he pretends to have beheaded his greyhound, though on further questioning he confesses. The mother's response seems as recognisable as it is pathetically inadequate, 'O what wilt thou do when thy father comes hame?' to which he metaphorically intimates his own suicide. In these examples the tone is by no means unsympathetic but what is to be made of the following? 'It is nae wonder,' said Brown Robyn,

> 'Altho I dinna thrive,
> For wi my mother I had twa bairns,
> And wi my sister five'. [57][17]

Is this admission supposed to generate shock, horror, revulsion or laughter? 'Brown Robyn' is, in any case, a most peculiar specimen in which Robyn's salvation is engineered by the Virgin Mary as a reward for his confession, a story which may well have been post-Reformation and comedic in intent. It may be rash to draw such inferences from such an uncertain example which, in any case, survives in only one version, but since clerics as far apart as Bishop Hay and the Covenanters in 1649 manifest something of a preoccupation with the subject of incest, both producing elaborate tables to indicate the forbidden degrees,[18] it may not be entirely fanciful to suggest that the ballad was intended to cock a snoop at the ecclesiastical authorities on behalf of a populace which did not share this particular obsession and which was perfectly capable, by itself, of policing such matters. It is also possible that the emphasis upon incest was part of an authoritarian campaign to destroy the kin-ties in general, an essential development, according to Eli Sagan, in the creation of all modern absolutist states.[19]

Incest of a different kind surfaces in the startling imagery of 'William and Lady Maisry' [70B], a ballad which bears some resemblance to 'The Bent Sae Brown' [71]; both have Scandinavian parallels and both were collected in north-east Scotland. Willie demands admittance to Maisry's chamber, 'tirling at the pin' of her bower, in a typically explicit sexual metaphor, rattling her latch prior to copulation. She is unaware that Willie has just dispatched her brother in the woods until she notices the 'cauld, cauld draps o blood' which fall from his 'trusty brand'. This startling penial image somehow subsumes Maisry's virginal blood as well and the metaphor is, so to speak, extended, when the girl's father runs Willie through as the lovers sleep. The revenge could hardly be more complete since, in the act of homicide Willie is symbolically and physically penetrated.

Rape is a much less common theme than might have been supposed. In two cases, 'The Bonnie House o Airlie' and 'Edom O Gordon', it is the implied concomitant of a castle under siege, an idea fairly common in medieval literature.[20] Explicit occurrences are, however, few. 'Prince Heathen' offers a clear example:

> He's taen her in his arms twa,
> Laid her between him and the wa,
> An ere he let her free again,
> Her maidenhead frae her he's taen. [104B]

Two versions of 'Bonny Baby Livingstone' depict Glenlion as a rapist [222B,C] and Rob Roy is similarly portrayed in the ballad to which he gives his name [225A,B]. There is a brutal example in the dubious 'The Wylie Wife of the Hie Toun Hie' [290]. Some of the cases of rape cited in the *Motif Index*[21] are not acceptable such as 'The Twa Magicians' [44A], which has many European parallels, and which is a sustained sexual parable liberally laced with fantastical inventiveness from the moment the blacksmith is introduced 'wi hammer in his hand'. As the shape-shifting begins what starts as a contest evolves into a magical courtship in which both partners are equally complicit. Neither is rape implied in 'The Knight and the Shepherd's Daughter' [110A,B] but it was planned from the beginning in 'Willie's Lyke-Wake' [25A] in which Willie arranged his own wake in order to obtain the object of his desire. When the maid came to pay her last respects (accompanied by her seven bold brothers at the insistence of her suspicious father) Willie, 'took her by the waist sae neat and sae sma / And threw her atween him and the wa', recalling the terminology of 'Prince Heathen'. Lady Maisry [70] concealed Willie at the side of the bed against the wall while she lay facing into the room whence she saw her vengeful father advancing. In 'Captain Wedderburn's Courtship' [46A,B] the refrain reiterates the theme that the captain wishes to bed his lady 'neist the wa', a position which she steadfastly refuses even when she marries him. It is thus clear that the natural position for the woman was the outside edge of the bed, otherwise she felt dominated, trapped or contained.

'Eppie Morrie' has been kidnapped by Willie, a highland cateran and when he gets her home the two are brought to bed. Eppie refuses to co-operate.

> 'Haud far awa frae me, Willie,
> Haud far awa frae me;
> Before I'll lose my maidenhead.
> I'll try my strength with thee'.
>
> She took the cap from off her head
> And threw it to the way;
> Said, 'Ere I lose my maidenhead,
> I'll fight with you till day'.

And she does just that. In the morning she is intact and Willie is labelled as a wimp throughout the length and breadth of Strathdon.

> Wally fa you, Willie,
> That ye could nae prove a man
> And taen the lassie's maidenhead!
> She would have hired your han. [223]

Whatever the precise meaning of the last line[22] it was not complimentary to the manhood of the would-be abductor.

There is not a great deal of evidence of cruelty to women in the Child corpus. Elopement with gypsy laddies could result in impoverished bliss or cruel exploitation depending presumably on whether the balladeers were partial or otherwise to the Romanies or 'Lords of Little Egypt' who maintained a significant presence in the Scottish borders from the sixteenth century onwards. 'The Gypsy Laddie' [200A,B] relates that the lady who went off with the raggle-taggle gypsies was under a spell and was cruelly treated by her new master, an inversion of the usual romantic alternative found in most gypsy ballads. Abduction often equated with elopement in a society which frowned upon freedom of action especially in opposition to parental wishes. Mary Queen of Scots set her subjects an appalling example when she made her futile dash for happiness with the Earl of Bothwell in 1567 under the cloak of abduction. In the ballad world abductors usually complied with the woman's wishes, that is, the couple lived happily ever after, or the lady was allowed to be rescued.

Almost the sole example of wife-beating in the ballads had its roots in a domestic dispute involving Lord and Lady Wariston.

> He spak a word in jest;
> Her answer wasna good;
> He threw a plate at her face,
> Made it a gush out o blood. [194A]

Jean Livingston married John Kincaid of Wariston in 1594; she was fifteen, he about twenty-four. As the ballad has it 'She's as jimp in the middle / As ony willow-wand'. There is a contemporary reference to at least one furious quarrel when Kincaid bit his wife's arm, striking her several times. They produced a child, Patrick, but Jean refused to tolerate her husband's abuse. She consulted her son's nurse, Janet Munro, who secured the services of Robert Weir, a horseboy employed by Jean's father, John Livingston of Dunipace. Janet had allegedly vowed that if Weir refused to assist she would take action herself, as in the ballad she is made to do. On the night of 1 July 1600 Jean made sure that Wariston drank deep and she personally conducted Weir into the house. The latter attacked the victim as he slept, throwing him from the bed, kicking him and eventually killing him by strangulation, Wariston struggling noisily until he was overcome. Weir escaped but the awakened household immediately presumed the wife's guilt, not surprisingly for according to her own testimony 'that I mycht seem to be innocent, I laboured to counterfeit weeping, but do what I could, I could not find a tear'. Initially unrepentant Lady Jean protested her innocence but she was eventually moved to confession and a profound religious experience by Mr James Balfour an Edinburgh minister who composed a moving 'Memorial' about her last few days of life. She was condemned to be strangled and burned, a sentence also passed on the nurse and two other servants.

In the eyes of contemporaries her crime was truly heinous, offending as it did Scotland's fundamental patriarchal order; technically it constituted hamesuckin – murdering a man in his own house, murder which furthermore was premeditated and cold-blooded. Jean's father was equally condemnatory but he used his influence to secure the more dignified sentence of beheading and contrived the execution for sunrise when fewer people would be around to witness it. To provide an additional diversion the servants were executed at the same hour on Edinburgh's Castle-hill. The murderess, comforted by her new-found faith, was disappointed that her audience was not larger but she died well, making a speech from the scaffold in which she admitted that she was the 'diviser' and so the 'committer' of the 'cruell murdering of mine own husband'.[23] The event was undoubtedly noteworthy and the ballad almost certainly originated at the time of the execution while the events it described were still hot news. Therein the Lady was led astray by the Devil himself which accretion adequately reflected the enormity of her crime and, furthermore, the assertion was believable because her original sentence was the same as that for convicted witches. The ballad also has her father urging her death, 'Gar mak a barrel o pikes / And row her down some lea' [194B] which is credible considering the disgrace and dishonour she had brought upon his family. Both the ballad and Balfour's 'Memorial' have Jean covering her eyes at the end. The sentence and execution were designed *pour encourager les autres* but the ballad concludes almost defiantly,

> 'Now a' ye gentle maids,
> Tak warning now by me,
> And never marry ane
> But wha pleases your ee',

hopelessly unrealistic advice at this period when many aristocratic marriages in particular were arranged for the betterment of the family and its fortune. The final stanza implies that the blame was all hers:

> 'For he married me for love,
> But I married him for fee;
> And sae brak out the feud
> That gard my dearie die'. [194A:10,11]

Very many ballads depict woman triumphant or women outwitting
their men. Lady Isabel dupes the 'Elfin Knight' on 1 May – Beltane – a
particularly significant date. He coaxes Isabel into the greenwood where
he announces that he has already killed seven princesses, on this very spot,
and that she will be his eighth victim. She charms him to sleep and,

> Wi his ain sword-belt sae fast as she ban him,
> Wi his ain dag-durk sae sair as she dang him.

> 'If seven king's-daughters here ye hae slain.
> Lye ye here, a husband to them a'. [4A]

Some of the subtle nuances of this ballad would be lost in a post-industrial
society. There is irony in the elfin knight's death because the 'gude
greenwood' is one of the prime locations in the ballads for the conception
of a male child.[24]

Beltane was a highly propitious date for the begetting of children,
associated as it was with fertility, fire, maypoles and flower-gathering, The
earliest documented evidence for Beltane festivals derives from St Andrews in
1432 and such observances survived in the Lowlands until well into the
eighteenth century. A king or queen of May was appointed to preside
over the celebrations though sometimes the *praeses* was the Abbot of
Unreason or the Abbot of Nae Rent. The latter by the early sixteenth
century had often been replaced by such figures as Robin Hood, Friar
Tuck and Little John, characters who seem to have represented the burghs
or guilds in mounting special plays and other events. Robin, clad in
vegetation or dressed in green, was clearly himself a fertility symbol and it
is quite possible that Robin Hood ballads, which are often considered to
have been purely English, were also recited or sung in Scotland – and just
possibly, danced. Henderson recorded two Robin Hood ballads on
separate occasions in the 1950s.[25] Andrew Wyntoun, Walter Bower and
John Mair, in their respective histories, treated Robin as a historical
character. There is a tantalising connection here because Robin frequently
turns out to be none other than the Earl of Huntingdon, a title acquired
by David I, king of Scots, in right of his wife, in 1114, and which continued to
be held by his successors until the mid-thirteenth century.[26] Later William
Wallace and William Douglas the knight of Liddesdale, both at different
times outlaws in Ettrick Forest, took on some of the attributes of Robin
Hood so suggesting a kind of reciprocity between the ballads and
historical personages though Maid Marian was apparently unknown in
Scotland. One rash Scot proclaimed that 'he believed as well a tale of
Robin Hood as any word is written in the Old Testament or New'.[27] It
may be presumed that his fate was as dire as that of the elfin knight.

The ballads preserve a number of other worthy women with the 'smeddum' to triumph over adversity. 'Kemp Owyne' is sweet-talked by a wood-nymph / monster into transforming her into 'as fair a woman as fair could be' [34A]. Lord Thomas tells his mistress 'Fair Annet' after a love session that he will never marry a woman – namely herself – against the wishes of his relatives, to which she spiritedly ripostes, 'If I binna gude eneuch for yer wife, / I'm our-gude for yer loun' [73I], – 'if I'm not good enough to be your wife, I'm too good to be your mistress'. A story remarkably modern in tone is related in 'The False Lover Won Back'. When John tries to ditch his lover for somebody else she responds thus:

> Now hae ye playd me this, fause love,
> In simmer, mid the flowers?
> I shall repay ye back again,
> In winter, mid the showers.
>
> But again, dear love, and again, dear love,
> Will ye not turn again?
> For as ye look to other women,
> I shall to other men. [218A]

Even if these stanzas were added in the eighteenth century, as Child's notes imply, they are still remarkable for their time. Furthermore the woman had her way for she eventually haunted her ingrate of a lover into submission.

Chaucer's 'Canterbury Tales', William Dunbar's 'The Twa Mariit Wemen and the Wedo', and the well-known ballad 'Get Up and Bar the Door' [275A] indicate that lusty, confident, clever women were no strangers to medieval literature; one of the finest and most attractive of them all features in the old ballad 'Tam Lin', the title of which was also applied to a tale and a dance in *The Complaynt of Scotland*, appearing as a tune in 1666. The ballad itself was first printed in London in 1558 while the most complete and most accomplished version, drawn from the oral tradition, was communicated by Robert Burns to Johnson's *Musicall Museum* (1792).[28] Janet is a bold beauty who kilts her green kirtle 'a little aboon her knee' and braids her yellow hair 'a little aboon her bree', hastening to the forbidden Carterhaugh, hoping to encounter the notorious Tam Lin who is infamous for stealing rings, mantles and maidenheads. Sure enough, although the act is decently censored in some versions, the enchanted and enchanting Tam relieves Janet of her prized possession. Back at her father's hall an ancient knight laments that he and others of the household would be blamed for Janet's predicament, but she is having none of it – 'Father my bairn on whom I will, / I'll father nane on thee'. When her father adds his voice to the general concern she reiterates her independence:

> 'If that I gae wi child, father,
> Mysel maun bear the blame;
> There's neer a laird about your ha
> Shall get the bairn's name.
>
> If my love were an earthly knight,
> As he's elfin grey,
> I wad na gie my ain true-love
> For nae lord that you hae'. [39A:14,15]

Returning to Carterhaugh Janet is accused by Tam of planning an abortion, which she does not deny, presumably because the father's supposed fairy origins gave her little option.

> Why pu's thou the rose, Janet,
> Amang the groves sae green,
> And a to kill the bonie babe
> That we gat us between? [39A:20]

Tam, however, is a mortal who has been abducted by the Queen of the Fairies,[29] and he fears that after a sojourn of seven years he has been earmarked as payment of the 'teind to hell'. Since the day is Hallowe'en he has one last chance to be rescued by his lover.

> Just at the mirk and midnight hour
> The fairy folk will ride,
> And they that wad their true-love win,
> At Miles Cross they maun bide. [39A:26]

Janet is given detailed instructions about how she will recognise Tam; as the procession passes she must pull him from his horse and hold on to him (literally) for dear life as he metamorphoses into a newt, an adder, a bear, a lion, a red-hot iron bar and lastly a burning ember before he re-materialises as a naked knight. She, of course, triumphs in the ordeal thus proving the strength of her love and her physical tenacity, qualities to be added to her sexual confidence. Above all, she outsmarts the queen of the fairies who curses her for having seized 'the bonniest knight in a my companie' [39A]. Janet is the most memorable heroine in all of ballad literature and, outstanding though she was, it is difficult to resist the conclusion that she represented, in all respects, ideal womanhood, in the minds of women as well as men.

Indeed it is not beyond the bounds of possibility that the ballads as much represent the world-view of women as they do of men. It is very doubtful if it is possible or legitimate to distinguish 'female topics' in the ballads since to do so would be to burden the past with the cultural values of the present. There is no reason to suppose that women would be any less interested in battle ballads than their men. All would equally enjoy the account of the battle of Ancrum Moor in 1544, at which it was said of the heroic 'Fair Maiden Lilliard' that 'Upon the English loons she laid mony thumps / And when her legs were cuttit aff she fought upon her stumps'.[30] Yet, perhaps illogically, it is harder to believe that men would have been responsible for concocting odd bits of information on such topics as childbirth or midwifery. Gender roles were discreet and distinctive, a point emphasised in 'Bonnie Annie' wherein the man says to his lover, 'What can a woman do, love, I'll do for ye', to which she replies, 'Muckle can a woman do, ye canna do for me' [24A]. Gillian Bennett has suggestively explored the role of women as tradition bearers, while Jan Vansina[31] has made some interesting observations about their place in African societies. There is a considerable amount of evidence to indicate that by the eighteenth century women were the major transmitters of the ballads,[32] but whether such a situation pertained in the earlier period is so far unknown, Symonds alone very tentatively hypothesising that perhaps singers and audience were primarily male in an earlier period of ballad production, giving way to females, notably after 1750.[33] That such a trend started earlier might be suggested by the comparative absence of certain topics in the ballad corpus such as witchcraft (or perhaps rather the witch-hunt), rape and wife-beating. If those absences are not simply an accident of later transmission and the predilections and preferences of later singers then it might be suggested that the ballads present something of woman's idealised view of her world with much of the pain expunged.

In this literature the symbolism is seldom ambiguous. When 'Hind Horn' [17A] gives his lady a wand with seven larks perched upon it there can be little doubt about what it is intended to signify; should confusion linger she reciprocates by giving him a ring. The balladeers were very comfortable with female imagery. 'Glenkindie', a variant of Chaucer's Glascurion and the Welsh Glas Keraint, was so great a harpist that,

> He'd harpit a fish out o saut water,
> Or water out o a stane,
> Or milk out o a maiden's breast,
> That bairn never had nane [67B],

though modern sensitivity is probably none too comfortable with this latter image, which nonetheless may be preferable, as emblematic of the life force, to the other great archetype of the ballads, which is blood.

When a man rejected his mistress in favour of a wife she died of grief and her ghost appeared at the foot of the nuptial bed to trouble his slumber.

> I dreamd a dream, my dear lady;
> Such dreams are never good;
> I dreamd my bower was full of red swine,
> And thy bride-bed full of blood. [74 A]

Another woman tended the corpse of her dead lover in 'The Dowy Houms o Yarrow'.

> She kissd his cheek, she kaimed his hair,
> As oft she did before, O;
> She drank the red blood frae him ran,
> On the dowy dens o Yarrow. [214E]

The stanzas of the ballads are literally soaked in blood. They reek of it. It drips from swords, it pours from corpses, from mutilated bodies, the blood of the innocent and the guilty, the blood of vengeance and reconciliation, young blood, virginal blood, wasted blood; the stench of gore is overwhelming. In numerous cases the sex act, however innocent and well intentioned, engenders violence which in turn leads inevitably and inexorably to death. The ballads were the product of societies under siege, societies which historically *were* bloody and which were literally dying of wounds partially self-inflicted but also savagely afflicted by aggressive new regimes intent upon imposing such notional concepts as civility and polity upon cultures whose values were already perceived to be anachronistic. The historical evidence provides ample corroboration for the images and outrages portrayed in the ballad world and the statements of official record are as blood-soaked and repellent as those of the ballads which provide a final articulation of societies in the process of deliberate and calculated destruction.

No discussion of this topic can avoid mention of perhaps the most horrific ballad in the entire canon and one which has been rather unconvincingly traced to historical events in thirteenth-century Northumberland and Fife.[34] 'Lamkin', despite his docile name, is a murderous mason who has not been paid for building Lord Wearie's castle. There is some implied criticism of the lord who cannot pay because he has chartered 'a bonny ship, to sail the saut sea faem'; the unthinkable alternative would be to sell his land. The marvellous, laconic sparseness of the ballad style conveys all sorts of possibilities in a very few lines. If Lamkin is a man of the New Age, a primitive accumulator pointed firmly in the direction of the future, Lord Wearie is equally a captive of the commercial world commissioning a redundant castle which he cannot afford, embarking upon the unaristocratic venture of a trading voyage, while abandoning his wife and his children to their own devices. It is indeed remarkable that so often in the ballads the lord of the castle is nowhere to be seen in times of danger, leaving his wife and children to suffer unspeakable agonies. Lamkin, however, as a man of the transition, understands enough of the old world to exact blood in lieu of money, shrewdly perceiving the values which would most surely impact upon Wearie. Others had killed for such familiar principles as love, honour, the obligations of kinship or parental duty but the mason is a rank materialist. The corruption at the heart of Lamkin's world is highlighted by his recruitment of the 'fause nourice', the treacherous wet-nurse, who should have been the most trustworthy member of the household, in pursuit of his despicable vengeance. To make sure the coast is clear he ascertains the whereabouts of the men, women and bairns of the house, all of whom 'ca me Lamkin', and who are presumably lulled by his gentle name into thinking him harmless in all respects and thus either exploitable or not taken seriously. Having established that only Lady Wearie is present he deliberately stabs her baby son in his cot. The intensity of the next five stanzas is searing.

> Then Lamkin he rocked,
> and the fause nourice sang,
> Till frae ilkae bore o the cradle
> the red blood out sprang.

> Then out it spak the lady,
> as she stood on the stair:
> 'What ails my bairn, nourice,
> that he's greeting sae sair?

> O still my bairn, nourice,
> O still him wi the pap!'
> 'He winna still, lady,
> for this or for that.'

> 'O still my bairn nourice,
> O still him wi the wand!' [rattle]
> 'He winna still, lady,
> for a his father's land.'

'O still my bairn, nourice,
O still him wi the bell!'
'He winna still, lady,
till ye come down yoursel.'

When the lady appears she not only discovers their crime but realises that she is to be their next victim as she begs for her life.

'O sall I kill her, nourice,
or sall I lat her be?'
'O kill her, kill her, Lamkin,
for she neer was good to me.'

The two villains debate whether they should catch the lady's blood in a basin, an image which recalls sacramental blood as well as the widespread practice of bleeding animals to make mealie puddings, the splicing of the ritual and the domestic combining to gruesome effect.

'O scour the bason, nourice,
and mak it fair and clean,
For to keep this lady's heart's blood,
for she's come o noble kin.'

'There need nae bason, Lamkin,
lat it run through the floor;
What better is the heart's blood
o the rich than o the poor?' [93A]

Such literary giants as Rabelais, Cervantes and Shakespeare had already decided that such a question admitted of only one answer and the composers of the ballads were reluctantly, if inevitably, coming to the same conclusion.

As this brief survey has hopefully indicated the ballad genre provides an entire cosmos with its own inherent system of checks and balances, as well as its own chaos since the human condition is essentially chaotic. What is most striking is that the picture painted by the ballad evidence departs at every critical juncture from the standard view of the submissive female enduring the patriarchal system. What this means is that the popular tradition enshrined in the oral literature of the ballads completely contradicts the 'official' view put forward by the church, government sources, and most contemporary historians and commentators, in short, the official historical record; yet that record has generally been followed by historians who have unwittingly, and perhaps dull-wittedly, manufactured yet another distortion of the past. When Douglas at Otterburn dreamed his dreary dream about the dead man winning the fight he provided a suitable concluding metaphor. The tradition represented by the ballads may be dead but the corpse, as in so many of the songs, still has a voice which, if heeded, may allow the dead to once again win the fight in the ongoing battle of competing histories.

NOTES

1 *Proposed Chair of Scottish History and Literature (Glasgow). Newspaper Extracts Chronologically Arranged.* The Scottish History and Literature Chair Committee (Glasgow 1908), 62.
2 J. Brown, 'Taming the magnates?' in G. Menzies (ed.), *The Scottish Nation* (London 1972), 46–59; J. Brown, 'The exercise of power', in J. Brown (ed.) *Scottish Society in the Fifteenth Century* (London 1977). See, too, J. Wormald, *Court, Kirk and Community. Scotland 1476–1625* (London 1981); and K. Brown, *Bloodfeud in Scotland 1573–1625 Violence, Justice and Politics in an Early Modern Society* (Edinburgh 1986).
3 N. Würzbach and S. M. Salz, *Motif Index of the Child Corpus: The English and Scottish Popular Ballad* (Berlin 1995) while useful, is disappointing overall.
4 A significant phrase ripe with meaning. See N. Z. Davis, 'Women on top', in her *Society and Culture in Early Modern France* (Stanford 1965), 124–51.
5 Hume of Godscroft's account of the battle reports Douglas's dying words – 'I die like my forefathers in a field of battle, and not on a bed of sickness. Conceal my death, defend my standard, and avenge my fall! It is an old prophecy, that a dead man shall gain a field, and I hope it will be accomplished this night': Walter Scott, *Minstrelsy of the Scottish Border*, ed. T. F. Henderson (4 vols., Edinburgh 1932), i, 277.
6 J. Reed, *The Border Ballads* (London 1973), 78–86; G. M. Fraser, *The Steel Bonnets: The Story of the Anglo-Scottish Border Reivers* (London 1971; repr. 1974), 198–200. Other useful works on Border history are: G. Ridpath, *The Border History of England and Scotland, deduced from the earliest times to the Union of the Crowns* (Berwick 1848; repr. Edinburgh 1979); J. Graham, *Condition of the Border at the Union* (Glasgow 1905); D. L. W. Tough, *The Last Years of a Frontier. A History of the Borders during the Reign of Elizabeth I* (Oxford 1928; repr. Alnwick 1928); and T. I. Rae, *The Administration of the Scottish Frontier 1513–1603* (Edinburgh 1966).
7 E. J. Cowan, 'Calvinism and the survival of Folk', in E. J. Cowan (ed.), *The People's Past* (Edinburgh 1980), 48–50. See also E. J. Cowan, 'The Angus Campbells and the origins of the Campbell-Ogilvie feud', *Scottish Studies*, xxv (1981), 25–38.
8 *Ordnance Gazetteer of Scotland: A Survey of Scottish Topography, Statistical, Biographical, and Historical*, ed. F. H. Groome (3 vols., Edinburgh 1886), iii, 448 note.
9 This version, 'from a manuscript written about the beginning of the nineteenth century, and now in the possession of Mr William Macmath', was first printed in H. L. Sargent and G. L. Kittredge (eds.), *English and Scottish Popular Ballads* (Boston 1904), 467–70.
10 R. Michison and L. Leneman, *Sexuality and Social Control Scotland 1660–1780* (Oxford 1989), 106–8, 128–9. Revised edition published in 2 volumes: *Girls in Trouble: Sexuality and Social Control in Rural Scotland 1660–1780*; and *Sin in the City: Sexuality and Social Control in Urban Scotland 1660–1780* (both Edinburgh 1998).
11 D. A. Symonds, *Weep Not For Me. Women, Ballads and Infanticide in Early Modern Scotland* (Pennsylvania 1997), *passim*; L. Stone, *Family, Sex and Marriage in England 1500–1800* (rev. edn, London 1979), *passim*.

12 *William Hay's Lectures On Marriage*, ed. Monsignor John C. Barry (Stair Soc., 1967), 111–13.

13 *Poems of the Vikings. The Elder Edda*, trans. P. Terry (Indianapolis 1969), 129–39.

14 Cf. 'Lord Thomas and Fair Annet' [73A] and 'Prince Robert' [87A,B].

15 Stone, *Family, Sex and Marriage*, 87–8. The notion that love between parents and children was uncommon has been challenged by J. L. Flandrin, *Families in Former Times. Kinship, Household and Sexuality* (Cambridge 1979), 160.

16 Würzbach and Salz, *Motif Index*, note 5 ballads on the theme of incest and 11 on infanticide, on which see Symonds, *Weep Not For Me, passim*.

17 Where were Dave Harker's gentrifiers when this one slipped by? See Intro. above.

18 *Hay Lectures*, 240–3; *Acts of the Parliaments of Scotland*, ed. T. Thomson and C. Innes (12 vols., Edinburgh 1814–75), VI, ii, 475–6.

19 E. Sagan, *At the Dawn of Tyranny: The Origins of Individualism, Political Oppression and the State* (New York 1985), xx.

20 E.g. Hrolf Gautreksson, *A Viking Romance*, trans. H. Pálsson and P. Edwards (Edinburgh 1972), cap 13.

21 Würzbach and Salz, *Motif Index*, 50.

22 Child glosses the expression as 'she would have paid you to do it' but it could also bear the meaning 'employed your servant'. It is left to the reader's discretion as to whether a further interpretation is permissible, for coarseness is certainly not alien to the ballad genre.

23 K. Brown, 'The Laird, his Daughter, her Husband and the Minister: unravelling a popular ballad', in R. Mason and N. Macdougall (eds.), *People and Power in Scotland. Essays in Honour of T. C. Smout* (Edinburgh 1992), 104–25; and 'Memorial of the confession of Jean Livingston, Lady Waristoun, with an account of her execution, July 1600', in C. K. Sharpe (ed.), *Lady Margaret Cunninghame, Lady Waristoun* (Edinburgh 1827).

24 D. Buchan, 'Folk medicine in the Scottish ballads: a medical perspective', in J. M. Kirk and C. Neilands (eds.), *Images, Identities and Ideologies. Papers from the 22nd International Ballad Conference, Belfast, 29 June–3 July 1992*, special issue of *Lore and Language*, xii (1994), 35–6, quoting D. Buchan (ed.), *Folk Tradition and Folk Medicine in Scotland: The Writings of David Rorie* (Edinburgh 1994). Greenwood conception of males is also found in 'Hind Etin' [41A] and 'Willie and Earl Richard's Daughter' [102A].

25 H. Henderson, 'The ballad and popular tradition to 1660', in R. D. S. Jack (ed.), *The History of Scottish Literature*: vol. I: *Origins to 1660 (Medieval and Renaissance)* (Aberdeen 1988), 273.

26 A. A. M. Duncan, *Scotland: The Making of the Kingdom* (Edinburgh 1975), 134, 524, 533.

27 A. J. Mill, *Medieval Plays in Scotland* (Edinburgh and London, 1927) 23n. For a useful overview of Robin Hood and the ballad tradition, see R. B. Dobson and J. Taylor, *Rymes of Robyn Hood. An Introduction to the English Outlaw* (London 1976; rev. and enlarged, Stroud 1997).

28 E. B. Lyle, 'The Burns text of "Tam Lin"', *Scottish Studies*, xv (1971), 53–65; E. J. Cowan, 'Burns and tradition', in K. Simpson (ed.), *Love and Liberty. Robert Burns: A Bicentenary Celebration* (East Lothian 1997), 229–38.

29 In both 'Tam Lin' and 'Thomas the Rhymer' the Queen of the Fairies is an abductress, a reversal of the usual situation.

30 *The New Statistical Account of Scotland*, ed. J. Sinclair (15 vols., Edinburgh 1845), iii, 244. Cf. 'The Hunting of the Cheviot' [162B] in which it is said of Witherington that 'when his leggs were smitten off/he fought upon his stumpes'.

31 G. Bennett, *Traditions of Belief. Women, Folklore and the Supernatural* (London 1987); J. Vansina, *Oral Tradition* (Harmondsworth 1973), 192.

32 D. Buchan, *The Ballad and the Folk* (London 1972; repr. East Linton 1997), 76; R. A. Houston, 'Women in the economy and society of Scotland 1500–1800', in R. A. Houston and I. D. Whyte (eds.), *Scottish Society 1500–1800* (Cambridge 1989), 140; M. E. Brown, 'Old singing women and the canons of Scottish balladry and song', in D. Gifford and D. McMillan (eds.), *A History of Scottish Women's Writing* (Edinburgh 1997), 44–57; Symonds, *Weep Not For Me*, 26–37. For an illuminating discussion of a traditional female ballad singer (Agnes Lyle of Kilbarchan), see W. B. McCarthy, *The Ballad Matrix. Personality, Milieu, and the Oral Tradition* (Bloomington and Indianapolis, 1990).

33 Symonds, *Weep Not For Me*, 18.

34 A. G. Gilchrist, 'Lambkin: a study in evolution', in M. Leach and T. P. Coffin (eds.), *The Critics and the Ballad* (Carbondale and London, 1961; repr. 1973), 204–24.

7

'Nouther right spelled nor right setten down': Scott, Child and the Hogg Family Ballads

VALENTINA BOLD

The quotation in my title is very well known but, to put it in context, I would like to quote the whole passage from James Hogg's *Familiar Anecdotes of Sir Walter Scott* (1834). Hogg is recalling an event which had happened thirty years earlier:

> One fine summer day of 1801 [actually July 1802], as I was busily engaged working in the field at Ettrick House, Wat Shiel came over to me and said, that 'I boud gang away down to the Ramseycleuch as fast as my feet could carry me, for there war some gentlemen there wha wantit to speak to me.' 'Wha can be at Ramseycleuch that want me, Wat?' 'I couldna say, for it wasna me that they spak to i' the byganging. But I'm thinking it's the Shirra an' some of his gang.' I was rejoiced to hear this, for I had seen the first volumes of the 'Minstrelsy of the Scottish Border,' and had copied a number of them from my mother's recital, and sent them to the editor preparatory for a third volume. I accordingly went towards home to put on my Sunday clothes, but before reaching it I met with THE SHIRRA and Mr William Laidlaw coming to visit me. They alighted and remained in our cottage for a space better than an hour, and my mother chanted the ballad of Old Maitlan' to them, with which Mr Scott was highly delighted. I had sent him a copy, (not a very perfect one, as I found afterwards, from the singing of another Laidlaw), but I thought Mr Scott had some dread of a part being forged that had been the cause of his journey into the wilds of Ettrick. When he heard my mother sing it he was quite satisfied, and I remember he asked her if she thought it had ever been printed; and her answer was, 'Oo, na, na, sir, it was never printed i' the world. For my brothers

an' me learned it frae auld Andrew Moor, an' he learned it frae auld Baby Mettlin, that was the housekeeper to the first laird o' Tushilaw.'

'Then that must be a very auld story, indeed, Margaret,' 'Ay it is that! It is an auld story! But mair nor that, except George Warton and James Steward, there was never ane o' my songs prentit till ye prentit them yourself, an' ye hae spoilt them a'thegither. They war made for singing, an' no for reading; and they're nouther right spelled nor right setten down.'

This should not be read on a literal level but considered, instead, as a vigorous anecdote from a great storyteller, reflecting the Hogg–Scott relationship as Hogg wished it remembered. By 1834, Hogg was an acknowledged authority on traditional culture, and he could not resist including information about performance practices (the 'chanting' mother) while implying the existence of a body of family texts. There is a retrospective dig at Scott's air-free collection in the observation that songs decay in print (Margaret Laidlaw continues, 'ye hae broken the charm noo, an' they'll never be sung mair'). This reflects Hogg's feelings about Scott's treatment of his family texts, given the hindsight of three decades of collecting, reworking and writing songs.[1] By examining a selection of Hogg's ballads, as they appear in manuscript, as well as in Scott's *Minstrelsy* and Child's *English and Scottish Popular Ballads* (1882–98), I aim to establish whether the Ettrick Shepherd's offended family pride was justified.

Community, and family experiences, had a direct bearing on Hogg's remarks. Hogg often emphasised the importance of song in the Ettrick Forest of his youth where 'we had singing matches every night'. The people of Selkirkshire, during Hogg's lifetime, enjoyed an enviable musical heritage although, by the nineteenth century, it was in transition. Manuscript collections made in 1815 and 1816, respectively, by Robert Pitcairn and Alexander Campbell (editor of *Albyn's Anthology*), testify to a rich tradition of piping, fiddling, lyrics and psalm-singing. Ettrick was familiar with Highland as well as Lowland melodies (related to droving contacts); Campbell was amazed, *en route* to Hogg's, to hear the 'Outlaw Murray' sung by an eighty-year-old tailor to the air, 'Mairi Bhan'.[2]

The second of four sons, in a family of multi-talented tradition bearers, Hogg enjoyed early and sustained exposure to orally transmitted song and music. Will o' Phaup, Hogg's grandfather, was a ballad expert, passing his repertoire on to his children, Margaret and William Laidlaw. Hogg was surprised, collecting for Scott, by the extent of his family repertoire. Margaret Laidlaw proved to be a 'living miscellany of old songs'. Her brother, William Laidlaw, provided several texts although he refused to sing ballads which he considered irreligious. Robert Hogg, the writer's father, is usually overlooked, but his family included fine singers. Campbell collected 'a few good melodies very old and entirely new to me' from Thomas and Frank Hogg, the Ettrick Shepherd's cousins. Hogg himself, of course, from the age of fourteen, enjoyed 'sawing over my favourite Scottish tunes' on the fiddle.[3]

In addition, by the time he met Scott in 1802, Hogg was *au fait* with literary traditions. Serving with the Laidlaws, first at Willenslee and from 1790 at Blackhouse, Hogg had access, for instance, to major Scottish works, such as Hamilton of Gilbertfield's version of Blind Hary's *The Wallace* (1722), and Ramsay's *The Gentle Shepherd* (1725). He already relished Burns, had formed a literary society and published lyrics like 'The Mistakes of a Night' (1794), and 'Donald MacDonald' (1801), as well as a book of *Scottish Pastorals* (1801). Such literary expertise meant Hogg was alert to the implications of Scott's canonised texts. Were his accusations, then, sour grapes?[4]

The Hogg family were actively sought by 'the Shirra' in his post-Ossianic quest for 'Tales which in elder times have celebrated the prowess and cheered the halls' of the 'gallant ancestors' of the duke of Buccleuch; a Borders' equivalent to Highland pretensions. William Laidlaw, who heard of the *Minstrelsy* through Scott's correspondent Mercer, made enquiries among his servants and discovered Hogg's family was known for their songs. Hogg subsequently transcribed many texts, mainly his mother's and uncle's, which were forwarded to Scott. They ranged from songs of love and chivalry from the Yarrow valley ('The Gay Goss Hawk', 'The Douglas Tragedy') to Ettrick's fairy traditions and cattle raids ('Tam Lin', 'Jamie Telfer').[5]

Some Hogg ballads were included in the third volume of the *Minstrelsy*, such as 'Old Maitland', 'The Battle of Otterburn' [Child 161], 'Clerk Saunders' [69], 'The Dowie Houms o' Yarrow' [214], 'The Duel of Wharton and Stuart', 'Erlinton' [8], 'The Gay Goshawk' [96], 'A Fragment on Cockburn's Death' [106], 'Lord William' [254] and the 'Lament of The Queens Marie' [173]. Hogg may, too, have provided 'Young Benjie' [86] and 'The Battle of Philiphaugh' [202]. The Hoggs provided Scott with several other ballads, such as 'Laminton' or 'Lochinvar' (which Scott retitled 'Katherine Janfarie'), 'Lamkin' [93], 'Lord Barnaby' [81], an untitled 'Johnny Scott' [99], 'Tushilaw's Lines', 'Jamie Telfer' [190], 'Johnny Armstrong's Last Goodnight' [169] and 'The Tale of Tomlin' [39]. Child included most of these, excluding only a few like 'Lord Barnaby', 'Johnny Scott' and 'Tushilaw's Lines'. Child also included references to Hogg fragments like the verse from 'The Queen's Maries' in volume four.[6]

Scott has often been accused of tampering with ballads. In line with current tastes, he certainly indulged in what has been called, 'that fine old Scottish practice of refurbishing traditional ballads'. Evelyn Kendrick Wells called Scott, 'neither philosophical nor scholarly'. However, the tendency to scoff at Scott as a collector should be tempered. Literary reworking, contrary to modern standards, was a respectable activity in the nineteenth century; it is within this context that Scott's (and Child's to a lesser extent) texts should be considered. Regarding the *Minstrelsy,* Scott paid lip service to responsible editorial policy, writing in 1801:

> I have made it an insatiable rule to attempt no improvements on the genuine Ballads which I have been able to recover. It will be necessary for me to be more particular in this respect because I shall give to the public many songs which have never before been published & some of which perhaps it may be now difficult to produce the reciters.[7]

Most of Hogg's texts are extant in manuscript, and I have chosen to look at three, listed in the appendix along with Scott's and Child's printed changes. Taken as a group, it is possible to see why Hogg remarked that these had been 'nouther right spelled nor right setten down'. Unfortunately, there are no tunes in the manuscript. Some of Hogg's sources, like his uncle William Laidlaw, sang all their songs to one melody, prompting Hogg to an observation about the importance ballad singers attach to texts: 'I find it was only the subject matter which the old people concerned themselves about, and any kind of tunes that they had, they always made one serve a great many songs.' This fascinating insight must be tempered with regret that William Laidlaw's tune was not recorded.[8]

The first item is one which Child, and Scott, accepted wholeheartedly: 'The Dowie Houms of Yarrow' [214], better known as 'The Dowie Dens of Yarrow'. This describes an unequal combat between a woman's lover (or husband) and her brothers. The outcome is predictably tragic, making another 'Border widow'. Scott borrows heavily from Hogg's notes to introduce the incident as referring to a duel, between John Scott of Tushielaw and Walter Scott of Thirlestane, noted in the Selkirk Presbytery Records for 1609. Hogg's text was one of three in Scott's composite ballad. One copy came from 'Nelly Laidlaw', another from Carterhaugh – probably both through William Laidlaw. Hogg provided an additional version (Child's M text).

It is not surprising that Hogg was annoyed by Scott's amendments.
They are mostly single word, or word ending, changes but, cumulatively,
alter the sound and tenor of the ballad. Hogg's version opens formulai-
cally, recalling 'Sir Patrick Spens' [58]:

> Late at e'en drinkin' the wine
>   Or early in a mornin'
> The set a combat them between
>   To fight it in the dawnin'.

Scott's additional 'gs' to words like 'drinkin' and 'mornin' makes this
harsher and less melodic, with direct effects on the 'chanting'. The tense
change in verse 5, from 'he's gane up yon high, high hill' to 'As he gaed
up' removes directness. A new reference to Tinnis compliments the duke
of Buccleuch (this was one of his estates) without enhancing the story.
Incremental repetition is lost in the sixth and twelfth verses – 'As oft she's
done', 'As ye hae doon', 'As aft she did' – which not only alters the
ballad's structure but detracts from the lovers' familiarity and poignantly
brutal separation. The change of 'noble' to 'leafu' lord, in verse 9, alters
audience perceptions and the gory line in verse 12, where Sarah drinks her
lover's blood, is replaced with a sanitised reference to kisses. The last two
verses become sentimental, as Scott reflects 'A fairer rose did never bloom
/ Than now lies cropped on Yarrow' and removes the final reductive
equation of the couple's sorrow with a love of gear: 'your ousen' (oxen).
A venomous Ettrick ending is thereby exchanged for romantic anguish.
Child's use of this Hogg version as his E text 'Braes of Yarrow' is more
'right setten down' than Scott's. There is some tidying, with punctuation
added to denote speech, for instance, but Hogg would have expected such
printed changes. The reading in Child differs, in one or two cases, from
my transcription, 'ir' for my 'in' in verse 6, for instance, gives a more
archaic flavour. Child's M text, also from a Hogg manuscript but not
apparently used by Scott, is more romantic, featuring picturesque wound
washing – she 'dried him wi the hollan' – and the woman dying, broken
hearted, in her father's arms. Child's J, K and L versions have the lover as
a servant lad from Gala, making the murder motive social rather than
economic. Child offers his E and M texts, as Hogg's, without overt
comment. Elsewhere, he adds snide remarks, for example about Hogg's
'Gay Goss Hawk': 'The Ettrick Shepherd sent Scott the following stanzas
to be inserted in the first edition at places indicated. Most of them are
either absolutely base metal or very much worn by circulation'. Perhaps
Child respected the 'Dowy Houms' as local, direct, and conforming to
nineteenth-century ideas, after Scott, of a 'classic' Border ballad. It has

certainly weathered well, recorded by many modern artists including Jean Redpath.[9]

It is tempting to speculate that Hogg might have preferred Scott's treatment of his thirty-verse 'Otterburn' to that of the 'Dowie Houms'. 'Otterburn' describes the battle of 5 August 1388 between the forces of James Earl of Douglas and Henry Percy ('Hotspur'), and is closely related to 'The Hunting of the Cheviot' [262]. It had particular resonance for the people of Ettrick Forest, long subject to Douglas control. Scott was determined to obtain a full copy, presumably comparable to Bishop Percy's seventy verses, and wrote to Laidlaw in 1803: 'I am so anxious to have a compleat Scottish Otterburne that I will omit the ballad entirely in the first volume hoping to recover it in time for insertion in the third'. Scott believed the *Minstrelsy* 'Otterburn', as he informed Bishop Percy in 1801, to be 'the Scottish account of the battle of Otterbourne; a ballad evidently much more modern than that published in the *Reliques* on the same subject'. Hogg himself tampered with the text, admitting minor changes to remedy transmission errors:

> As for the Scraps of Otterburn which I have got They seem
> to have been some confused jumble made by some person
> who had learned both the songs which you have and in time
> had been straitened to make one out of them both. But you
> shall have it as I had it saving that as usual I have sometimes
> helped the measure without altering one original word.[10]

The *Minstrelsy* follows Hogg's version fairly closely. Scott adopts Hogg's suggestion that 'Almon Shire' (verse 3) is a corruption of Bamborough-shire (verse 2), as corroborated by Bishop Percy's ballad. Small spelling alterations are made: 'wha's' for 'whaes', 'hundred' for 'hunder' and Scott punctuates Hogg's text heavily. The present tense is sometimes favoured over the past, adding immediacy: 'rue it' rather than 'rued it' (verse 1) for instance. Elsewhere Scott subtly remakes phrases, perhaps, to better suit the period: 'right furiouslie' for 'most furiouslie' (verse 7); the gentle 'Lammas tide' for Hogg's term-day 'Lammas time' (verse 1). More substantial changes include the deletion of verse 9, which effectively reiterates verse 8, presumably based on the notion that a repeated verse can be boring in print, even if powerful in performance.

Scott alters the ballad's plot-line to make it more romantic. The last two lines of verse 21 are altered, where Douglas makes for the battlefield to meet Percy. Scott exchanges 'Where he met wi' the proud Piercy / And a' his goodley train' for 'But he forgot the helmet good, / That should have kept his brain' – a change which makes Douglas's defeat by Percy excusable. Furthermore, to maintain the illusion of chivalry, and patriotism, Scott alters Douglas's backward flight to 'he fell on the ground' (verse 23). Scott, then, treats a text like this with a mixture of respect (by mainly minor alterations) and contempt (by deleting verses).

Child chooses to follow the *Minstrelsy*, not the manuscript. Perhaps Scott's 'correct' language, like 'Percy' for Hogg's 'Piercy' (although the 'ee' sound is characteristic of oral ballads), and knightly protagonists appealed. Some Scott 'corrections' do enhance the aesthetic appeal of the text; the rhythm becomes regular; there is new earthiness in the 'helmet' that would have preserved Percy's 'brain'. Scott heightens the drama, too, in the final confrontation.

My third example examines Hogg's own 'setten down' of texts. 'Old Maitland' was not accepted by Child. In the *Minstrelsy*, though, Scott remarked that, despite its 'present appearance', 'Old Maitland' was 'the most authentic instance of a long and very old poem' he had encountered in oral tradition:

> It is only known to a very few old people upon the seques-
> tered banks of the Ettrick, and is published as written down
> from the recitation of the mother of James Hogg, who sings,
> or rather chants it, with great animation. She learned the
> ballad from a blind man, who died at the advanced age of
> ninety ... the language of this poem is much modernised, yet
> many words, which the reciters have retained without
> understanding them, still preserve the traces of its antiquity.
> Such are the words *springals* (corruptedly pronounced
> *springwalls*), *sowies*, *portcullize*, and many other appropriate
> terms of war and chivalry, which could never have been
> introduced by the modern ballad-maker. The incidents are
> striking and well-managed, and they are in strict conformity
> with the manners of the age.

Hogg's employer, Laidlaw, heard the opening verses in Blackhouse from a servant girl; she revealed Hogg's grandfather knew the whole. Excited by 'a ballad not even hinted at by Mercer in the ... list of desiderata which he had sent from Scott', Laidlaw requested a full 'Auld Maitland' from Hogg:

> In a week or two I received his reply with the ballad as he
> had copied it from the recitation of his uncle Will of Phawhope,
> corroborated by his mother, and that both said they had
> learned it from their father (a still elder Will of Phawhope),
> and an old man named Andrew Muir, who had been servant

to the famous Mr Boston of Ettrick [Minister of Ettrick and author of *Human Nature in its Fourfold State* (1720)].

Exactly in this state it was published by Scott, and when he himself and Leyden called, I rejoiced that I had 'Auld Maitland' ready for them ... as Hogg had sent it written in his own hand from his uncle's and his mother's recitation ... Instantly, both he and Leyden, from their knowledge of the subject, saw and felt that the ballad was undoubtedly ancient, and their eyes sparkled as they exchanged looks. Mr Scott read with great fluency *con amore*, and with much proper emphasis and enthusiasm, all which entirely gained my heart. Leyden was like a roused lion. He paced the room from side to side, clapped his hands, and repeated after Mr Scott such old expressions as echoed the spirit of hatred to the Southerns as struck his fancy.

Despite their initial, patriotic, excitement the collectors grew suspicious. As the men rode out, Laidlaw assured Leyden that Hogg would not offer Scott 'old ballads' of his own composition: 'he would never think of any such thing, and neither he would at that period of his life'.[11]

Scott was convinced the ballad was genuine, alerting George Ellis in 1802 to, 'the preservation of ... Auld Maitland by oral tradition probably from the reign of Edward 2d or 3d'. Hogg wrote to Laidlaw in 1801: 'I believe I could get as much from these traditions as to make good songs myself. But without Mr. Scott's permission this would be an imposition, neither would I undertake it without an order from him.' As seen in his notes to 'Otterburn', Hogg makes no attempt to supply stanzas when verses are forgotten but usually offers a summary of the missing information. Unkindly, it could be added that 'Old Maitland' is one of the less exciting ballads in the Hogg set; the Ettrick Shepherd could have produced a more entertaining, plausible, piece. To forge 'Old Maitland' would have required elaborate scheming, and collaboration with an uncle, mother and Laidlaw's servant informant.[12]

Andrew Lang thought Hogg was innocent. On 9 November 1902 Lang wrote to the Selkirkshire antiquarian Thomas Craig-Brown: 'I don't think it was a hoax of Hogg's for he would have bragged of it sooner or later, moreover his mother probably neither could nor would get up a long poem by heart to cheat Sir Walter.' The argument that Hogg would have boasted of forgery rings true, as his later pride in 'Donald MacGillavry' indicates. On 14 November, Lang wrote to Craig-Brown: '"Auld Maitland" is a copy by an educated man, of 1560–1600, based on a ballad or legend, as,

I think, is "The Outlaw Murray".' On 20 December Lang added 'Baby Mattlin was about 2 generations before old Mrs. Hogg. She was a distant source of the ballad. Would that she had got into trouble ... it is impossible to track her – if she did not'. As Lang points out in *Sir Walter Scott and the Border Minstrelsy* (1910), the story of Old Maitland was only available in manuscripts which Hogg could not obtain. Furthermore, 'the style is not that of Hogg when he attempts the ballad'. To pursue this point, Hogg's later ballad-style poems, such as 'Sir David Graeme', are heavily romanticised.[13]

The lack of corroborative texts, though, is a persuasive argument against the ballad being genuine or, at best, not well known. In a letter of 30 June 1802 to Scott, Hogg denied the text was a 'modern forgery', stressing 'most of the old people' locally were familiar with 'Old Maitland' and demonstrating a sophisticated understanding of oral transmission processes as 'the feats of ... ancestors recorded in songs' passed down, between generations, through repeated performances:

> had a copy been taken down at the end of every fifty years, there must have been some difference, occasioned by the gradual change of language. I believe it is thus that many very ancient songs have been gradually modernized to the common ear, while, to the connoisseur, they present marks of their genuine antiquity.[14]

I think it unlikely Hogg forged 'Auld Maitland' but probable that he touched up the text. Given contemporary practices, for Leyden and Scott to doubt Hogg is like the pot calling the kettle black. Child had a more valid reason, if only the lack of corroboration, for rejecting the ballad. Overall, the balance favours Hogg's integrity in 'setting down' texts.

This becomes apparent if Hogg's 'right spelled' and 'right setten' version is consulted over the *Minstrelsy*. By indulging in the sort of changes already indicated, Scott made it difficult to take the uncorroborated ballad seriously. Scott's changes to Hogg's manuscript range from altered tenses – 'lived a King' for 'lives a king' (l.1), – to spelling – 'hight' for 'hicht', 'fatherlesse' for 'fatherless' – and replacing words – 'Gin' for 'if' (l.73), 'trayne' for 'main' (l.160) – and phrases – 'up and down' for 'towr and town' (l.31) to avoid repeating 'town' in the rhyme. Extra lines are added such as 'Who marching forth with false Dunbar, / A ready welcome found' after line 27. Hogg included these in the manuscript, with the proviso they could be inserted at any point; he implies the reciters forgot where the lines occurred. Scott makes the ballad scan better, adding words: 'And they are on to [King] Edwards host' (l.84), for instance. Hogg provided an extra verse, the first two lines of which were his own, as Scott acknowledged: 'Remember Piercy, aft the Scot / Has cower'd beneath thy hand / For every drap of Maitland blood, / I'll gie a rig of land' after line 175. Hogg's claim to have found an additional stanza to the original transcript may be evidence, of course, of innocence, or of his skill in the ruse. Scott excluded several Hogg texts from the *Minstrelsy*. 'Lamkin', for instance, was not used but is in Child's 'Additions and Corrections'. Presumably Child, like Scott, thought this a second-rate text. Neither Scott nor Child use Hogg's 'Lord Barnaby' [81], a ballad of betrayal, although Scott's marginal notes show he was intrigued to find a Scottish version. In a similar vein there is an untitled 'Johnie Scott' [99], thematically like 'Willie o' Winabury' [100]. Hogg was unimpressed by 'Johnie Scott' commenting, 'you might find any trace of its being founded on fact because if it is not it hath little else to reccomend [sic] it'.[15] Scott, presumably, agreed, perhaps objecting to the piece's ambiguous morality. Scott, then, edited Hogg's texts in several ways. Overall, he showed respect. The majority of changes are of single words, often well matched to the ballad idiom. These constitute the sort of alterations a singer might make. Scott also made more substantial cuts, pruning away what he perceived as superfluous verses, to please literary tastes. In general the tone is made more romantic and chivalric. Hogg's earthier texts are not published in the *Minstrelsy*. Damningly, bloodthirsty sections in pieces like 'The Dowie Houms' are removed, changing a vigorous ballad into an insipid whole. Scott had no more regard for Hogg's ballads than for his other sources, fusing parts into composite renditions.

Even if his family ballads were 'nouther right spelled nor right setten down', *The Minstrelsy* indirectly inspired Hogg. Being 'dissatisfied with the imitations of the ancient ballads', Hogg 'selected a number of traditionary stories, and put them in metre by chanting them to certain old tunes'. These early works, Hogg stated, were 'more successful than in any thing I had hitherto tried, although they were still but rude pieces of composition'.[16] Perhaps 'Old Maitland' was one of these flawed attempts. Ultimately, Scott's techniques provided a dubious model for Hogg's collecting enterprises, like *The Jacobite Relics of Scotland* (1819–21). Hogg emulated Scott's manner of obtaining songs, composite texts, historical notes and appendices. However Hogg notably differed from Scott in realising the need for musical transcripts (helped by William Stenhouse) to permit a full appreciation of his texts.

Hogg was substantially correct in having his mother state family texts were 'nouther right spelled nor right setten down' by Scott, and right to anticipate further reconditioning. However, though Scott could sometimes be heavy handed, his literary adeptness, and inspirational qualities, ensured the survival of texts like those of the Hogg family. Child's less intrusive tidying served a similar purpose. Scott, like Child, is only culpable of period-centred practices. More importantly, the literary editing of Scott and Child placed the oral Hogg family ballads into a transmission chain. The 'setten down' ballads allow the modern reader to appreciate a tradition in transition. Such a lasting contribution, ultimately, outweighs the problems relating to family ballads being 'nouther right spelled nor right setten down'.

APPENDIX

The Hogg Family Ballads

The following selection of ballads is transcribed from Hogg's manuscript texts in 'Scotch Ballad Materials', National Library of Scotland [NLS] MS. 877, folios 250, 243–4 and 144–5 respectively. Scott's changes, in the *Minstrelsy of the Scottish Border*, are in square brackets, as is matter deleted in, or omitted from, the manuscript. Scott's heavy punctuation is not indicated as including this would make the text virtually unreadable.

'The dowy houms o' Yarrow' [214]

Tradition placeth the event on which this song is founded very early that the song hath been written near the time of the transaction appears quite evident altho like others by frequent singing the language is become adapted to an age not so far distant The bard does not at all relate particulars but only mentions some striking features of a tragical event which every body knew this is observable in many of the productions of early times at least the secondary hands seem to have regarded their songs as purely temporary.

The Hero of the ballad is said to have been of the name of Scott and is called a knight of great ?mery. He lived in Ettrick some say Oakwood others Kirkhope but was murderously slain by his brother in law as related in the ballad who had him at ill will because his father had parted with the half of all his goods and gear to his sister on her marriage with such a respectable man the name of the murderer is said to be Annand a name I believe merely conjectural from the name of the place where they are said both to be buried which at this day is called Annan's Treat a low-muir lying to the west of Yarrow church where two huge tall stones erected below which the least child that can walk the road will tell you the two lords are buried that were slain in a duel.

Late at e'en drinkin' [drinking] the wine
    Or early in a mornin'
[And ere they paid the lawing]
The [They] set a combat them between
    To fight it in the dawnin' [dawning]

O stay at hame my noble lord
    O stay at hame my marrow
My cruel brother will you betray
    On the dowy [dowie, *passim*] houms o' Yarrow

O fare-ye-weel my lady gaye
    O fare-ye-weel my Sarah
For I maun gee Tho' [though] I ne'er return
    Frae the dowy banks o' Yarrow

She kiss'd [kissed, *passim*] his cheek she kaim'd his hair
    As [oft] she had done before O
She belted on [him with] his noble brand
    An' he's awe to Yarrow

O he's gane up yon high high hill
    I wat he gae'd wi' sorrow
An' in a den spie'd nine arm'd men
    I' [In] the dowy howms o' Yarrow
[As he gaed up the Tennies bank, / I wot he gaed wi' sorrow, / Till, down in a den, he spied nine arm'd men, / On the dowie houms of Yarrow.]

O in ye come to drink the wine
    As ye hae coon before O
Or in ye come to wield the brand
    On the bonny banks o' Yarrow
["O come ye here to part your land, / The bonnie Forest thorough? / Or come ye here to weird your brand, / On the dowie houms of Yarrow?"]

I im [I'm, *passim*] no come to drink the wine
    As I hae coon before O
[I come not here to part my land, / And neither to beg or borrow]
But I im come to wield the brand
    On the dowy houms O'Yarrow

[The *Minstrelsy* version has another stanza here: the challenger comments on the unequal odds of nine to one]

Four [has] he hurt an' [and] five he [has] slew
    On the dowy houms o' Yarrow
    [On the bloody braes of Yarrow]
Till that stubborn knight came him behind
    An' ran his body thorrow [bodie thorough]

Gae hame gae hame Good-brother John
    An' [And] tell your sister Sarah
To come an' [and] lift her noble [leafu'] lord
    Who's [He's] sleepin' sound on Yarrow
Yestreen I dream'd a dolefu' dream,
I kend there wad be sorrow
[I fear there will be sorrow!]
I dream'd I pu'd the heather green
    On the dowy banks o' Yarrow,
[Wi' my true love, on Yarrow.]

[Scott's composite version has two extra stanzas: Sarah sends a kiss
to her lover in the first; in the second she realises her knight is slain]

She gae'd up [As she sped down] yon high high hill
I wat she gae'd wi' sorrow
[She ga'ed wi' dole and sorrow,]
An' in a den spy'd nine dead men [ten slain men]
On the dowy housl banks] o' Yarrow

She kiss'd his cheek she kaim'd his hair
As aft she did before O
[She search'd his wounds all thorough,]
She drank the red blood free him ran
[She kiss'd them, till her lips grew red,]
On the dowy houms o' Yarrow

O [Now] haud your tongue my douchter [daughter] dear
    For what maeds a' this sorrow
    [For a' this breeds but sorrow;]
I'll wed you on [ye to] a better lord
    Than him you [ye] lost on Yarrow

O haud your tongue my father dear
    An' dinna grieve your Sarah
    [Ye mind me but of sorrow]
A better Lord was never born
    Than him I lost on Yarrow

[A fairer rose did never bloom
    Than now lies cropped on Yarrow".]

Tak hame your ousen tak hame your kye
    For they have bred our sorrow
I wiss that they had a' gene mad
    Whan they cam first to Yarrow
[Scott omits this final stanza]

'The Battle of Otterburn' [161]

It fell about the Lammas time [tide]
    When the muir-men won [win] their hay
That [omitted] the doughty carl [omitted] Douglas went
    Into England to catch [drive] a prey

He chose the Gordons and the Graemes
    With the [them] Lindsays [Lindesays] light and gay
But the Jardines wadna wi' him [wald not with them] ride
    And they rued [rue] it to this day

And he has burnt [burn'd] the dales o' [of] Tine
    And part of Almon Shire [Bamboroughshire]
And three good towers on Roxburgh fells
    He left them all on fire

Then [And] he march'd up to Newcastle
    And rode it round about
O whaes [wha's] the lord of this castle
    Or whae's [wha's] the lady o't

But up spake proud lord Piercy [Percy, *passim*] then
    And O but he spak hie
I am the lord of this castle
    And [omitted] my wife's the lady gaye

If you are [thour't the] lord of this castle
    Sae sweet [weel] it pleases me
For ere I cross the border again [fells]
    The ane [tane] of us shall die

He took a lang spear in his hand
    Was made [Shod] of the metal free
And for to meet the Douglas then [there]
    He rade most [rode right] furiouisly [furiouslie]

But O how pale his lady look'd
    Frae off [aff] the castle wa'
When down before the Scottish spear
    She saw brave [proud] Piercy fa'

How pale and wan his lady look'd
    Frae off [aff] the castle hieght
When she beheld her Piercy yield
    To doughty Douglas might
[Scott omits this stanza]

Had we twa been upon the green
    And never an eye to see
I should have [wad hae] had ye [you] flesh and fell
    But your sword shall gae wi' me

But gae you [ye] up to Otterburn [Otterbourne, *passim*]
    And there wait dayes [dayis, *passim*] three
And if I come not ['at' deleted in MS.] ere three dayes end
    A fause lord [knight] ca' ye me.

The Otterburn's a bonny [bonnie, *passim*] burn
    'Tis pleasant there to be
But there is naught [nought] at Otterburn
    To fend my men and me

The deer rins wild owr [on] hill and dale
    The birds fly wild frae [from] tree to tree
And [But] there is neither bread nor kale
    To feed my men and me

But [Yet] I will stay at Otterburn
    Where you shall welcome be
And if ye come not ere [at] three days end
    A coward [fause lord] I'll ca' thee

Then gae your ways to Otterburn
    And there wait dayes three
And if I come not ere three days end
    A coward ye's ca me
[Scott exchanges this for a less repetitive stanza: "'Thither
will I come,' proud Percy said,/ 'By the might of Our
Ladye!' – / 'There will I bide thee,' said the Douglas, / 'My
trowth I plight to thee.'"]

They lighted high on Otterburn
  Upon the bent so [sae] brown
They lighted high on Otterburn
  And threw their pallions down

And he that had a bonny boy
  Sent his horses [out his horse] to grass
And he that had not a bonny boy
  His ain servant he was

But up then spak [spake] a little page
  Before the peep of the [omitted] dawn
O waken ye waken ye my good lord
  For Piercy's hard at hand

Ye lie ye lie ye loud liar [liar loud]
  Sae loud I hear ye lie
The Piercy hadna [had not] men yestreen
  To dight my men and me

But I have seen [hae dream'd] a dreary dream
  Beyond the isle o' Sky
I saw a dead man won the [win a] fight
  And I think that man was I

He belted on his good broad [braid] sword
  And to the field he ran
Where he met wi' the proud Piercy
  And a' his goodley train
[Scott substitutes, for the two last lines, 'But he forgot the
helmet good, / That should have kept his brain'.]

When Piercy wi' the Douglas met
  I wat he was right keen [fu' fain]
Thy swakked their swords till sair they swat
  And the blood ran them between [ran down like rain]

But Piercy wi' [wish] his good broad sword
  Was made o' the metal free
  [That could so sharply wound]
Has wounded Douglas on the brow
Till backward he did flee
[Till he fell on the ground]

Then he call'd on his little page [foot-page]
And said run speedily
And bring my ain dear sisters son
Sir Hugh Montgomery

This ballad which I have collected from two different people a crazy old man and a woman deranged in her mind seems hither to considerably entire but now when it becomes more interesting they have both failed me and I have been obliged to take much of it in plain prose however as none of them seemed to know any thing of the history save what they have learned from the song I took it the more kindly any few verses which follow are to me unintelligible.

He told Sir Hugh that he was dying and ordered him to conceal his body and neither let his own men nor Piercy's know which he did and the battle went on headed by Sir Hugh Montgomery and at length.

[The *Minstrelsy*, at this point, adds six stanzas: in the first Douglas tells the dream to his nephew, in the second, third and fourth his corpse is hidden beside the bush. In the fifth, by moonlight, the Scots slay many of the English; in the sixth the 'Gordons good' steep their shoes in English blood, while the Lindsays 'fly like fire' for the rest of the fray.]

When stout Sir Hugh wi' Piercy met
    I wet he was right fain
They swakked their swords till sair they swat
    And the blood ran down like rain
[The Percy and Montgomery met, / That either of other were fain; / They swapped swords, and they twa swat, / And the blude ran down between.]

O yield thee Piercy said Sir Hugh
    O yield or ye shall die
Fain wad I yield proud Piercy said
    But ne'er to loun like thee
["Yield thee, O yield thee, Percy!" he said, / "Or else I vow I'll lay thee low!" / "To whom shall I yield," said Earl Percy, / Now that I see it must be so?"]

Thou shalt not yield to knowe nor lown [lord nor loun]
    Nor shalt thy [yet shalt thou] yield to me
But yield ye [thee] to the breaken [bracken] bush
    That grows on yonder [upon yon lilye] lee

I will not yield to bush nor brier [to a braken bush]
    Nor [yet] will I yield to thee [to a brier]

But I will [would] yield to Lord [Earl] Douglas
    Or Sir Hugh Montgomery
    [Or Sir Hugh the Montgomery, if he were here.]

Piercy seems to have been fighting devilishly in the dark indeed! my reciters added no more but told me that Sir Hugh died on the field but that He left not an Englishman on the field.

* * *

That he hadna either killtd or ta'en
    Ere his hearts blood was cauld.
[Scott has two final stanzas to Hogg's one; Piercy surrenders to Montgomery, who raises him by the hand, then the deed is placed at Otterbourne and Douglas buried]

Almon Shire may probably be a corruption of Banburghshire but as both my relations called it so I thought proper to preserve it The towers on Roxburgh fells may not bee [sic] so improper as we were thinking there may have been some strengths on the very borders.

'Old Maitland a very ancient Song'

There lives [lived] a king in southern land
    King Edward hicht [hight, *passim*] his name
Unwordily he wore the crown
    Till fifty years was [were] gane
[Scott splits the ballad into four-line stanzas]
He had a sisters son o's ain
    was large o' [of] blood and bane
And afterwards [afterward] when he came up
    Young Edward hicht his name
One day he came before the king
    And kneeld low on his knee
A boon a boon my good uncle
    I crave to ask of thee.
To [At] our lang wars i' [in] fair Scotland
    I lang hae lang'd to be
    [I fain hae wished to be]
If fifteen hunder [hundred, *passim*] wale [waled] wight men
    You'll grant to ride wi' me
Thou sal [sall, *passim*] hae thee thou sal hae mae
    I say it sickerly [sickerlie]

And I mysel [mysell] an auld grey [gray] man
    Array'd your host sal see
King Edward rade King Edward ran
    I wish him dool and pain [pyne]
Till he had fifteen hunder men
    Assembled on the Tyne
And twice as many at North Berwick
    Was [were] a' for battle bound
[Scott includes Hogg's extra lines here:
    'Who, marching forth with false Dunbar, / A ready
welcome found']
They lighted on the banks of Tweed
    And blew their coals see het,
And fir'd [fired] the Merce [Merse] and Tevidale [Teviotdale]
    All in an evning [evening] late
As they far'd up o'er Lammermor [Lammermore]
    They burnt baith towr and town
    [They burned baith up and down]
Till [Untill] they came till [to] a dirksome [darksome] house
    Some call it Leaders town [Leader-Town]
Whae [Wha, *passim*] huds [hauds] this house young Edward cry'd
    Or whae gae's't [giesit] owr to me,
A grey [gray] heir'd knight set up his head
    And cracked [crackit] right crousely
Of Scotlands king I haud my house
    He pays me meat and fee
And I will keep my gaud [gude] auld house
    While my house will keep me
They laid their sowies to the wall
    Wi' mony [a] heavy peal
But he threw owr [ower, *passim*] to them again
    Baith pick [pitch] and tar barille [barrel]
With springs:wall [springwalds] stanes and gaod of
        ern [gads of airn]
    Amang [Among] them fast he threw
Till many [mony, *passim*] of the English men
    About the wall he slew
Full fifteen days that braid host lay
    Sieging old Maitland [auld Maitland, *passim*] keen
then [Syne] they hae left him safe and hale [hail and fair]
    Within his strength o [of] stane:

Englands our ain by heritage,
    And whae [what] can us gainstand [withstand]
When [Now] we hae conquer'd fair Scotland
    Wi bow buckler and brande:
[Scott reverses the order: the preceding four lines
are interchanged with the following four lines. The last line
becomes 'With buckler, bow, and brand']
Then fifteen barks all gaily good
    Mett [met] them upon a day,
Which they did lade with as much spoil
    As they could bear away
Then they are on to the land o' France
    Where auld king Edward lay
burning each town and castle strong
[Burning baith castle, tower, and town]
    that ance [he] came [met] in his way
untill he came unto that town
    Which some call Billop-Grace
There were Old Maitland's sons, a' three
    Learning at school alas
The eldest to the others [youngest] said
    Oh see you [ye] what I see
if [Gin] all [a', *passim*] be true [trew] yon standard says
    Were fatherless a' [all] three
For Scotland's conquer'd up and down
    Landsmen we'l [we'll, *passim*] never be
Now will ye go my brethren two
    And try some jeopardy
Then they hae saddled two [twa, *passim*] black horse
    Two black horse and a grey,
And they are on to [King] Edward's host
    Before the dawn [break] of day
When they arriv'd before the host
    They hover'd on the ley [lay]
Will you [thou] lend me our kings standard
    To carry [bear] a little way
Where was [wast] thou bred Where was [wast] thou born
    Wherein [Where or] in what country
In the north of England I was born
    What [It] needed him to lie

A knight me got [gat] a lady bore
　　　I'm a squire of high renowne
I well may beer't to any king
　　　That ever [yet, included by Scott, crossed out
　　　　　　　　　in MS.] wore a crown
He ne'er came of an English man
　　　Had sic an ee or bree
But thou art [the] likest auld Maitlin
　　　That ever I did see
But sic a gloom on ae brow head
　　　Grant I ne'er see again
For many of our men he slew
　　　And many put to pain
When Maitlan heard his father's name
　　　An angry man was he
Then lifting up a gilt dager
　　　Hung low down by [upon] his knee
He stab'd [stabb'd, passim] the knight the standard bore
　　　He stabb'd him cruelly [cruellie, *passim*]
Then caught the standard by the neuk
　　　And fast away rade [rode] he
Now is 'tna time brothers he cried
　　　Now is 'tna time to flee
Aye [Ay] by my sooth they baith reply'd
　　　We'l bear you company
The youngest turn'd him in a path
　　　And drew a burnish'd [burnished] brand
And fifteen o' the formost [foremost] slew
　　　Till back the leve did stand
He spurr'd the grey unto [into] the path
　　　Till baith her [his] sides they bled
Grey thou maun carry me away.
　　　Or my life lies in wed [wad]
The captain lookit ower the wall [wa']
　　　Before [About] the break o day
There he beheld the three Scots lads
　　　Pursued alongst [along] the way
Pull up portculzies [portcullize] down draw briggs [draw-brigg]
　　　My nephews are at hand
And they shall [sall] lodge with [wi'] me to night
　　　In spite of all England

When e'er they came within the gate
    They thrust their horse them free
And took three lang spears in their hands
    Saying here sal [sall] come nae mae
Then [and] they shott [shot, *passim*] out and they shots in
    Till it was fairly day
When many of the Englishmen
    About [Along] the drawbrigg lay
Then they had yoked carts and wains
    To ca' their dead away
And shot auld dykes aboon the leve
    In gutters where they lay
The king in [at] his pavilion door
    Was heard aloud to say
Last night three o' the lads o' France
    My Standard stole away
Wi' a fause tale disguis'd they came
    And wi' a fauser train [trayne]
And to regain my gaye standard,
    These men were a' down slaine
It ill befits the youngest said
    A crowned king to lie
But or that I taste meat or [and] drink
    Reproved shall [sall] he be
He went before King Edward straight [strait]
    And kneel'd low on his knee
I wad hae leave my liege [lord] he said
    To speak a word wi' thee
The king he turn'd him round about
    And wistna what to say
Quo' he man thou's hae leave to speak
    Though thou shaud [should] speak a' day
You said that three young lads o France
    Your standard stole away
Wi' a fause tale and fauser main [trayne]
    And many men did slay
But we are nane the lads o' France
    Nor e'er pretends [pretend] to be
We be [are] three lads o' fair Scotland
    And Maitlin's sons a' three [sons are we]

Nor is there men in a' your host
> dare [Daur] fight us three to three

Now by my sooth young Edward cry'd [said]
> Well [Weel] fitted sall ye be [ye sall be]

Piercy shall [sall] wi' the eldest fight
> And Ethert Lunn wi' thee

William of Lancaster the third
> And bring your fourth to me

[Scott adds Hogg's 'modern' lines: 'Remember Piercy, aft the
Scot / Has cower'd beneath thy hand' and, to complete the
stanza, adds, 'For every drap of Maitland blood, / I'll gie a
rig of land'.]

He clanked Piercy owr the head
> A sharp stroke [deep wound] and a sair

Till a' the blood [Till the best blood] o' his body
> Came rinnin owr [rinning down] his hair

Now I've slain [Now I have slayne ane;] one slaye ye the twa
> And that's good [gude] company

And tho' [if] the two [twa, *passim*] should [suld, *passim*]
> slay ye both
> Ye's [Ye'se, *passim*] get nae [na] help o' me

But Ethert Lunn a baited bear
> Had many [unaltered] battles seen

He set the youngest wonder sair
> Till th' [the] eldest he grew keen

I am nae king nor nae Sic thing
> My word it sanna [shanna] stand

For Ethert shall [sall] a buffet bide
> Come he aneath [beneath] my brand

He clanked [clankit] Ether owr the head
> A sharp stroke and a sair
> [A deep wound and a sair]

Till a the blood o' his body
[Till the best blood of his bodie]
> Came rinnin [rinning] owr his hair

Now I've slain two slay ye the ane
> Isna that good company [companye]

And though [tho'] the ane should slay
> ye both [ye baith]
> Ye's get nae help o' me

The twa-some they hae slayne the ane
      They maul'd them cruelly
Then hung them owr [over] the draw bridge
      That a' [all] the host might see
They rade their horse they ran their horse
      Then hover'd [hovered] on the ley
We be three lads o' fair Scotland
      We [That] fain wad fighting see
This boasting when Young Edward heard
      To's uncle thus said he
      [An angry man was he]
I'll take [tak] yon lad I'll bind yon lad
      And bring him bound to thee
But [Now] God forbid King Edward said
      that ever thou should try
Three worthy leaders we hae lost
      And you the fourth shall be
      [And thou the fourth wad lie]
If thou wert hung owr [shouldst hang on] yon draw bridge
      Blythe wad I never be
But wi the pole axe in his hand
      Out owr the bridge [Upon the brigg] sprang he
The first stroke that young Edward gae
      He struck wi' might and main [mayn]
He clove the Maitlins [Maitlan's] helmet stout
      And near had pierc'd his brain
      [And bit right nigh the brayn]
When Matlin saw his ain blood fa'
      An angry man was he
He let his weapon frae him fa
      And at his neck [throat] did flee
And thrice about he did him swing
      Till on the ground he light
Where he has hadden [halden] Young Edward
      Though [Tho'] he was great in might
Now let him up Young Edward [King Edward] cry'd
      And let him come to me
And for the deed that ye hae [thou hast] done
      Ye shall [Thou shalt] hae earldoms three
Its ne'er be said in France nor Ire [e'er]
      Nor [In] Scotland when I'm hame

That Edward ance was [once lay] under me
    And yet wan up again
    [And e'er get up again]
He stabb'd him thro' and thro' the heart
[He pierced him through and through the heart]
    He maul'd him cruelly
Then hang [hung] him owr the drawbridge
    Beside the other three
Now take from [frae] me that featherbed
    Make me a bed o' strae
I wish I nee'r had seen [hadna lived] this day
    To make my heart see wee
If I were ance at London town [tower]
    Where I was wont to be
I never mair should gang free hame
    Till borne on a bier tree.

You may insert the two following lines any where you think it
needs them or else substitute two better

And marching south with curst Dunbar
    A ready welcome found

NOTES

1 Reprinted in James Hogg, *Memoir of the Author's Life and Familiar Anedotes of Sir Walter Scott*, ed. D. S. Mack (Edinburgh 1972), 61–2.

2 James Hogg, 'On the changes in the habits, amusements, and condition of the Scottish peasantry', *The Quarterly Journal of Agriculture*, iii (1831–2), 256–7. See A. Campbell, 'Fragments of two journals, 1802 and 1816', Edinburgh University Library [EUL} MSS. La. II. 378. R. Pitcairn, 'Collection of Ballads' (3 vols.), National Library of Scotland [NLS] MSS. 2913–15.

3 James Hogg, 'Odd characters', *The Shepherd's Calendar* (Edinburgh and London 1829); Campbell, 'Fragments of two journals', 4. See E. Petrie, 'Odd characters: traditional informants in James Hogg's family', *Scottish Literary Journal*, cx (1983), 30–41.

4 See James Hogg, 'Memoir of the Author's Life', in Hogg, *The Mountain Bard* (Edinburgh and London, 1807; rev. and expanded edn, Edinburgh and London, 1821) – further revised and expanded in *Altrive Tales* (London 1832).

5 See Scott's introduction to *Minstrelsy of the Scottish Border* (3 vols., Edinburgh 1802–3); W. Laidlaw, 'Recollections of Sir Walter Scott', *Trans. Hawick Archaeological Soc.* (1905), 67. Hogg's texts appear in 'Scotch ballad material of the Borders', NLS MS. 877. See, in particular, fos. 133, 144–5, 243–6, 250, 256–7. I would like to thank the Trustees of the National Library of Scotland for permission to quote from this material.

6 See *The English and Scottish Popular Ballads*, ed. F. J. Child (5 vols., Boston and London, 1882–98), iv, 513.

7 See C. Zug, 'Scott's "Jock of Hazeldean": the re-creation of a traditional ballad', *Journal of American Folklore*, lxxxvi (1973), 152; E. K. Wells, *The Ballad Tree* (New York 1950); Walter Scott, *The Letters of Sir Walter Scott, 1787–1807* (12 vols., New York 1971), i, 120.
8 James Hogg, quoted in E. Batho, *The Ettrick Shepherd* (Cambridge 1927), 26.
9 J. Redpath, *The Song of the Seals* (1970) (Brig o' Turk, Callander, 1977), SRCM 160.
10 Scott, *Letters*, i, 173; NLS MS. 877, fo. 243.
11 Laidlaw, 'Recollections', 67–8.
12 Scott, *Letters*, xii, 31; James Hogg, quoted in Batho, *Ettrick Shepherd*, 20.
13 A. Lang, 'Letters', Selkirk Archives SC/S/16/2/15–16; A. Lang, *Sir Walter Scott and the Border Minstrelsy* (1910, repr. New York 1968), 40.
14 'Letters to Scott', NLS MS. 3874, fo. 114.
15 NLS MS. 877, fo. 257.
16 Hogg, *Memoir of the Author's Life*, 16.

8

Sound and Song in the Ritual of Popular Protest: Continuity and the Glasgow 'Nob Songs' of 1825[1]

CHRISTOPHER A. WHATLEY

Popular culture in Scotland in the early modern era is relatively under-researched.[2] Hardly surprisingly then that the place of song and verse in popular protest in pre-Victorian Scotland is a topic about which cultural historians have had little to say. There have been some exploratory probes into the subject but the efforts of those concerned to uncover a hidden tradition of plebeian protest song or poetry in Scotland in the eighteenth and early nineteenth centuries have only been partially successful.

In a richly documented, seminal study of political and protest songs in the eighteenth century, Thomas Crawford reported that trade union verse and 'urban songs of protest' did not become common until later in the nineteenth century and early in the twentieth; their production, born of greater suffering, was facilitated by increased literacy and cheap publishing.[3] A popular poetic or song tradition of 'gritty realism' might have existed but few traces of it can be found, nor can songs or ballads which contained 'threats of direct violence'. Crawford's impressions were largely confirmed by Kenneth Logue who concluded that there was 'a notable dearth of folk songs referring to the many instances of popular direct action [in the eighteenth century]'.[4] Both Crawford and Logue were convinced that the nineteenth-century songs of the working class must have had eighteenth-century precursors, but neither was able to produce much supporting evidence, other than that prototypes in the form of English broadsides 'of general plebeian social protest' were in circulation and evidently used by poets such as Robert Burns.[5]

There were songs and poems in the eighteenth century which were concerned with political issues. The Darien scheme of the 1690s was celebrated in music and verse, while opponents as well as supporters of the Union of 1707 were able to call on a repertoire of songs and poems to sustain their respective points of view. So too could Scottish Whigs.[6] As in early Hanoverian England much anti-establishment verse and song appears to have been grounded in the catch-all rhetoric and imagery of Jacobitism.[7] The allegation that most Jacobite songs – 'brilliant fakes' – were written long after Culloden[8] has been convincingly refuted. The *sentimental* songs were composed later but Murray Pittock has pointed to the existence of a sizeable body of active and aggressive contemporary popular Jacobite song which was transmitted in the vernacular in broadside or oral form, most commonly in ale-houses and by street-singers.[9] Thereafter however, with few exceptions, Jacobite poems and songs lacked the harder edge of their Irish counterparts in which the longed-for return of the Stuart dynasty was conjoined with and eventually supplanted by the iconography of nationalist struggle.[10] Although Burns in his patriotic poetry and songs drew on 'features of Jacobite ideology such as the corrupting power of gold' and applied a Jacobite critique within the Jacobin context, his genuinely felt Jacobitism had effectively become a lost cause.[11]

The discovery of a stronger tradition of popular oppositional Jacobite song up until the mid-1700s notwithstanding, it is difficult to disagree with the received view, that in early modern Scotland songs and ballads were the 'shared property of king and commoner', even though the treatment of shared sentiments could differ. The eighteenth century, it has been argued, 'saw the rise and maturity of a lyric culture in which practically everybody took part'.[12]

One explanation which has been advanced to account for the absence of a canon of popular literature of protest is that Scotland was socially 'backward'.[13] This is a variant of the traditional view of Scottish society during this period, in which is depicted a quiescent lower class, whose obedience and passivity was ensured through strict Kirk control and a system of criminal law which was relatively heavily weighted against the accused. The 'dispersed nature of Scottish rural settlement' may also have militated against group action in the countryside where landowners exercised considerable power in their baron courts, while social change is judged to have taken place relatively slowly in a society in which paternalism predominated.[14] For a variety of reasons the 'uninflammable' Scottish people were little moved by events such as the French Revolution and even the so-called 'Radical War' of 1820, which failed to arouse the passions of more than a minority, let alone act as conduits for insurrection.[15] Popular culture within Lowland Scotland has also been presented as lacking in passion, and as both ritually and relatively impoverished. Of particular relevance for this chapter is the observation that outside the Northern Isles and the north-east Lowlands, where a ballad tradition flourished, the Scots were 'less musical' than their English, Welsh and French counterparts after the Reformation.[16]

There is another less sanguine interpretation of the nature of social relations in eighteenth- and early nineteenth-century Scotland, which has a bearing on popular culture. This is based on the identification of tensions which lay beneath the relatively calm exterior of Scottish society observed by many historians, and places greater emphasis on the incidence of various forms of popular protest including overt if generally non-fatal violence, as in riots for example and, the specific focus of this paper, industrial disputes and disturbances in the early 1800s.[17] In this view the Kirk and the other agents of social control which it has been assumed produced a peculiarly passive people who readily adapted to the dictates of modernising and industrialising society were less effective than their advocates have supposed.[18] Kirk proscription of traditional festivities may have been effective in the middling decades of the seventeenth century but the Restoration brought music back on to the public stage and popular social events such as the ubiquitous 'penny wedding' (of which music was an integral component) continued to take place. Indeed judging by the vehemence of presbytery exhortations that these should be curtailed – as in Fife in 1719 – they appear to have flourished far beyond the confines of the north-east of Scotland.[19] It was been argued elsewhere that although the opportunities for communal recreation and release in early modern Scotland were fewer than in England, they were not curbed altogether but instead found alternative outlets, as on the 'drunken, disorderly, abandoned ... cruel, violent, fiery, irreverent' occasion of the monarch's birthday.[20]

In this paper it will be suggested, firstly, that there is now firmer evidence of a popular culture of oppositional song and verse than was available to the earlier contributors to the subject in the later 1970s and 1980s. Tom Leonard's *Radical Renfrew*, a collection of mainly working-class poems and songs from Paisley and Renfrewshire from the 1790s to the First World War, demonstrates that, while the search for such material is necessarily time-consuming, it need not be in vain.[21] Weaver poets and others of mainly artisan status in this 'rich ballad region' produced an extensive body of poetry and song, much of it written either wholly or partly in the vernacular.[22] Within it the themes of political rights, opposition to oppression and class feeling can be clearly identified. Many of the ballads collected in 1825 by William Motherwell from Agnes Lyle (b. *c.*1775), a weaver's daughter from Kilbarchan, were firmly located within the particular social and political conflicts of the 1820s. Handloom weavers were avid readers, as well as being especially good customers of the numerous hawkers of chapbooks, penny histories and ballads which were 'found in almost every house' in and around Glasgow in the early

1800s. No ballad seller 'ever visited the weavers shop', one contemporary recalled, 'without disposing of one or more of his ballads or histories'.[23]

The potency of the handloom weaver versifier is highlighted in the case of the Paisley weaver Alexander Wilson, author in 1790 of 'The Hollander', a savage attack on a local silk manufacturer, and in 1792 of the 'Lang Mills Detected', or 'The Shark', a barely concealed reference to William Sharp, also a silk manufacturer.[24] 'Weaver blades' were urged to 'Defend yourselves! Tak sicker heed!' as 'SHARK's resolved, wi' hellish greed / To gorge us a' the gither'. A copy of the poem which it was alleged would 'create discord betwixt a manufacturer and his workers and stir up combination, opposition and violence', was sent anonymously to Sharp, along with an offer to destroy the manuscript if five guineas were paid within three hours. A warrant was issued ordering the arrest and trial of Wilson and banning the printers from publishing further copies of the poem. In February 1793 Wilson himself had to burn the poem on the steps of Paisley Tolbooth.[25]

There is sufficient evidence to suggest that song and music formed an integral part of the ritual of the protesting crowd, and is deserving of greater attention than has been paid to it by historians. Whatever the peculiarities and supposed shortcomings of popular culture in Scotland, Lowland Scots, it seems, had a good ear for music and a particular enthusiasm for dancing: trumpets, drums 'touking' and 'men, women and children dancing and drinking' formed part of the festivities in Edinburgh which marked the restoration of King Charles II in 1661, while the term 'dance revolution' has been applied to the early 1700s.[26] A visitor to Glasgow in 1811 observed that while the fair there was duller by comparison with England in terms of the type and variety of goods on sale, the public-houses were filled with 'holiday people, who dance till day-light, to the sound of the bagpipe', while at the Martinmas market in November 1822 such was the energy which was expended on 'penny reels' that it was 'as if it had been the last night these places [public houses in the Saltmarket] were to be appropriated for such purposes'.[27] Music mattered more in the lower echelons of society than some commentators have allowed, and musical provision may have been more extensive, as in Dundee in 1719 where there was no shortage of 'vilers', Alexander Neilsone and George Morrisone, both burgesses, complaining that country players, of whom there were many at a time when the status of the musician was not high, were taking away their business at weddings within the burgh.[28]

Of particular relevance for this paper is the role of music and song within the workplace. These were not solely the preserve of the articulate and politically conscious 'independent' handloom weaver working in a room attached to his place of residence. Fiddle music was played in the first mills to enliven tired workers' spirits and to encourage further effort. In the regimented handloom weaving factory of the early Industrial Revolution, songs were described by one contemporary as 'the dew drops that gathered during the long night of despondency', and acted as providers of a moral code which the church was no longer capable of supplying.[29] Paternalistic employers recognised the emotional bonding potential of music, as in the loyal airs and songs which were played by the band and sung at the outing laid on for their workers by the proprietors of Ruthven Printfield near Perth on the King's birthday in June 1814.[30]

The third strand of the argument concerns the role of women in the transmission of what can with some justification be termed an oral tradition of protest. Female literacy rates in early modern Scotland, particularly those of women from the labouring classes, were relatively low compared to those of their male counterparts.[31] Nevertheless there are grounds for believing that females were vital conduits which linked past and present, old and new. But their role was not simply passive. Rather it was active, adaptive and creative, as it was in the cases of several Scotswomen from the ranks of the aristocracy and gentry who enjoyed higher levels of literacy than their sisters of the lower orders, and who collected, preserved and reworked traditional ballads, poems and songs in both English and Gaelic.[32]

The core of this chapter is a case study which is constructed from evidence drawn from a set of Lord Advocate's papers which were generated during legal proceedings which resulted from a strike in the Glasgow cotton industry in 1825, and the subsequent shooting of John Graham, a mule spinner at Dunlop & Co.'s Broomward cotton mill in Calton, Glasgow. Graham was shot – in the back – on his way home from work on 30 March. In what must be a classic case of clinical understatement, a Dr Corkindale, who examined him on 3 April, reported that every symptom was favourable, 'except the paralytic state of his limbs and bladder'.[33] The 'murderous assault' outraged Archibald Alison, Crown Counsel and a future Sheriff of Lanarkshire, and in April 1825, one of Graham's assailants, John Kean, a cotton spinner, was tried, convicted and sentenced to transportation for life after, strapped tightly to a wooden cross, he had endured a public whipping of eighty 'stripes' or lashes.[34]

The shooting was one of an intermittent series of 'outrages' which occurred as a result of tensions within the cotton industry. Lasting from the early 1820s and culminating in the momentous strike of 1837, industrial relations disputes spilled out on to the streets and tested to the limits the inadequate policing resources of Glasgow and Lanarkshire. The cotton industry had expanded rapidly from around 1780, and was increasingly concentrated in Glasgow and Paisley. From the later 1790s virtually all new spinning mills built in Scotland were confined to the Glasgow area.[35] From the early 1800s, however, the industry faced intensifying competition not only from Lancashire mills but also continental Europe. Masters in the west of Scotland therefore sought to rationalise production methods and cut costs.

Various approaches were adopted by the cotton factory and mill proprietors. New technologies were introduced. The powerloom was one which, worked in pairs and operated by females, resulted in substantial cost savings; between *c*.1815 and 1820 the cloth dressing machine doubled production per employee and reduced the cost of each piece of cloth by two-thirds.[36] Another approach, allied to the masters' determination to regain control of the day-to-day operation of their mills, was to replace highly paid male mule spinners with new men and where possible with females. During the era of expansion, male mule spinners, many of whom were Irish, had established a remarkably tight hold over the industry.[37] (John Kean and those accused with him of attacking Graham were Irishmen.) They were able, for example, not only to restrict entry to the trade but also to determine who should train as a mule spinner and thus succeed them, and to demand that their masters appoint only supervisors of whom they approved. The 1810s, 1820s and 1830s were riven with disputes, processions, strikes and lock-outs as masters sought to get the upper hand and as the established work-force struggled to maintain what control it had over the work process.

Much has been written about this crucial period in Scottish economic and labour history.[38] Most writers, however, have presented the conflict as one between masters and men and men against female intruders. Considerable emphasis has been placed on physical intimidation and the level of violence.[39] Not only was recourse had to firearms but there were also numerous instances of the 'diabolical' practice of vitriol (sulphuric acid) throwing which resulted in burned clothes, skin and blindings.[40] Largely confined to the cotton industry, not unusually the victims were females who were employed in place of male spinners.

There is nothing factually incorrect about this outline of the main features of the situation. Indeed that Dunlop & Co. had been the first company in Glasgow (in 1818) to attempt to introduce female spinners into their works gives it even greater credence. From an early date Broomward Mill was the site of mobbing, a fire (in January 1820 when pitch and gunpowder were thrown through the windows), and at least one shooting on the part of the threatened male spinners.[41] In December 1819 two females, Elizabeth Kelly and Elizabeth Lafferty, along with some other workers from the mill (most of whom were female), were struck and 'severely wounded' by a 'gang' of 'Villains' which was allegedly connected to the Glasgow Cotton Spinners' Association.[42] Yet in reality the picture is more complicated. Few writers have paid any attention to the role of females as actors in the disturbances, or to the specific parts they played in defending the *status quo*, not only at Broomward but elsewhere in the west of Scotland textile industry. It is this which is the focus of the rest of this chapter.

As has been indicated, Broomward cotton mill at which John Graham was employed was owned by the Dunlop family. The Dunlops were leading masters in the Glasgow cotton trade and had often featured in the disputes which had dominated industrial relations since early in the second decade of the century. Along with the Houldsworths the Dunlops were considered by the Spinners' Association to be the two employers who were most hostile to their organisation and the most determined to loosen its grip.[43] A series of confrontations (in 1803, 1806, 1819, 1822 and 1823) culminated in the conflicts of 1824 and 1825 and the shooting of John Graham.

Graham and his four children, two sons and two daughters, had been recruited to Broomward Mill from Balfron around 20 December 1824. They were joined by other blacklegs, or 'Nobs'. From the time of their appearance in Glasgow, Graham and the other new workers had been more or less constantly taunted and exposed to various forms of intimidation, including stone and brick throwing and threats that they would be assassinated. They were particularly at risk when the machinery was stopped and during meal times when they left the comparative safety of the mill, and as they walked home after their shift. Early in March, however, shots were fired at the mill, into the flat in which Graham and the new workers were employed; on Wednesday 30 March as he made his way home at about a quarter to eight in the evening he was shot, at the corner of Barrowfield St. and Clyde St. He and the other blacklegs were easy targets, even though they were escorted by special constables employed by the Dunlops to protect them; they all appear to have been housed in and around McAuslan's Land in Stevenson St. in Calton and were readily followed.

Thus far women and to a lesser extent children, as well as the part played by song during the confrontation, have been deliberately excluded from the account of the attack on Broomward Mill. But both inside it, where several of the 'old' hands were still employed (but in separate rooms or flats) and outside, Graham and his fellow newcomers were subjected not only to the abuse and threats referred to above, but also to what can justifiably be described as a fearsome cacophony of sound. According to one witness, once inside the mill the old hands would 'hurra, Shout and make a noise, and ... Sing what they called "Nob Songs"'. On the night that Graham was shot, another witness recalled that as soon as Graham and the others left the mill 'a great Crowd of women and girls, and a number of men farther off and behind them kept up a loud Shout and continued making a great noise and some of them called "there comes the Nob buggars"'. Their tormentors were also singing.

That women and girls should have been at the front of the crowd outside Broomward Mill should occasion no surprise. It has long been established that as far as food riots were concerned for example, women were 'highly visible ... and ... frequently involved', but they swelled the size of the protesting crowds on other occasions too. It was not unusual for females to be singled out by observers for their excessive 'turbulence' or particularly boisterous or licentious behaviour.[44] Investigation into the composition of crowds in Scotland has not taken place on the English and European scale but such published work as is available points in a similar direction.

In Kenneth Logue's study of popular disturbances in Scotland between 1780 and 1815 some 15% of those charged with offences connected with direct action were women, although much higher proportions of females were involved in patronage and food riots.[45] As females were much less likely to be prosecuted such figures are misleading and understate the real extent of female participation. Qualitative evidence from earlier in the century confirms this, with women being reported as outnumbering men in certain types of disturbance in some parts of the country – assaults on customs and excise officers in Dumfries and Galloway for instance. It was dirt thrown by 'some idle women and boys' at excise officers who were inspecting malt kilns at Hamilton which inaugurated the Malt Tax riots which swept Scotland in the summer of 1725.[46] In the Highlands from 1782 at least, females were frequently either in the forefront or comprised a sizeable and prominent element of crowds who confronted the military, sheriff's officers and other agents of 'improving' landlords as they fought to resist clearance.[47] Within the working-class communities of the villages which comprised the mushrooming Glasgow region in the 1820s, in which handloom weavers predominated, women were ferocious defenders of the trade (in which growing numbers of them were being employed) and the agreed list of prices. According to one contemporary account of a march and attack on a Camlachie handloom weaver who had received four new webs (and who was also accused of having failed to turn out during the 'Radical War'), women were not only numerous but also 'particularly active' in the effigy-carrying, stone-throwing crowd of 7–800 people.[48] Women had much to lose, either as weavers in their own right, or as guardians of the household economy. The Radicalism of 1819 and 1820, which had touched Broomward Mill along with the rest of the spinning industry in the west of Scotland, was not gender-specific. Although reports of the responses of the crowd which watched during John Kean's whipping in May 1825 are ambiguous about the extent to which the sound of disapproving hissing was drowned by the sound of cheering as the executioner drew blood, there is no doubt that large numbers of females were in attendance.[49]

Apart from the concept of 'rough music', which was both loud and deliberately tuneless, much less is known about sound and the incorporation of music within the 'ritual of revolt', but it is clear that aural stimulation had an important place in crowd activity both north and south of the border.[50] In early Hanoverian England, drums and violins were played by opponents of King George I.[51] In Scotland it was not unusual in the early stages of a disturbance for the instigators to take possession of drums and either handbells or townhouse or church bells, the means normally used by the burgh authorities to attract the attention of the community. Their appropriation by the protesting mob not only called out the inhabitants in support of their cause but also represented a symbolic if temporary transfer of one part of the apparatus of power. At Errol in Perthshire in 1801 the first signs that a meal riot was taking place were when a 'parcel of children [and] half grown lads' seized the village officer's handbell, which was normally used for 'publishing advertisements through the town' but on this occasion it was rung to 'proclaim' a mob.[52] Later the ringing of the bell was accompanied by 'a person beating upon a weight' as the crowd marched to the door of a farmer from whom it was hoped to obtain some meal. Musical instruments of one sort or another – drums, flutes and fifes were the most usual – accompanied Radical processions which wound their way round the villages of Anderston, Calton and elsewhere in the sprawling Barony parish *en route* for the centre of Glasgow during the winter months of 1819–20. In June 1823 it was by 'tuck of drum' that the inhabitants of the villages of Parkhead, Camlachie, Westmuir and Tollcross were called to march to Westhorn estate to pull down a recently erected dyke which was blocking a footpath alongside the river Clyde.[53] The resonance which the drum beat had for the working-class inhabitants of Scottish towns in the early decades of the nineteenth century is to be seen in the repetition of the opening line, 'Rubadub, rubadub, row-de-row', in the weaver-poet William Thom's 'Whisperings For The Unwashed'.[54]

Rhythmic chanting and dancing could also give expression to a cause and unify the participants in their endeavour. The incantatory and even the magical qualities of rough rhyming verse or doggerel were noted by E. P. Thompson.[55] Something of this sort was apparent during a food riot at Dysart in Fife in 1720, recorded for posterity in a crudely composed, near-contemporary poem, published as a broadsheet, which lauds the 'Valiant Wives of Dysart'. On their way to the shore it was recounted that:

> The Lasses Skiped down [to ?] the Gate,
> And pass'd throw the Kirk-Yeard,
> Calling where is that stinking Beast,
> The Ugley Swine the Laird?

Thereafter, led by a bayonet-carrying woman, the crowd attacked the burgh's magistrates and disarmed a party of soldiers.[56]

Songs were written especially for such events, both during the period of confrontation and afterwards, to commemorate a particularly successful action. An example survives from Fraserburgh in the form of the 'Fraserburgh Meal Riots' (probably of 1813) of which two versions survive, one of which may have been written shortly before the riot ('Charlie, Charlie, rise and rin') while the other was clearly penned afterwards. Charles Simpson, a grain dealer, had fled 'O'er the dyke' and 'Doon the road', hence 'Charlie we'll nae mair pursue', 'the meal will be roon in the mornin'.[57] Other songs were deemed fit for purpose without adaptation, for instance the stirring martial air, 'Scots Wha Hae', which featured in a Radical demonstration near Paisley in 1819. Partly as a result of news breaking that the magistrates there had imprisoned the band which had been playing it, the tune was adopted as the movement's anthem, and 'played at all public meetings ... sung by the ballad singers in the streets ... and whistled by workmen passing to & from their work'. 'Rule Britannia', the 'Sprig of Shillelah [sic]' and 'Hey Johnny Cope' (played on the bagpipes) were also included in the Radical repertoire, while those attending Radical rallies marched to the music of trade societies' bands.[58]

Just what the females at Broomward Mill were singing is uncertain as two of the witnesses disagreed on this point. What is clear, however, is that there were five or six of the so-called 'Nob Songs'. These, it was reported, were sung not only outside in the streets but also inside the mill itself. According to Isobel Kingsberry, a twelve-year-old fly frame worker who was occasionally asked to make bobbins for the spinners, she had 'frequently' joined in the singing of one song in particular. This she declared, which had been sung, 'along with the rest of the girls in the Carding rooms', was 'The Rock and the Wee Pickle Tow'.

Purely fortuitously the words to this 1825 version of what was a popular song have survived, amongst the legal papers in the case against Graham's assailants. They may not be entirely accurate inasmuch as they were recalled by young Isobel Kingsberry in the presence of legal officers during the precognition process, but Kingsberry did testify that she had heard the words often enough to remember them:

> We are the braw chiels that belongs to the wheel
> That earns their bread by the spinning o't
> Ne'er let your hearts tumble down to your heels
> But stand on your feet for the spinning o't
> Let spinning & winning all go to pot
> There's Corn in Egypt still to be got,
> Never give way to a scheme or a plot
> But tak aff a plack o' the Spinning o't.
> It was in eight hundred & just twenty four
> Some Mills man he was the beginning o't
> He's name has gone farther than Scotia's fair Shore
> That first put a stop to the Spinning o't.
> Them that would go 'tween brother & trade
> Would deceive all the masters that ere' gave them bread
> I think they would tak both the quick & the dead
> And howk up a Corpse for the Skinning o't.
> Their houses are Shinny their children are braw
> Their tables are costly, their privies warst of a'
> But when they go on they will soon get a fa'
> And wha will they be the beginning o't.

In common with many songs composed by workers elsewhere in Britain in the period, this song celebrates a trade and confidently declares a craft pride.[59] The themes of worker independence, class solidarity and hostility towards blacklegs are also prominent, while the incorporation of a Biblical allusion is not only indicative of elevated literary pretensions but also of the moral high ground upon which the spinners stood.[60] The righteousness of the working-class cause and the belief that the idle and ostentatious rich would receive their just rewards in the hereafter is a recurring theme in popular ballads in the nineteenth century.[61]

The second song the words of which have survived is the shorter of the two, and was sung to the tune 'Nid Nid Nodding':

> Mr Dunlop how do ye do
> How many Nobs have ye, if your
> > fifth flat were fu'
> Blin' Jock, blin & blin' may he be
> He'll ne'er quit his nobbing till
> > he'll lose his t'other 'ee
>
> And we are a' a nobbing, nob
> > nob nobbing
> Ti see auld Graham with his Short
> > white coat
> And wasn't he a fool to come
> > out & be Shot

The words of this song are even more clearly located in time and place than the first and refer explicitly to the Broomward Mill: 'Blin Jock' was John Cameron, a seventeen-year-old spinner who had been employed from early in 1825 as one of the 'new' hands, while 'auld Graham' is a reference to John Graham. It is an angry song, laced with venom, an acknowledgement of the force of direct action and very much the product of the bitter circumstances in which it was created.

What is the provenance of these songs? Both were sung to traditional tunes. The appropriation of popular melodies and the provision of new words and meaning to serve particular purposes was a regular feature of plebeian political song-craft. 'Johnny Cope' was the tune which the Fraserburgh meal riot songsters adopted, for example.[62] 'Nid Nid Nodding' or 'We're A' Nodding' was apparently a fairly well-known song in the eighteenth century, with a version being collected and adapted by Burns under the title of 'Gudeen to you kimmer'.[63] More than this however, it was a spinning song, with a rhythm which accorded with the movement of a spinning wheel. One version is much blander than that of 1825 (Burns's version includes a hint of marital infidelity and is distinctly light-hearted), but even so the words suggest a strong element of gender awareness.

The tune for 'The Rock and the Wee Pickle Tow' may have originated in the seventeenth century, although the words took several forms. Like much Scottish vernacular poetry of the eighteenth century it was drawn from the 'life of the living community' and has a dancing rhythm.[64] The best-known version humorously but also shrewdly relates the trials and tribulations of hand-spinning; these can best be understood in the context of the spectacular rise of the yarn and linen industries in Scotland in the seventeenth and eighteenth centuries.[65] The words most commonly published are attributed to Alexander Ross, a parish schoolmaster and moderately successful eighteenth-century poet and violin player. Ross however did spend a considerable part of his life in Forfarshire, where female hand-spinning was widespread and from whence, with Fife and Perth, between half and two-thirds of Scottish linen cloth stamped for sale was made between 1730 and 1790. Ross's best poetry is considered to have been that which drew on 'the manners and conversation of the lowest part of the people'.[66] Most of Scotland's rural domestic spinners, working for low wages which more often than not were essential to supplement the subsistence income levels of the majority of Scottish households until the later 1700s, were usually drawn from precisely this section of society.[67]

Thus it seems entirely reasonable to suppose what we may be tapping into in the case of the two 1825 songs is a long-established creative oral tradition at the heart of which were female hand-spinners. This is indicated in George Penny's *Traditions of Perth*, first published in 1836 and in which Penny recollects events over the previous half century or so. Before around 1780, Penny implied that 'A great many of our old Scotch songs were sung, chiefly picked up by the ear from maids at the wheel.'[68] Alexander Ross was evidently one person who had listened to them.

There is some evidence to suggest that within the domestic or putting-out system in eighteenth-century Scotland female hand-spinners worked not alone but in groups – not in mills or factories or capitalised centres of production – but rather in a household or quasi-household environment, with clusters of four, five or six spinning wheels. These informal units of production, comprising mainly household members, daughters and servants, or a group of females gathered together from neighbouring fermtouns, could be headed by the mother of the household, the 'manager of her own little spinning mill'.[69] These working arrangements, which overlapped into the social life of both household and community, acted as a 'grand Theatre' of courtship, with young males attracted to the spinning sessions, in search of the best spinners. As elsewhere in Europe it was also the locus of much camaraderie – and song.[70]

Certainly the first of the features of the household spinning units reported here can be found in an eighteenth-century version of one of the two songs in question. Thus in 'We're A' Nodding' there are the lines 'And we're a' noddin, nid, nid, noddin / And we're a' noddin at our house at hame / The cats like milk and the dogs like broo / The lads like lasses, and the lasses lads too.' Yet there is more to it than this. Contained within the songs there is a sense of revolt, or at least of complaint, which is at odds with the idealised and sentimentalised portrayals of the spinner's situation and circumstances as presented by contemporary painters such as

Thomas Gainsborough or David Allan, or a poet like Robert Burns.[71] Sung by women, that such songs should reflect a lower level of contentment makes sense within the material historical context in that although they were rare, there are traceable instances when female spinners acted collectively to resist wage reductions in the first half of the eighteenth century, and to oppose the new flax spinning mills in the 1780s and 1790s.[72] Alexander Ross's 'The Rock and the Wee Pickle Tow', which was apparently an abridged version of a longer poem, cut for singing purposes, contains couplets which register regret at the coming of hand-spinning, or at least of relentless hand-spinning. Another tune for what was a similar song was 'The Weary Pound of Tow'. It is possible that this reflects the fact that as the eighteenth century wore on, and as demand for hand-spun yarn burgeoned relentlessly, the hours worked by hand-spinners increased considerably and even by the middle of the eighteenth century had risen to twelve hours a day, not unusually for five or six days a week.[73] Thus the 'auld wife' who had taken up spinning: '... choked and boaked, and cried like to mang, / Alas for the dreary spinning o't!', and later exclaims: 'The spinning, the spinning, it gars my heart sob / When I think upon the beginning o't.' Sentiments like this are recorded in another mid-eighteenth-century song reported by Thomas Crawford, on the theme of the soldier laddie, and the advantages of being a soldier's wife or partner. Ironically, one is that it allows a woman to escape from the drudgery and exploitation of hand-spinning. Hence:

> With rinning and spinning, my head was unsteady,
> But now I will go with my sodger laddie,
> My sodger laddie ...[74]

This song, in common with most folk songs, had long roots and went through many metamorphoses. What is being proposed here is that during the eighteenth and early nineteenth centuries spinning songs underwent such a change, perhaps as female domestic workers grew in status as independent earners and as a 'female consciousness' developed.[75] This can be demonstrated in the case of 'The Rock and the Wee Pickle Tow' which in Ross's version begins:

> There was an auld wife and a wee pickle tow,
> And she wad gae try the spinning o't;

By 1824 or 1825 that first couplet, following the same rhyme pattern, had become:

> We are the braw chiels that belongs to the wheel
> That earns their bread by the spinning o't.

Feminisation and the addition of a woman's point of view has been identified as a significant feature of the development of the street ballad in eighteenth-century Britain.[76] Certainly 'The Rock and the Wee Pickle Tow' had become the possession of the females of Broomward Mill, adapted once more for their immediate purposes. Like the spinning industry itself, which had formerly been located in the countryside, in fermtouns and small villages, the locus of the song had been removed from its rural situation where Ross had found it and been transplanted into the urban environment, the world of the three- and four-storey water- or steam-powered mill of the Industrial Revolution. Until recently this version of the song had been lost from sight, its distinctly short-lived nature causing it to be unknown or overlooked by nineteenth-century collectors. Almost certainly there were others like them.

What should be emphasised is that lower levels of literacy and the heavy expense of publishing before the middle of the nineteenth century did not mean that songs which conveyed a plebeian perspective and oppositional songs were not composed and sung. As was suggested earlier these were to be heard in the later nineteenth century. Eleanor Gordon has shown that within Dundee's jute mills song played a major role in underpinning solidarity amongst female workers, and could act as a powerful vehicle for expressing collective feelings about their status or conditions of employment, or unpopular individuals. In this Dundee was by no means alone: there is, according to one historian of work in the nineteenth century, 'a good deal of evidence that factory workers [in many parts of Britain] used song as a way of commanding, or signifying the command of space within the workplace'. This, it is argued, 'had particular significance for women workers'.[77]

This chapter, however, has been concerned with an earlier period. The fragments of evidence which have been adduced here may represent segments of a fragile bridge which connects the oral culture of the largely rural female hand spinners of the eighteenth century with the much better-known strike and other work songs of the textile towns of the later nineteenth and twentieth centuries. There is continuity outside the workplace too: the description of a strike in Dundee in 1874 when female workers paraded through the town, hooted and shouted and threw missiles, and manifested their enthusiasm 'by singing and dancing wherever they went', or an occasion when they 'indulged in shouting and singing, the latter being a peculiar sort of march', bear a notable resemblance to what happened in Dysart in 1720, some 160 years earlier.[78]

This short chapter makes no claim to be definitive. It is exploratory, its main purpose being to draw attention to a neglected aspect of popular culture which may well take on a different appearance in the light of recent revisionist conceptions of Scottish society in the eighteenth and early nineteenth centuries. It also goes some way towards confirming the suspicions of earlier writers on the subject. Further research however is required to substantiate the claims made herein. If, as has been suggested, cultural productions which represented a more distinctly plebeian point of view (rather than 'socially harmless' ballads and love songs) were not recorded by the compilers of folk-song collections as they may have found offence in works which attacked the higher social classes from which they tended to be drawn, or simply because they lacked interested 'mediators', the chances of uncovering them must be slight.[79] However, while deeper delving into Court of Session papers, the voluminous records of the sheriff courts, burgh minute books and court records, and a careful reading of contemporary eye-witness material, newspapers and collections of broadsheets would take time, the indications are that such an investigation would greatly enrich our understanding of a period from which the sense of sound is all too often missing.

NOTES

1 An earlier and shorter version of this paper was published in the *Scottish Labour History Soc. Journal*, xxviii (1993), 71–6.

2 R. A. Houston and I. D. Whyte, 'Introduction: Scottish society in perspective', in R. A. Houston and I. D. Whyte (eds.), *Scottish Society 1500–1800* (Cambridge 1989), 33.

3 T. Crawford, 'Political and Protest Songs in eighteenth-century Scotland I, Jacobite and Anti-Jacobite'; and 'Political and Protest Songs in Eighteenth-Century Scotland II, Songs of the Left', *Scottish Studies*, xiv (1970), 112–13; see also J. Purser, *Scotland's Music* (Edinburgh 1992), 242.

4 K. Logue, 'Eighteenth-century Popular protest: aspects of the people's past', in E. J. Cowan (ed.), *The People's Past* (Edinburgh 1980), 109.

5 Crawford, 'Political and Protest Songs II', 116–17; T. Crawford, *Society and the Lyric: A Study of the Song Culture of Eighteenth-Century Scotland* (Edinburgh 1979), 159.

6 Crawford, 'Political and Protest Songs I', 22–3; W. Donaldson, *The Jacobite Song: Political Myth and National Identity* (Aberdeen 1988), 38–47.

7 N. Rogers, 'Riot and Popular Jacobitism in early Hanoverian England', in E. Cruickshanks (ed.), *Ideology and Conspiracy: Aspects of Jacobitism, 1689–1759* (Edinburgh 1982), 71, 76; M. G. H. Pittock, *The Invention of Scotland: The Stuart Myth and the Scottish Identity, 1638 to the Present* (London 1991), 48–9.

8 Donaldson, *Jacobite Song*, 3–4.

9 M. G. H. Pittock, *Poetry and Jacobite Politics in Eighteenth-Century Britain and Ireland* (Cambridge 1994), 4–5, 147, 169–70.

10 See B. Ó Cuív, 'Irish language and literature, 1681–1845', in T. W. Moody and W. E. Vaughan (eds.), *A New History of Ireland*, vol. IV: *Eighteenth-Century Ireland, 1691–1800* (Oxford 1986), 374–423.

11 Pittock, *Poetry and Jacobite Politics*, 215–22; Donaldson, *Jacobite Song*, 88–9.

12 J. Purser, *Scotland's Music* (Edinburgh 1992), 19; for a fuller development of this argument, see T. Crawford, 'Lowland Song and Popular tradition in the eighteenth century', in A. Hook (ed.), *The History of Scottish Literature*, vol. II: *1660–1800* (Edinburgh 1987), 123–39.
13 Crawford, 'Political and Protest Songs II', 113.
14 Houston and Whyte, 'Introduction', 25–7.
15 T. C. Smout, *A History of the Scottish People 1560–1780* (London 1969; 1981 edn), 303–10; 412–20; for an explanation for the apparent weakness of Scottish radicalism in the 1790s, see T. M. Devine, 'The failure of Radical reform in Scotland in the late eighteenth century: the social and economic context', in T. M. Devine (ed.), *Conflict and Stability in Scottish Society 1700–1850* (Edinburgh 1990).
16 Houston and Whyte, 'Introduction', 34.
17 W. H. Fraser, 'Patterns of protest', in T. M. Devine and R. Mitchison (eds.), *People and Society in Scotland*, vol. I: *1760–1830* (Edinburgh 1988), 277–91.
18 There is a growing literature on this topic but for a summary, see C. A. Whatley, 'An uninflammable people?', in I. Donnachie and C. A. Whatley (eds.), *The Manufacture of Scottish History* (Edinburgh 1992).
19 University of St Andrews Archives, CH2/82/5, Cupar Presbytery Minute Book, 1715–23, 179, 142.
20 C. A. Whatley, 'Royal Day, People's Day: the monarch's birthday in Scotland, c.1660–1860', in R. Mason and N. Macdougall (eds.), *People and Power in Scotland: Essays in Honour of T. C. Smout* (Edinburgh 1992), 185.
21 *Radical Renfrew: Poetry from the French Revolution to the First World War*, ed. T. Leonard (Edinburgh 1990).
22 W. B. McCarthy, *The Ballad Matrix* (Indiana 1990), 23.
23 University of St Andrews Archives, Aitken-Mackinnon MSS.; see also N. Murray, *The Scottish Hand Loom Weavers 1790–1850* (Edinburgh 1978).
24 Leonard, *Radical Renfrew*, 8–9.
25 Paisley Public Libraries, A. Crawford, *Lochwinnoch Matters*, IV, Petition, W. Sharp to the Sheriff Depute of Renfrewshire, 23 May 1792; Warrant against A. Wilson, 23 May 1792; Libel, Sheriff of Renfrewshire against A. Wilson, 27 Jun. 1792.
26 Whatley, 'Royal Day, People's Day', 176; D. Johnston, *Music and Society in Lowland Scotland in the Eighteenth Century* (Edinburgh 1972), 121.
27 E. I. Spence, *Sketches of the Present Manners, Customs and Scenery of Scotland* (2 vols., London 1811), i, 97; *Glasgow Courier*, 28 Nov. 1822; 17 Jul. 1824.
28 For authoritative comments on this issue, see Johnston, *Music and Society*; and Purser, *Scotland's Music*; Dundee City Archives, General Petitions to Dundee Town Council, 1719.
29 W. Thom, *Rhymes and Recollections of a Handloom Weaver* (London 1845), 14–15.
30 *Dundee, Perth and Cupar Advertiser*, 10 Jun. 1814.
31 R. A. Houston, *Scottish Literacy and the Scottish Identity* (Cambridge 1986), 57–70.
32 H. Henderson, 'The Ballad, the Folk and Oral Tradition', in *The People's Past*, 106; *An Anthology of Scottish Women Poets*, ed. C. Kerrigan (Edinburgh 1991), 6; Crawford, 'Lowland Song', 126–7, 133; Purser, *Scotland's Music*, 157.
33 Scottish Record Office [SRO], AD14/25/192, Case against John Kean and others, 1825. Unless otherwise stated all information relating to this case is drawn from this source.
34 A. Alison, *Some Account of My Life and Writings: An Autobiography* (2 vols., London 1883), i, 382; *Glasgow Courier*, 12 May 1825.
35 J. Shaw, *Water Power in Scotland, 1550–1870* (Edinburgh 1984), 330.
36 C. A. Whatley, 'Labour in the industrialising city', in T. M. Devine and G. Jackson, *Glasgow*, vol. I: *Beginnings to 1830* (Manchester 1995), 366.

37 W. H. Fraser, 'The Glasgow cotton spinners, 1837', in J. Butt and J. T. Ward (eds.), *Scottish Themes* (Edinburgh 1976).

38 J. Butt, 'Labour and industrial relations in the Scottish textile industry during the Industrial Revolution', in J. Butt and K. Ponting (eds.), *Scottish Textile History* (Aberdeen 1987); see too Fraser, 'Glasgow cotton spinners'; and the same author's *Capital and Class: Scottish Workers 1700–1838* (Edinburgh 1988), 114–20, 151–62.

39 See, e.g., J. T. Ward, 'Textile trade unionism in nineteenth-century Scotland', in *Scottish Textile History*, 131–4. But for a reassessment of these disputes which was published after this chapter was written, see A. Clark (ed.), *The Struggle for the Breeches: Gender and the Making of the British Working Class* (Berkeley, CA, 1997), 119–40.

40 Fraser, 'Glasgow cotton spinners', 85; *Glasgow Courier*, 30 Dec. 1823.

41 Fraser, 'Glasgow cotton spinners', 84.

42 *Glasgow Courier*, 29 Jan. and 1 Feb. 1820.

43 Fraser, 'Glasgow cotton spinners', 91.

44 See E. P. Thompson, *Customs in Common* (London 1991; 1993 edn), 305–36; J. Bohstedt, *Riots and Community Politics in England and Wales 1790–1815* (Harvard 1983), 153.

45 K. Logue, *Popular Disturbances in Scotland 1780–1815* (Edinburgh 1979), 199–203.

46 C. A. Whatley, 'How tame were the Scottish Lowlanders during the eighteenth century?', in Devine, *Conflict and Stability in Scottish Society*, 8, 13.

47 E. Richards, *A History of the Highland Clearances* (London 1982), 249.

48 *Glasgow Courier*, 8 Sep. 1824.

49 *Glasgow Courier*, 12 May 1825.

50 M. Ingram, 'Ridings, Rough Music and the "Reform of Popular Culture" in early modern England', *Past and Present*, cv (1984); for a discussion of the role of the ballad as an effective expression of 'the struggles and emotions that animated the body of the people' in mid-nineteenth-century England, see P. Joyce, *Visions of the People: Industrial England and the Question of Class, 1848–1914* (Cambridge 1991), 235.

51 Rogers, 'Riot and Popular Jacobitism', 76.

52 SRO, JC 26/313, Declaration by Mary Jackson, 11 Nov. 1801.

53 *Glasgow Courier*, 24 Jun. 1823; Whatley, 'Labour in the industrialising city', 389.

54 Thom, *Rhymes and Recollections*, 72–3.

55 E. P. Thompson, 'The crime of anonymity', in D. Hay and others (eds.), *Albion's Fatal Tree: Crime and Society in Eighteenth-Century England* (London 1988), 303.

56 National Library of Scotland [NLS], Ry.III.c.36 (141), 'An Exact List of the Battle of Dysart, which was Fought by King Georges Forces, and the Saltors and Suttors and Coliars, with a List of the Killed and Wounded' (Edinburgh 1720); Whatley, 'How tame were the Scottish Lowlanders', 17.

57 *The Greig-Duncan Folk-Song Collection*, ed. P. Shuldam-Shaw and E. B. Lyle (7 vols., Aberdeen and Edinburgh, 1981–95), ii, 240, 546.

58 University of St Andrews Archives, Aitken-MacKinnon MSS.; *Glasgow Courier*, 26 Oct. 1819.

59 M. Vicinus, *The Industrial Muse: A Study of Nineteenth-Century British Working-Class Literature* (London 1974), 12.

60 Thompson, 'Crime of anonymity', 301–2.

61 Joyce, *Visions of the People*, 247–55.

62 Shuldam-Shaw and Lyle, *Greig-Duncan Folk Song Collection*, 546.

63 *The Poems and Songs of Robert Burns*, ed. J. Kinsley (3 vols., Oxford 1968), ii, 880–1; iii, 1516–17.

64 K. Wittig, *The Scottish Tradition in Literature* (London 1958), 162.

65 A. Durie, *The Scottish Linen Industry in the Eighteenth Century* (Edinburgh 1979), 22–31.

66 *The Scottish Works of Alexander Ross*, ed. M. Wattie (Edinburgh 1938), xv–xvi.

67 A. J. S. Gibson and T. C. Smout, *Prices, Food and Ages in Scotland, 1550–1780* (Cambridge 1995), 291, 354–6.

68 G. Penny, *Traditions of Perth* (Perth 1836, repr. Coupar Angus 1986), 117.

69 University of Dundee Archives and Manuscripts Department, MS.11/5/14, C. Mackie, MS. 'History of Flax Spinning from 1806 to 1866', 16–18; see also A. Fenton, 'The people below: Dougal Graham's chapbooks as a mirror of the lower classes in eighteenth-century Scotland', in A. Gardner-Medwin and J. Hadley Williams (eds.), *A Day Estivall: Essays on the Music, Poetry and History of Scotland and England and Poems previously unpublished* (Aberdeen 1990), 75.

70 P. Burke, *Popular Culture in Early Modern Europe* (Aldershot 1978; 1988 edn), 50.

71 C. A. Whatley, 'Burns: Work, Kirk and Community in later eighteenth-century Scotland', in K. Simpson (ed.), *Burns Now* (Edinburgh 1994), 99.

72 C. A. Whatley, 'The experience of work', in *People and Society*, vol. I, 242.

73 Durie, *Scottish Linen Industry*, 76.

74 Crawford, *Society and the Lyric*, 160–2.

75 D. Valenze, *The First Industrial Woman* (Oxford 1995), 122–6.

76 Vicinus, *Industrial Muse*, 9.

77 C. Behagg, 'Narratives of control: informalism and the workplace in Britain, 1800–1900', in O. Ashton, R. Fyson and S. Roberts (eds.), *The Duty of Discontent: Essays for Dorothy Thompson* (London 1995), 132.

78 E. Gordon, *Women and the Labour Movement in Scotland 1850–1914* (Oxford 1991), 133; C. Bull, 'Who are the Subalternists? A Study of the Dundee Millworkers from 1850–1885' (St Andrews University, M.Phil. thesis, 1989), 34.

79 Crawford, 'Political and Protest Songs II', 113.

9

In Praise of Mountains and the Freedom to Roam: Some Mountaineering Songs and Verse from the Cairngorms, 1850–1960

ROBERT A. LAMBERT

> May your heart keep true to the peaks above;
> May your feet be sure on the hills you love;
> May the summer mist and the winter storms
> Never hide your path to the High Cairngorms.[1]

In the early part of the twentieth century Seton Gordon published the first book that aimed to capture the charm and spirit of the Cairngorms. A writer, hill-walker, naturalist and photographer, he also sought to examine humankind's relationship to these mountains from an emotional and spiritual viewpoint. Gordon fully appreciated the role that song and verse could play in this study in praise of the 'Cairngorms experience'. Writing in 1925 from his home in Aviemore (at that time a small Highland town expanding around the focus of the railway station), he was not shy in using his own verse and Gaelic rhyme and song from a variety of writers to convey to his readership 'chapters [that] may give pleasure to the many lovers of the High Cairngorms'.[2]

Writing in praise of mountains and what they can offer the human eye, the mind or the legs, is nothing new in the history of Scotland's literature, verse and song. Of particular note is the nation's heritage of Gaelic poetry in praise of landscape and nature, and according to the late John Lorne Campbell, this rich tapestry of verse within the Gaelic oral tradition is one that we ignore at our own risk, especially if we seek to define our cultural relationship to the natural world.[3] Duncan Ban Macintyre gained much of his visual inspiration from the journeys he regularly made through the Highlands and Islands in the middle of the eighteenth century and he was, by choice or by chance, a wanderer, known and loved in the communities he visited as *Donnchadh bàn nan òran* (a maker of songs to sing). His poetic vision was comprehensive, taking in both landscape and the individual components of natural history that made the wider picture, thus creating a sympathetic observation of the countryside. It was regularly to the wild places that he was drawn, to capture both landscape and nature untamed, though at times he can appear to speak with the tongue of an early twentieth-century campaigning recreationalist:

> ... to be tramping on the hillsides,
> at the hour the sun was rising,
> and the deer would be a-bellowing.
>
> The clean rain and the air
> on the peaks of the high mountains,
> helped me to grow, and gave me
> robustness and vitality.

For his work in praise of mountains we need look no further than the epic poem in 'Praise of Ben Dobhrain', where corries and crags, springs and streams are named affectionately, though the poet is mainly interested in the deer that roam over this, one of the hills of his home.[4] Ironically, many English and Lowland writers of hill-walking and travel guides for the Scottish Highlands in the 1920s, 1930s and 1940s, would draw upon (and quote liberally from) this tradition of Gaelic verse and song. It was commonplace for them to quote various poets in Gaelic, with an accompanying English translation.[5]

The writers of the mountaineering club songs from the era of the First World War and the 1920s, also gained much inspiration from the Gaelic tradition of praise poetry, not least in the production of songs that could be learned and sung. They also found a background for their work in other traditions. One such inherited type of verse-making was that of tinkers or travelling people in the Highlands, whose songs spoke of freedom and a love for the open road. It is a small step to take from the individual liberty displayed in the song 'Come A' Ye Tramps An' Hawkers', to that sense of spiritual independence sought by the working-class male climbers from Glasgow in the early 1930s.

> I've seen the high Ben Nevis, awa' toorin tae the mune,
> I've been by Crieff an' Callander an' roon by bonnie Doon;
> I've been by Nethy's silvery tides and places ill tae ken,
> Far up intil the stormy north lies Urquhart's fairy glen.
> But I'm happy in the summer time beneath the bright blue sky,
> Nae thinking in the morning at nicht whaur I'm tae lie,
> Bothies or Byres or anywhaur, or oot amang the hay.
> And if the weather does permit I'm happy a' the day.[6]

Next to the songs of the vagrant travellers and wanderers,[7] stands the similarly inherited tradition of childhood nursery rhymes in an era before the popular use of television and radio, when a school playground would echo to young voices singing in union and repetition.[8] A love for communal song was carried quite naturally into adulthood. Of more immediate relevance to the north-east of Scotland where the Cairngorms have had their most direct economic and social impact, are the bothy songs and ballads of Aberdeenshire and the surrounding counties. Collections of such songs and ballads in the region reveal the popularity of this immense oral tradition, that is both unique to the north-east and thoroughly tied to the agricultural practices of that region. Most of these bothy songs were a communal product and concern themselves with everyday affairs in the countryside, depicting the hired labourer's life with its lights and its shadows, its daily toil, amusement, recreations, its joys and its sorrows.[9] These native north-east bothy songs are also known as 'corn-kisters', because their rhythm was often tapped out by those sitting on corn chests, with the banging of heels against the wood.[10] These ballads and bothy songs gained a wide circulation in the nineteenth century as the hired bachelor labourers moved on when a term of service had ended; by the First World War, the bothy system itself was dying out under the general amelioration of farm labourers' working and living conditions, and the songs that were once in vogue fell rapidly into disuse. In 1889 a newly founded mountaineering club, the Cairngorm Club, based itself in Aberdeen and the subsequent verse-makers and songwriters within its membership may have taken some inspiration from the particular oral song tradition of the surrounding countryside.[11]

Although the events that became known in the nineteenth century as the Battle O' Glen Tilt took place in late August 1847, the infamy of the occasion was not recorded for posterity until 1850, when Douglas Maclagan, Emeritus Professor of Medical Jurisprudence and Public Health at the University of Edinburgh (and a keen hill-walker) published his sole, notable contribution to mountaineering literature, in the ballad of the same name.[12] It stands today, widely admired as not only a well-constructed and humorous piece of doggerel lampooning the actions of the duke of Atholl and his estate staff but also as a major contribution to the rights of way campaign in Scotland from 1850 to 1900. Originally composed for the entertainment of a social medical club in Edinburgh it has assumed a much wider importance. When Maclagan died in April 1900, the Cairngorm Club saw fit to publish the full ballad in tribute in the July edition of their journal.[13]

The ballad celebrated the successful resistance of Dr Balfour, the Professor of Botany at the University of Edinburgh, and a group of his botany students, to the attempts made by the duke of Atholl and his staff to exclude them from Glen Tilt:

> The Duke cam' o'er
> Wi' gillies four,
> To mak' a stour,
> An' drive Balfour,
> Frae 'yont the Hielan' hills, man.

The dispute centred around the absolute refusal of the duke to recognise Glen Tilt as an ancient drove road, and thus right of way, between Braemar and Blair Atholl. The case assumed legal importance, when the Association for the Protection of the Public Rights of Roadways in Scotland which had been founded in 1847 (to become the Scottish Rights of Way Society in 1884) became immediately involved in the provision of financial backing to take the issue to the Court of Session in December 1849.[14] The case rumbled on and was heard in the House of Lords in June 1852; meanwhile, in August 1850 the duke of Atholl chose to evict two Cambridge undergraduates as they were descending into Glen Tilt.[15] In 1886, a similar rights of way dispute erupted when 'Jocks Road', a hill path from Glen Doll, by the Tolmount and on to Auchallater near Braemar, was closed. No verse poked fun at Duncan Macpherson's attempt to obstruct the right to roam; Maclagan's ballad stands alone, and became popular when sung to the air 'Shirra Muir'.

> The battle it was ended then,
> Afore't was focht ava', man;
> An' noo some ither chaps are gaen
> To tak' the Duke to law, man.
> Ochon! Your Grace, my bonny man,
> An' ye had sense as ye ha'e lan',
> Ye'd been this hour
> Ayont the po'er
> O' lawyers dour,
> An' let Balfour
> Gang through your Hielan' hills, man.[16]

However, the so-called 'Battle of Braemar' in 1891, when the laird of Invercauld attempted to close a track which led from the Glen Clunie road to the Braemar–Ballater road, did produce some doggerel verse, often composed by the summer visitors to the town who were entertained by the frequent weekly restorations and demolitions of the Clunie road fence.[17]

F. S. Smythe could claim to understand mountaineers and their sport, 'the struggle of man with the mountain' as it was once described.[18] In the 1930s he wrote extensively on the lure of mountaineering in many continents, and became the recognised literary champion of those who sought to challenge themselves in the hills of Scotland, the Alps or the Himalayas:

> Mountaineers are gregarious, argumentative creatures. Their gregariousness leads to clubs, and clubs lead to dinners and speeches, and their argumentativeness leads to committees and club journals, in which other club journals are adversely reviewed.[19]

Undoubtedly, he was writing at a time of enormous interest in the sport of mountaineering; the spirit of the hills was touching a new breed of adventurer in Scotland (some of them working-class men of Glasgow) but the recreational interest in mountains had its roots in the mid-nineteenth century.

British climbing began in the Alps; by 1850 around one hundred Alpine peaks had been conquered, mostly by British climbers who were destined to 'make this realm ... so completely and brilliantly their own'. However, these early ascents were completed by a band of scattered enthusiasts (seen as eccentrics) and over a long period of time. The 'Golden Age' of mountaineering began in 1854, when that summer saw a throng of ambitious and accomplished climbers enter the Alps; numbers increased over 1855 and 1856. The British Alpine Club was founded in London in 1857. By the 1860s the cumulative result of these individual climbing exploits, was the birth of modern mountaineering.[20] These Alpine and later Himalayan climbing adventures did produce a comprehensive array of mountaineering verse and prose well into the twentieth century but it appears from these sources that they walked in silence and certainly did not sing.[21]

Between 1849 and 1890, Scotland saw the formation of several outdoor clubs which devoted themselves to the sport of climbing, rather than focusing on rambling or countryside walking. Most were based in the cities of Glasgow, Edinburgh and Aberdeen. They included the Cobbler Club, a fellowship of outdoor lovers, in 1866; the Glasgow-based Scottish Mountaineering Club (SMC) in 1889; and the Cairngorm Club in Aberdeen in 1889. Like their Alpine forefathers these early Scottish mountaineers were mostly professional men, with ample leisure time to devote to the sport, backed by healthy financial resources. When Sir Hugh

Munro published his first *Tables* of the 3,000 ft. mountains of Scotland in 1891, he could hardly have foreseen the impact that this would have on the sport of mountaineering. It laid down a challenge to all, and indirectly, broadened the appeal of the sport. The first man to achieve the complete list, and thus the first Munroist, was Rev. A. E. Robertson in 1901.[22] Why then did the members of these clubs not produce club songs and verse to be sung on outings into the hills, until after 1910?

Smythe contends that the change in attitude that produced the club songs came from a turn of the century 'age of humour' within the sport, that was linked to annual dinners, an increased membership across the middle class and a contrast in levels of climbing expertise. The gregarious nature of the early twentieth-century climbers saw the climbing club develop into a strong community, built upon a shared sense of humour, a common danger that moulded a common thought, a common hardship and thus a common philosophy; the perfect mountain friendship.[23]

The song of the SMC, sung to the air 'The Golden Slippers', reflects how outdoor recreation was seen as a universal cure-all, a test of character and of taste, a victory of true values over materialism.

> For the best of the Club will then be afoot,
> From the President down to the last recruit,
> And a merry band you'll find us, as we leave the town behind us,
> When we go up to the mountains in the snow.

The importance of having good equipment featured in the often repeated chorus:

> Oh, my big hobnailers! Oh, my big hobnailers!
> Memories raise of joyous days
> Upon the mountain side!

However, this particular song returned again and again to the sense of unity and superiority that membership of the SMC offered. As a group on an outing, members were to be solid, dependable and hardy:

> Good comrades we, of the SMC,
> We're a jolly band of brothers, tho'
>   we're sons of many mothers;
> And trouble, strife, and worry —
>   Gad! They quit us in a hurry
> When we go up to the mountains in the snow
> ... And from Caithness down to Arran, on the
>   mountains big and barren,
> You can trace our little footprints in the snow.[24]

The writing of a club song mirrors the wider popularity in Scottish society of the Student Song Books, that first appeared in 1891 but saw their greatest and most widespread usage in the four decades up to 1940. The 1891 edition has few references to songs about hiking, climbing or outdoor recreation,[25] but by 1915 the situation had changed. The *Fellowship Song Book* was written 'for Indoor and Open-Air Singing', and was to be passed amongst 'branches which frequently meet for social intercourse'. The compilation was brought together on behalf of the National Adult School Union, the Co-operative Holidays Association, the Holiday Fellowship, the Home Music Study Union, the Workers Educational Association and it was to be 'Songs of Faith, Nature and Comradeship' for the 'General use of Clubs, Social Unions and Public Schools'. The compilers felt that 'a good Song Book will be appreciated ... at public meetings, co-operative holidays, tramps on moor and shore'. Song 82, 'The Open Road', was to be sung 'Heartily and Swiftly':

'Tis the open road for me, Where I wander fancy free
Away to the purple hills, Or down to the dancing sea
... And all whom I pass I greet, for every face is a friend's
... The Song wells up as I go, And my feet to the tune keep time.[26]

The 1937 book *Student Songs for Camp and College* had an even greater focus on health-giving outdoor recreation in Scotland, being dedicated to, 'Students, Beloved Vagabonds, Pilgrims and Strangers, Who Wander By Hill and Loch, Moor and River, Highway and Byway, And All Who Carry A Song in Their Heart'. Hiking, rambling and mountaineering was becoming so popular in the late 1930s, especially within Scottish universities, that the Student Representative Councils of these universities urged that the Scottish Student Song Book Committee should produce, 'a compact selection of songs convenient for the pocket or knapsack', paying heed to the fact that, 'young people sing not only indoors round the piano, but also out-of-doors tramping the highways, the hills and the woodlands'.[27] Mountaineers and hill-walkers often carried anthologies of song and verse with them on their travels. The mountaineer Ben Humble hoped that his Skye-inspired collection could, 'be a fitting companion for many a journey, and find a home in many a knapsack and many a heart'.[28] Catherine Loader has shown how the youth of Scotland in the late 1940s not only carried songs about the Cairngorms with them, but were so inspired by a stay at Glenmore Lodge, that they often composed verse and song in the evenings about their experiences, friendships and challenges out in the mountains. Some were even written and then read aloud as

contributions to the Friday ceilidh evenings at this Scottish Centre for
Outdoor Training which had opened in September 1948.[29]

The SMC had another song in this pre-World War One era, and it again
emphasised the bonds that tied the club together, whilst revealing a firm
sense of insider superiority; the 'out group', the non-walkers, those that
remained at 'sad sea-level', were thoroughly ridiculed:

> I sing of a Club, and a jolly good Club,
> And its Members frank and free,
> Professors and Proctors — Divines and Doctors —
> And Duffers like you and me: —
> And the singular thing about which I sing
> Is the unanimitee-ee-ee
> Of all and each to practice and preach
> The creed of the SMC.

This song was to be sung to the popular air 'Ten Thousand Miles Away',
and it concluded thus:

> I've proved in rhyme you all must climb
> If happy you would be.
> For all delights belong to the heights
> Without any doubt — you see-ee-ee
> I give you the toast to please you most,
> The toast of the SMC.[30]

Smythe noted this love in mountaineering circles for ridiculing the
outsider in song or verse or speech, whether he be a rambler, a skier or
someone who preferred to stroll along in the floor of the glen: 'And if we
get bored, we vent our spleen on the pot-hunting skiers ... and the skiers
reply with spirit, and call us prigs and snobs and so on ... just *pour passer le
temps*.'[31] Robert Aitken has another theory; that these songs were the
product of men, who he labels the: '... bolshies of the Golden Age ... the
advocates and exponents of Rights of Way and Access to Mountains, the
deer-disturbers and signpost-erectors ...'[32] The rope had cemented a union
of sympathy and understanding, and a degree of radical thought and
humour. Writing in 1950, the climber W. K. Richmond was worried
about how his own book on mountaineering would be received by his
peers; he feared their response would be negative: '... he ranks no better
than a hiker, or worse, a tourist ... he might be classified as a member of
that tame, villatic species, the hill-walker. Pah! The fellow is an impostor.
Away with him'.[33]

Perhaps Richmond detected that by 1950 mountaineering had lost its jolly image, and was determined to distance itself from other, less hardy users of the hills. Just as the technological advances made in the car industry and the construction of roads to some facilitated easier access to an area like the Cairngorms, so others remained thoroughly tied to the turn of the century values of their club.

> But soon when all are flying and dependent on the hub,
> There'll still be Johnny Walker and the Cairngorm Club.

> O, Hills o' Caledonia, may you be ever free
> From fiendish record-breakers as they scorch from sea to sea;
> When roadways twine among you and invade your calm retreat,
> Still keep a patch o' moorland for those ancient things called feet.[34]

The years of the Depression brought the most profound change to mountaineering and hill-walking in Scotland. The first democratic or proletarian climbing clubs were formed, such as the Creagh Dhu in 1930 in Clydebank, and they became a vehicle by which young men could leave the squalor of the cities and the hardships of unemployment and discover a wonderful tonic in the hills.[35] They travelled north from Glasgow by foot, by cycle or by hitch-hiking (which had become respectable in the mid-1930s) for weekends away in Glencoe or the Arrochar Hills. They later reached the Cairngorms for a week's holiday by rail or stuffing a car with as many bodies as it would take.[36] Prior to these trips, the Glasgow men often met around the Craigallion fire, 'in a secluded pine-fringed hollow near Craigallion Loch, Milngavie'. Here they would swap yarns, make plans and sing together; by the late 1930s these songs were often taken from America, upbeat hill-billy tunes such as 'The Brave Engineer', that described vast open spaces and pioneering adventure. They also read the poetry of Robert W. Service. 'Amongst all of these Glasgow men was a desire to live like a hard man or a tramp'; when they were up in the hills many scorned the new fashion for youth hostel accommodation which had come to Scotland in 1931, happy to sleep in caves, barns, bothies or what they called tramp's howffs. Witness Alastair Borthwick: 'The cave was a very sociable place where everyone was made welcome. Many a night large companies gathered and sing-songs started ...'[37] Borthwick described bothy, howff and youth hostel life in his popular hill-walking book *Always A Little Further*, first published in the opening year of the Second World War. He noted that the Creagh Dhu Mountaineering Club out of Clydebank sang hill-billy songs and cowboy tunes:

Everybody sang ... they instinctively avoided the modern
Tin-Pan Alley versions of the old tunes and confined them-
selves to those ... songs with twenty verses apiece about
cowboys who want to be buried out on the lone prairee; and
engine drivers, generally called Casey Jones, who are killed,
round about verse eighteen, in train smashes.

He cited a diverse range of widely liked songs, such as 'Frankie and
Johnnie', 'The Wreck of the Ninety-Nine', 'The Dying Mountaineer',
'Rock of Ages', 'Greenland's Icy Mountains', 'Minnie the Moocher', 'The
Eriskay Love Lilt', 'An t'Eilean Muillach', 'The Cockle-Gatherers', and
'Banks of Loch Lomond'. Climbers from the north-east of Scotland
brought the bothy ballads out of Buchan and the Mearns, 'grand songs,'
into the cave where they were treasured and thus preserved, and the
climbers agreed that a 'rowdy and satisfactory' art was being lost as the
Students' Songbooks fell out of regular use. Mouth organ music and the
Jew's harp often accompanied these songs, and a fine story-telling tradi-
tion persisted in these mountain retreats. In the more international
atmosphere of a Scottish youth hostel, Borthwick recorded that a Euro-
pean song culture existed, with a nationalistic (including Gaelic) and
creative song exchange amongst overseas and domestic climbers and hill-
walkers. In the earliest years of a distinct Scottish youth hostel movement
in the early 1930s, Borthwick himself picked up Boer folk songs from
South Africans in Glen Nevis and heard an exquisite *Volkslied* from four
German girls at Arrochar. Alastair Borthwick remains one of the most
perceptive writers on the inter-war outdoor movement in Scotland, and a
vocal champion of the youth hostelling movement of the 1930s, which he
famously described as 'one of the more important social innovations of
this century'. He also realised that so much of the survival of this tradition
of song depended upon individual climbers and their respective personali-
ties, believing that 'the story of the open air in Scotland, whoever should
tell it, is not a novel or a biography: it is a collection of short stories each
with its own characters.'[38]

In 1962 Tom Patey wrote of the most famous of the Cairngorm bothies
and howffs and of the people that patronised them. At each of the
individual bothies, be it Luibeg, Lochend, Gelder Shiel, Bynack, the
Geldie Bothies, Altanour, Corrour and the much-loved Shelter Stone,
members of the climbing fraternity were assured friendly company;
amongst the north-east climbers of the 1950s everybody knew everybody
and formal introductions were unnecessary. Celebrated Cairngorm illegal
retreats included the Kincorth Club's subterranean 'Howff' opened in
1954, Charlie's Howff, Freddy and Sticker's Howff, and Mac's Howff

(dating back to 1949 and of Shelter Stone proportions). It was in such places that impromptu song sessions began, and songs were composed and sung by the characters, and 'diversities of opinion and ideals that characterised the bothy set, and stamped each of its members as a genuine eccentric, uninhibited by the conventions of society' flourished. Other bothies became the home hut of an identified group of climbers in this period, and so the 'brigands of the bothy' were born, proud of their 'usual unpleasantness to strangers'. The Lochend Bothy near Lochnagar was the domain of the Boor Boys (a group of unruly youngsters from Aberdeen Grammar School), later known as the Corrour Club.

Patey also recalls how on the Friday afternoon bus out to Deeside from Aberdeen in the early 1950s, climbers strummed on guitars on the back seat, whistled some obscure *aria* or argued about New Orleans trumpeters. The 'nonconformists' of the Etchachan Club poked fun at the Cairngorm Club by taking lines from the club's circular and weaving them into a West Indian Calypso tune; 'Members are requested not to ring the Meets Secretary at his residence' enjoyed a fair measure of popularity when sung on buses or in a bothy. The Aberdeen University Lairig Club stopped for beer and singing at such places as the Inver Inn, the Etchachan Club stopped at any pub on the route, whilst the Cairngorm Club were known to sometimes 'wine and dine' and sing in the Fife Arms in Braemar. These clubs were made up of 'real mountaineers,' not mere hill-bashers. They spoke of, 'icy vigils and gigantic ice falls, routes that finished long after dark, remote bivouacs in faraway corries, riotous nights in bothies, late-night dances in Braemar, and brimming tankards in the Fife Arms'.[39] Tom Patey is right; it was impossible to dissociate the Cairngorm mountains from those who climbed upon them, a compact group of peaks loved by a closely knit community of north-east climbers. Good climbing and good company went hand in hand, each being essential to the full enjoyment of the other. In the Cairngorms in the 1940s, the 1950s and the early 1960s they were inseparable. From 1960 onwards mountaineering and hill-walking in Scotland have become thoroughly egalitarian pastimes; the supply and provision of equipment can be big business and sponsorship can guarantee overseas climbing for those that seek it at a far more challenging level than that found in Scotland.

One wonders whether Scottish climbing groups abroad burst into song now. In the mid-1940s, Tom Patey used song as a navigational aid when approaching Bob Scott's bothy at Luibeg, near Derry Lodge on the Braemar side of the Cairngorms. To him it was still a part of the fabric of the sport: 'Often, as you approached the rickety shelter which adjoined the house, you would hear song and laughter, the camaraderie of climbers ...'[40]

Not all song and verse written about the Cairngorms in the period
from 1850 to 1950, falls directly into the category of a mountaineering
club song. Other writers, whilst regarding their source of inspiration as
the glens and mountains of the region, wrote as outsiders from the world
of the mountaineering club. In 1906, Thomas Sinton brought together a
collection of the poetry and prose of Badenoch, believing that he had the
privilege to live, 'among the children of song who poured forth their lays
of joy and sorrow attuned to the rippling waters of the Spey and to the
variable sounds of nature around ...' The collection included both written
verse, and song transcribed from the oral tradition of the area. The first
part of the book, the 'Songs of Feeling', included verse about Glen Feshie,
Cairn Gorm and Carn Eilrig.[41] An earlier verse was included in a personal
letter written by an unknown author to his sister, from Honeybarrel,
Kildrummy. It described 'a few days rambling among the hills' in October
1870, and celebrates in particular the Lairig Ghru:

> Yet thou, lone Lairig Ghru, 'tis delightful to con
> The wild frowning glories that desolate thee,
> Where from thy limpid well through a rampart of stone
> At the foot of Braeriach springs swift-running Dee.[42]

Such praise of a mountain environment and experience, harks back to
Duncan Ban Macintyre, but this anonymous writer's work conforms to a
romantic view of mountainous landscape seen with a Victorian eye and
sensibilities. This immense defile in the Cairngorms, is later described as
both bleak and gloomy, as well as wild and enchanting. This was a para-
dox that was to be a feature of Victorian tourist poetry and verse on the
region; there was a silence like death to be found in the mountains, yet to
wander in the hills and glens was spiritually invigorating, a cleansing
experience. The most infuriating aspect of analysing this nineteenth- and
early twentieth-century desire to publish and thus pass on the enjoyment
of holidays in the Cairngorms, is that when the writer quoted poetry in
the text, only very rarely was a source given.[43]

Two very different types of mountain experience have been communi-
cated by the use of verse. On 2 January 1928, Hugh Barrie lay dying of
exposure in Glen Einich and he composed a poem that begged that his
body would not be buried in the dark earth, but that his friends would:

> Find me a wind-swept boulder for a bier,
> And on it lay me down,
> Where far beneath drops sheer the rocky ridge ...
> So may I know,
> The swiftly silent swish of hurrying snow,

The lash of rain,
The savage bellowing of stags,
The bitter keen-knife-edge embrace of the rushing wind;
and still the tremulous dawn will touch the eyeless sockets
    of my face ...

J. P. Grant of Rothiemurchus gave permission for a cairn to be erected at Whitewell in Rothiemurchus, as a memorial to Barrie and his companion on that fateful hill-walking expedition in late December 1927 into the very heart of the Cairngorms.[44]

In direct contrast to the pathos of this verse, is the humour generated in numerous pieces of poetry and song that appeared after Professor Norman Collie disclosed to an astonished public in Aberdeen in 1925, the ghostly apparition that he had observed whilst climbing alone on Ben MacDhui in 1891. He believed that he had seen *Ferlas Mhór*, the Big Grey Man of Ben MacDhui; suddenly, a whole host of people had heard footsteps behind themselves in the Cairngorms, and had fled in fear from the Lairig Ghru. Some of the doggerel from the late 1940s was delightfully wicked:

If ever ye gang through the Lairig Ghru —
(Abominable Snowman's there the noo!)
Dinna produce a Hielan cromach —
Or try to poke him in the stomach.
For he is 'fifty' round the chest,
And wears a lang robe for a vest.
So if ye hike through Lairig Ghru,
(Grasping claymore and skean dubh),
Gie him a greeting, like Sir Hugh,
But try the Gaelic, nae Urdu.[45]

Some early twentieth-century poets of landscape who wrote of the Cairngorms are deserving of mention, not least Nan Shepherd whose 1934 collection *In The Cairngorms*, used verse to capture the sense of loneliness one can feel in these hills. She chose to have no written explanation at the foot of each poem, wishing each piece to stand alone. Her poetic imagination continually returns to favoured locations such as Loch Avon, Glen Einich, Braeriach and Corrie Etchachan.[46] William Jeffrey's long poem 'Rothiemurchus' from the mid-1940s was admired to the extent that extracts from it were chosen to head each chapter of the Forestry Commission's National Forest Park Guide to Glen More.[47]

Photography and verse combined in the late 1920s in *The Scots Magazine*, as it sought to lead a public campaign within Scotland to have the Cairngorms designated as a National Park. If created, the proposed National

Park for Scotland would offer the Scottish population a sense of freedom, 'in a great uncharted magnificence like the Cairngorm Mountains, where are to be found the origins of so many national spiritual values'.[48] Verse that was used to reveal the virtues of this 'ideal National Domain', stressed its special landscape qualities and the solitude of a walk within the mountains, but more often than not, no clue was provided to identify the writers of such poetry.[49]

By 1950 the mountaineering club song was dead and buried though not the verse-making tradition. It had fallen out of fashion in both mountaineering club journals and in books on the subject of climbing and hill-walking; after the Second World War, writers in this field preferred to offer their readership a vision of the future, not of the past, and one that was linked to the new era of technological advances that were being made in the sport.[50] A new mass age of popular recreation was about to begin in the Cairngorms, based around the development of Cairn Gorm itself as a centre for British skiing, with a chairlift opening in 1961, after a ski road had been built from Glenmore up into Coire Cas in 1960. Principal Shairp of the University of St Andrews had predicted such an invasion of tourists and recreationalists into the Scottish Highlands almost a hundred years earlier. Recognising that the newly opened Highland Railway would act as a catalyst for the development of a holiday industry based upon Scotland's scenery and landscape, he composed the ballad 'A Cry from Craigellachie' after travelling north to Inverness on this rail line in 1864:

> Land of bens and glens and corries
> Headlong rivers, ocean floods!
> Have we lived to see this outrage
> On your haughty solitudes.
> Cherished names! How disenchanted!
> Hark the railway porter roar –
> Ho! Blair Athole! Dalna-spidal!
> Ho! Dalwhinnie! Aviemore!
>
> ... In and in must Saxon wriggle,
> Southern, cockney, more prevail?

He probably chose this title, as the battle cry of Clan Grant was 'Standfast, Craigellachie!' The rock of Craigellachie, which lies just behind Aviemore, was declared a National Nature Reserve in 1960. Is it possible that Shairp even had a vision of a road bridge over to Skye ...?

> If e'en these should fail, I'll get me
> To some rock roared round by seas.

There to drink calm Nature's freedom
Till they bridge the Hebrides.[51]

Collections of songs and verse about other glens or mountains or even towns in Scotland do exist, whether it be Glenesk,[52] Schiehallion[53] or Kilbarchan,[54] but perhaps only Skye and its Cuillin range can compete with the Cairngorms in the breadth and variety of mountain literature, song and verse that has been generated by the landscape. The tradition of verse-making, however, did not die in 1950, and continues into the 1990s through contributions on the Cairngorms from Colin Lamont,[55] William Montgomerie[56] and the blind mountaineer and poet Syd Scroggie.[57]

Donald William Ross shepherds at Leault of Kincraig and can still be persuaded to recite verse that he has written over the last four decades in praise of the Cairngorm and Monadhliath mountains, and his homeland of Badenoch.

You may speak about the Coolins which rise far off in Skye,
Schiehallion of Perthshire, so majestic to the eye.
The rocky hills of Ross-shire or the green slopes of the north,
But the hills of Bonnie Badenoch are the hills that are of worth.[58]

NOTES

1 S. Gordon, *The Cairngorm Hills of Scotland* (London 1925), frontispiece.
2 Ibid., vii.
3 J. Hunter, *On the Other Side of Sorrow: Nature and People in the Scottish Highlands* (Edinburgh 1995). Interview, John Lorne Campbell, Canna House, Isle of Canna, dated 28 Mar. 1995. *Fear Chanaidh* died in Italy on 25 Apr. 1996, as I was writing this piece, but I was privileged to spend an enthralling afternoon in his company and in his Gaelic library on Canna in March 1995, and for that opportunity I am extremely grateful.
4 *The Songs of Duncan Ban Macintyre*, ed. A. Macleod (Scottish Gaelic Texts Soc., 1952).
5 See esp. E. Baker, *The Highlands With Rope and Rucksack* (London 1923); E. Baker, *On Foot in the Highlands* (London 1933, first publ. 1932); M. Marshall, *The Travels of Tramp-Royal ...* (Edinburgh 1933); and C. Plumb, *Walking in the Grampians* (London 1935).
6 Anon., 'Come A' Ye Tramps an' Hawkers', as sung by Jimmy MacBeath: *The Penguin Book of Scottish Verse*, ed. T. Scott (Harmondsworth 1970).
7 H. G. Gallacher, *Rhymes of the Road and Ballads of Ben Venue* (Oban 1927); E. MacColl and P. Seeger, *Travellers' Songs from England and Scotland* (London 1977). A recent newspaper article on this oral song tradition is, T. Neat, 'Secret Language of the Travellers' Tales', *The Sunday Times,* Ecosse Section 11, 7 Jul. 1996, 2.
8 *Sandy Candy and Other Scottish Nursery Rhymes*, ed. N. and W. Montgomerie, (London 1948).

9 See esp. G. Greig, *Last Leaves of Traditional Ballads and Ballad Airs, Collected in Aberdeenshire* (Aberdeen 1925); and J. Ord (ed.), *The Bothy Songs and Ballads of Aberdeen, Banff and Moray, Angus and the Mearns* (Paisley 1930).

10 H. L. Edlin, 'Poetry and literature', in H. L. Edlin (ed.), *Forests of North-East Scotland* (Edinburgh HMSO 1976).

11 J. Alison (ed.), *The Poetry of North-East Scotland* (Edinburgh 1978).

12 For the original version of this ballad, see D. Maclagan, *Nugae Canorae Medicae: Lays by the Poet Laureate of the New Town Dispensary* (Edinburgh 1850), 54–61.

13 D. Maclagan, 'The Battle O' Glen Tilt', *The Cairngorm Club Journal*, iii (15) (Jul. 1900), 185–9.

14 The archives of the Scottish Rights of Way Society are held in the Scottish Record Office [SRO], at GD335. See GD335/1, Papers Relating to the Formation of the Scottish Rights of Way Society, 1847–1885.

15 T. Stephenson, *Forbidden Land: The Struggle for Access to Mountain and Moorland* (Manchester 1989), see ch. 5, 118–30.

16 Maclagan, *Nugae Canorae Medicae*, 54, 61.

17 S. Anton, 'Battles for Cairngorm rights of way', *The Cairngorm Club Journal*, xx, (102) (1991), 23–9.

18 F. Younghusband, 'Foreword', in F. S. Smythe, *Kamet Conquered* (London 1932), xv.

19 F. S. Smythe, *The Spirit of the Hills* (London 1938; first publ. 1935), 245.

20 J. R. Ullman, *High Conquest: The Story of Mountaineering* (London 1942), 40–3.

21 See esp. A. Le Blond, *Adventures on the Roof of the World* (London 1907; first publ. 1904); J. Keay, *When Men and Mountains Meet: The Explorers of the Western Himalayas, 1820–1875* (London 1977); H. Spender, *In Praise of Switzerland: Being the Alps in Prose and Verse* (London 1912).

22 D. Bennet (ed.), *The Munros: The Scottish Mountaineering Club Hill-walkers Guide* (Scottish Mountaineering Trust, East Kilbride, 1986).

23 Smythe, *Spirit of the Hills*, 242–53.

24 J. G. Stott, 'Song of the Scottish Mountainering Club', *The Scottish Mountaineering Club Journal*, xii (71) (Jun. 1913), 291–2.

25 Scottish Students' Song Book Committee, *Scottish Students' Song Book* (Glasgow 1891): Song 70, 'Climbing, Climbing, Climbing'; Song 130, the Gaelic air 'Gabhaidh sinn an rathad mor' (We will up and march away).

26 H. W. Davies (ed.), *The Fellowship Song Book* (London 1915): Song 82, 'The Open Road', by William C. Braithwaite.

27 A. G. Abbie and others (eds.), *The British Student's Song Book* (Glasgow 1930); A. G. Abbie (ed.), *Student Songs for Camp and College* (Glasgow 1937).

28 B. H. Humble (ed.), *The Songs of Skye: An Anthology* (Stirling 1934): see 'Introduction' by Lauchlan MacLean Watt.

29 C. M. Loader, *Cairngorm Adventure at Glenmore Lodge: Scottish Centre of Outdoor Training* (Edinburgh 1952). For the original poems written by the children who visited Glenmore Lodge in 1948: 49–52.

30 J. G. Stott, 'Song', *The Scottish Mountaineering Club Journal*, xii (69) (Oct. 1912), 151–2.

31 Smythe, *Spirit of the Hills*, 250–1.

32 R. Aitken, 'Stravagers and marauders', *The Scottish Mountaineering Club Journal*, xxx (166) (1975), 351–7.

33 W. K. Richmond, *Climber's Testament* (London 1950), 4.

34 M. A. Skakle, 'Club Song', *The Cairngorm Club Journal*, xi (66) (Jan. 1928), n.p.

35 R. Smith, 'The playground of the future', in M. Magnusson and G. White (eds.), *The Nature of Scotland: Landscape, Wildlife and People* (Edinburgh 1991), 196–210.

36 I. McMorrin and W. Noyce, *World Atlas of Mountaineering* (London 1969), 64.

37 I. MacLean, 'Mountain men', in B. Kay (ed.), *Odyssey: Voices from Scotland's Recent Past* (Edinburgh 1980), 79–87.

38 A. Borthwick, *Always a Little Further* (Stirling 1947; first publ. 1939), 54, 65–6, 132–7.

39 T. Patey, 'Cairngorm commentary', *The Scottish Mountaineering Club Journal*, xxvii (153) (May 1962), 207–20.

40 R. Else and C. McNeish, *The Edge: One Hundred Years of Scottish Mountaineering* (London 1994), 85.

41 *The Poetry of Badenoch: Collected and Edited*, ed. T. Sinton (Inverness 1906), p. xxxvii.

42 Anon., 'Lairig Ghru', anonymous poem and letter written at Honeybarrel, Kildrummy in Oct. 1870, *The Deeside Field*, 2nd ser. (5) (1966), 28–9.

43 See W. A. Smith, 'The Cairngorms in summer', *The Scottish Mountaineering Club Journal* (3) (Sep. 1890), 106–14; W. A. Smith, 'A visit to the Cairngorms in 1875', *The Scottish Mountaineering Club Journal*, xiv (3) (Jun. 1917), 224–34; and G. M. Lawson, 'The Cairngorms: an appreciation', *The Scottish Mountaineering Club Journal*, xxv (89) (Apr. 1920), 233–40.

44 M. H. Scarlett, *In the Glens Where I Was Young* (Milton of Moy 1988), 57–8.

45 A. Gray, *The Big Grey Man of Ben MacDhui* (Edinburgh 1994; first publ. 1970), 51–2.

46 N. Shepherd, *In the Cairngorms* (Edinburgh 1934).

47 The extracts can be found in J. Walton (ed.), *Glen More: Cairngorms* (National Forest Park Guide, Edinburgh HMSO, 1960; first publ. 1949). The original poem was published in W. Jeffrey, *Sea Glimmer: Poems in Scots and English* (Glasgow 1948), 7–11.

48 A. Graeme, 'Hills of Home: the spiritual claim for a National Park', *The Scots Magazine*, new ser., x (2) (Nov. 1928), 89–96.

49 A. I. McConnochie, 'The national nature of the Cairngorms', *The Scots Magazine*, new ser., x (3) (Dec. 1928), 178–83. A map accompanies this article describing in detail the boundaries of the Cairngorm Area and the proposed National Domain.

50 For technical mountaineering texts from this period, see Association of British Members of the Swiss Alpine Club, *Mountaineering Handbook: A Complete and Practical Guide for Beginner or Expert* (London 1950); and J. E. B. Wright, *The Technique of Mountaineering* (London 1955).

51 A. Macpherson, *Glimpses of Church and Social Life in the Highlands and Olden Times* (Edinburgh 1893), 10–11.

52 G. Michie (ed.), *A Glen Anthology* (Glenesk 1959).

53 J. Sinclair (ed.), *Schiehallion: A Posy of Rannoch Poesy* (Stirling 1905).

54 C. P. Lyle, *Poems and Ballads of Kilbarchan* (Glasgow 1929 and 1931).

55 D. Glen (ed.), *Akros Verse, 1965–1982: An Anthology fom Akros, Nos. 1–49* (Nottingham 1982). Colin Lamont's poem 'Rothiemurchus', written in 1980, is found on page 39.

56 G. Bruce and F. Rennie (eds.), *The Land Out There: A Scottish Land Anthology* (Aberdeen 1991). Much of this collection contains verse and prose celebrating the landscape of Scotland. William Montgomerie's poem 'To The Mountain' is found at pages 245–6.

57 S. Scroggie, 'Wild Land' (poem), in J. Crumley and R. Smith (eds.), *Cairngorms at the Crossroads* (Edinburgh 1987), 42–3; S. Scroggie, *Cairngorms Scene and Unseen* (Edinburgh 1989).

58 D. W. Ross, 'Bonnie Badenoch', unpublished poem by Donald William Ross of Leault of Kincraig, no date. I have had the pleasure of hearing this poem recited from memory by Donnie Ross Snr, both in Kincraig and in Glen Feshie. I would like to thank his daughter, Eileen Ross for providing me with a much tamer written version of the poem from her father's collection in the loft at Leault.

Index of Ballads, Songs and Poems

General Index